Second Edition

Inviting Transformation

Presentational Speaking for a Changing World

Sonja K. Foss
University of Colorado at Denver

Karen A. Foss
University of New Mexico

WAVELAND
PRESS, INC.
Prospect Heights, Illinois

For information about this book, contact:
Waveland Press, Inc.
P.O. Box 400
Prospect Heights, Illinois 60070
(847) 634-0081
www.waveland.com

CONTENTS

ACKNOWLEDGMENTS

We never intended to write a public speaking book. In fact, for years, we steadfastly refused even to consider the possibility because we did not believe the world needed another public speaking textbook. There came a time, however, when we felt we had something to say about public speaking that had not been said before and that maybe needed to be. We decided that we wanted to write a book on the subject so that we no longer would have the experience of lecturing on a concept in a public speaking class, turning to write it on the board, and finding ourselves thinking, "I don't believe this anymore; this doesn't fit my experience." The result is *Inviting Transformation*. Our primary intent with this book is to expand the options for public speaking—or what we prefer to call *presentational speaking*—so that all of us are better prepared for the changing world in which we live.

Once we decided we wanted to write a book on presentational speaking, the writing was helped along by many others. Our publishers, Carol Rowe and Neil Rowe, have been extremely patient and supportive through both editions of this book. Thank you for trusting us and our vision for this book. Special thanks to Sally Miller Gearhart and Sonia Johnson for sharing with us their notions of transformation that are at the heart of this book. Ongoing conversations with several others about these ideas also were invaluable: Karen Carlton, Deborah Fort, Cindy L. Griffin, Josina M. Makau, Steve Moore, and Ann Skinner-Jones. Sonja's advisees at Ohio State supplied valuable insights about translating theory into practice: Kimberly Barnett Gibson, Gail J. Chryslee, Debra Greene, D. Lynn O'Brien Hallstein, Cristina Lopez, Helene Shugart, and Catherine Egley Waggoner.

Our thanks also go to those who read the book in manuscript form and offered honest feedback and valuable ideas. Robert Trapp and Gail J. Chryslee read the first edition, and Judith A. Hendry, Ann Skinner-Jones, Stephen W. Littlejohn, Melissa McCalla Manassee, and Barbara J. Walkosz read the second.

We tried out versions of this book on students at Ohio State University, Humboldt State University, the University of Colorado at Denver, and the University of New Mexico. Our students provided important feedback as well as allowing us to use their speaking plans and speeches as models. Teaching assistants in public speaking at the University of New Mexico and instructors at the University of Colorado at Denver, coordinated by Barbara J. Walkosz, provided syllabi, exercises, exams, and insights. Instructors using the book at the International College at Beijing of the University of Colorado at Denver—Victoria DeFrancisco, Jennifer Gruenewald, Laura K. Hahn, Cheris Kramarae, and Sharon M. Varallo—were helpful in addressing multicultural dimensions. We are especially grateful for the confirmation all of you offered that we are on the right track.

Others helped behind the scenes in various ways. Kelly M. O'Connor served as a research assistant, and Marcel Allbritton and Joseph Milan helped with the instructor's manual. Sally Thee created the diagrams in chapter 5 and chapter 10. Eric Berson provided companion passes on United Airlines to make the process of getting together to write this book easier.

Finally, as always, our thanks to Anthony J. Radich and Stephen W. Littlejohn for enduring yet another book with patience, humor, and love.

TING
TRA RMATION

Our world is cha
enable us to connect
New technologies su
Internet enable us to
not met and with wh
nologies. The increas
their home communi
are exposed to new p
munities with practic

The tearing dov
exponentially increa
world to connect w
ized by globalizatio
and information. A
that we are encount
at the world in very

Many of us w
encountered peopl
pretty much the sar
and values, but this
ethnic minorities n
2050, that percent
Americans, Hispai
Americans togethe

redible speed. Many of these changes
ith more people throughout the world.
ones, e-mail, and chat rooms on the
instantaneously with people we have
would have contact without these tech-
our culture enables individuals to leave
ocate again and again. As we move, we
deas, and we "pollinate" the new com-
rought from our previous locales.
in Wall and the end of the Cold War
ities for groups in different parts of the
er. The modern landscape is character-
le, and greater access to transportation
s for connection increase, we discover
vho are different from us and who look
s.

homogeneous communities, where we
essional and personal lives who were
and who agreed with us on basic issues
he case. In the United States, racial and
bout one third of the population, and by
d to rise to almost 50 percent. African
mericans, Pacific Islanders, and Native
ore than half of the population of several

metropolitan areas in the United States, including Los Angeles, Miami, San Antonio, and Honolulu.[1] As of 2001, Caucasians officially became a minority in California, amounting to a little less than half the population of the state, a trend that is expected to continue in the near future in states such as Florida, New York, and Texas.[2]

Increasing diversity is evident not only in demographics related to race and ethnicity but in other areas of our lives as well. Nearly a million women and men in the United States identified themselves as members of same-sex couples in the 2000 census.[3] Changes in the average age of the U. S. population also contribute to increasing diversity. Projections show that the percentage of the population between the ages of 20 and 64 will decline after 2010 and that the percentage of people over age 65 will increase dramatically. As a result of changes such as these, we all have many more opportunities for encountering people whose perspectives differ from our own.

This book is designed to provide you with a framework for responding effectively to diverse perspectives. As we encounter worldviews that differ from our own, we have two major choices: We can engage in communication that isolates and protects us from those perspectives, or we can embrace challenges to our thinking as opportunities for growth and change. We believe that this latter option is the most effective one for responding to the changes that are going on around us. When we make use of diverse perspectives to facilitate our own growth, we discover many opportunities for stimulation, expansion, adventure, joy, and wonder. An openness to the growth that comes from engaging and grappling with perspectives different from our own enables us to have more satisfying relationships, to be more effective and successful in our professional lives, and, simply, to have much more fun.

In this book, you will be learning a framework that you can use for enjoying, cultivating, responding to, and contributing to the diverse perspectives you encounter. The options in this framework are drawn from the speaking practices and values of many different cultures. As you are introduced to a variety of communication practices, you will be able to respond in ways that put others at ease and that give you confidence when entering into interactions with people who differ from you.

The options presented to you as part of this framework are much broader than those usually included in the purview of public speaking. When you think about giving a speech or making a presentation, a standard image probably comes to mind: One person standing behind a lectern, looking out at an audience of many people. In this conception of public speaking, the speaker does all the talking, and any participation by the audience is limited to asking questions at the end of the speech. You probably associate this kind of speaking event with public settings such as lecture halls, classrooms, senate chambers, courts of law, churches, and campaign rallies.

We do not limit [
these kinds of speaki
more broadly. Most of
spectives do not occu
speeches. Most of us g
we develop communi
that traditionally are [
communicate in the v

We have chosen t
ing to describe the cc
term suggests that we
but they are not all ta
ask us about our vie
called *mini-presentatio*
nication in which we
The tools offered in [
contexts in which co

Presentational s[
coach who gives a
introduces herself a
mon, and a public c
are involved when a
presents ideas to he
preparation for rem
party, a potential e
student talks with a
situations, a messag
constructed delibera
the interaction.

We began this c
tic of our contempo
ment with that char
notion of transform
ing in this book. V
that is exciting and
as we communicat

We have noted
book is designed to
spectives more abl
transformation. Th
initiate communic
your audience op
the form of a pres
the world in new
presentational spe

of communication in this book to
and conceptualize public speaking
in which we encounter different per-
re listening to or presenting formal
of speeches relatively infrequently. If
lat only enable us to speak at events
ic speaking, we will be ill equipped to
ions we encounter today.

ational speaking instead of *public speak-*
that is the subject of this book. This
many presentations during the day,
public, formal settings. When people
ing, we respond with what might be
e through our day, we initiate commu-
ve are and what we believe to others.
iseful in all of the diverse settings and
)ccurs.

ncludes the communication used by a
wrestling team, a new manager who
meeting, a minister delivering a ser-
campaign speech. Presentations also
ative meets with a client, an employee
iomeowner interviews a contractor in
chen, friends engage in small talk at a
:rs questions at a job interview, and a
he classes she is taking. In all of these
very short, sometimes longer—is being
plish a goal the communicator has for

about change. Change is a characteris-
id openness to growth through engage-
is a healthy and effective response. The
concept in the framework we are offer-
ng change as a condition of our world
nd we are privileging a desire to change
iments produced by that change.

work for presentational speaking in this
encounter and interact with diverse per-
fectively—to contribute to and manage
pens in one of two ways. One is that you
iers because you believe you can offer
growth. By offering your perspective in
nvite the audience to see and experience
ond possibility for transformation from
vhen you are open to learning from the

perspectives that others present as you engage with them. You enter an interaction seeking to share your perspective with others, you compare it with the perspectives that audience members offer you, and you may choose, as a result, to engage in a process of questioning and rethinking your own viewpoint. Your communication also should encourage others with whom you are interacting to do the same.

Transformation as a result of presentational speaking can range from the dramatic to the subtle. You may emerge from an interchange with another—either as a speaker or an audience member—having changed your opinion on an issue, having gained information about a subject you did not have before, or having adopted a new behavior. Transformation also includes the subtle kind of change that occurs when you incorporate new information into your systems of thought. The information incubates, and you find yourself making use of it later to develop and refine your ideas.

In the model of presentational speaking presented in this book, you enter an interaction with a goal of transformation. You encourage growth and change in your audience and are open to opportunities for growth and change for yourself. This receptivity to transformation by both speaker and audience is facilitated when the interaction assumes the form of an invitation. We now turn to an explanation of this key concept, which we call *invitational rhetoric*, starting with the idea of modes of rhetoric.

Modes of Rhetoric

There are many different forms, patterns, or modes of communication that can serve as frameworks for presentational speaking. An explanation of all of the options available to speakers is a useful starting point for understanding invitational rhetoric. The five basic rhetorical modes that can serve as frames for presentational speaking offer distinct ways of managing, negotiating, and addressing our changing world. They are: (1) conquest rhetoric; (2) conversion rhetoric; (3) benevolent rhetoric; (4) advisory rhetoric; and (5) invitational rhetoric.[4] The term *rhetoric* may be unfamiliar to you as it is being used here. *Rhetoric* is an ancient term for what we now usually call *communication*. The term comes from the classical Greeks, who were the first in the Western tradition to study rhetoric in a systematic and formal way. Both terms—*rhetoric* and *communication*—mean the same thing: the study of how humans use symbols to communicate.

Conquest Rhetoric

Conquest rhetoric has winning as its goal. In this kind of rhetoric, you are successful if you win the argument, your view prevails, or you get your way. The purpose of this mode of interaction is to establish your

idea, claim, or argum
tions. Conquest intera(
to end with a winner and

Conquest rhetoric
It is an inherent part (
legislative, and judici;
making. These system
discover the truth abc
controversial issues. I;
individuals to live tog

In political, legis
directed at determini;
or positions. Conque;
ple, when presidentia
winner and a loser is
constitutes conquest ;
Congress, passage of
that opponents have
or not guilty is anot
the defense or the pr(

: one from among competing posi-
1e basic rule: *"Every disagreement has*

1on form of rhetoric in U. S. culture.
most cherished American political,
>ublic communication and decision
to uphold the rights of individuals,
and arrive at judgments concerning
they provide mechanisms that allow
ifferences, in civil ways.
licial systems, conquest rhetoric is
>osition and rejecting opposing ideas
ed in the political context, for exam-
>ate, an event in which determining a
>art of the process. The election itself
one candidate wins, and one loses. In
at supporters of the bill have won and
n by a jury to find a defendant guilty
f conquest rhetoric. One side—either
1s, and the other loses.

Conversion Rhet(

Conversion rhet
perspectives on an i;
designed not to defe
the rightness or s;
involved in conversi
sales are examples
conversion rhetoric
do. Activists in gro;
Awareness Campa;
their efforts at pers;
ute in various ways
when you and a fri
version rhetoric to ;
action film you wa;

1nication designed to change others'
ge how they behave in some way. It is
or a position but to convince others of
1 perspective. The primary method
ersuasion. Advertising, marketing, and
rhetoric. Religious groups engage in
to persuade others to believe as they
Sierra Club or the National Abortion
conversion rhetoric when they direct
lic to adopt their views and to contrib-
es. In the interpersonal context, such as
1g to see a movie, your friend uses con-
> see a romantic comedy rather than the

Benevolent Rhe

Benevolent rh(
out of a genuine d(
cation, the speake
for their well-being
to others that they
they want to learı

ed to provide assistance to individuals
eir lives better. In this type of communi-
ge audience members out of a concern
umes the form of providing information
ir lives in some way. Those who decide
subject and possibly make a change in

their lives have the opportunity to secure more information about the proposed change. The primary goal in this mode is to benefit others, in contrast to conquest and conversion rhetoric, in which the primary goal is to benefit the speaker in some way.

Health campaigns are examples of benevolent communication. A campaign that encourages workers in outdoor settings to use sunscreen is designed to alert individuals to the dangers of skin cancer and to suggest health practices that will reduce the likelihood of its development. In an interpersonal context, when you see someone doing a task in a way that seems inefficient and suggest another way for her to do the task, you are using benevolent rhetoric. The individual may choose to adopt the suggestion or not, but the communication is created from a genuine desire to make that person's life easier or better.

Advisory Rhetoric

Advisory rhetoric is communication designed to provide requested assistance. It is developed in response to an implicit or explicit request for advice or information from others. Individuals who are the recipients of advisory rhetoric are interested in learning, growing, and changing. They deliberately seek out interactions with or information from individuals who can help them accomplish these goals. In advisory rhetoric, communicators provide guidance by offering new ideas that encourage others to broaden their understanding in some way.

Counseling and education are the paradigm cases of advisory communication. Individuals who choose to see a counselor to work through difficulties in the hope of leading happier lives or who choose to develop themselves through education deliberately expose themselves to new perspectives they believe will be useful to them. You benefit from advisory rhetoric when you ask a friend who is highly knowledgeable about cars for her advice on what kind of car to buy. Likewise, when someone asks a clerk in a Motor Vehicles Department how to go about getting a driver's license, he is requesting that the clerk engage in advisory rhetoric, and he willingly accepts the advice or assistance she offers him about what he needs to do to get a license. Advisory rhetoric is marked by someone's request for assistance, unlike conquest, conversion, and benevolent rhetorics, in which the information given is unsolicited.

Invitational Rhetoric

Invitational rhetoric is rooted in the notion of an invitation.[6] An invitation is a request for the presence or participation of someone. When you issue an invitation, you ask someone to come somewhere or to engage in some activity with you. In the case of presentational speaking, you invite your audience members to see the world as you do and to consider your

perspective seriously. T
reached as communi(
words."[7] The goal is n
to achieve understandi
invitational rhetoric, tl
tribute to thinking abo
understanding of the s

Ultimately, the re
understanding of an i:
sarial framework estal
of the participants the
rhetoric, a professor m
ments for a course as
explanation of why h
able. Both would con
also would understa
clearer idea of the m
tives and actions.

itational rhetoric is understanding,
in a "sharing of worlds through
ve superiority but to clarify ideas—
pants involved in the interaction. In
audience jointly consider and con-
at everyone involved gains a greater
, and complexity of that issue.
nal rhetoric is often more than an
f the nonjudgmental and nonadver-
nteraction, a greater understanding
cur. For example, using invitational
a student why she structured assign-
en listens carefully to the student's
signments are unfair and unreason-
anderstanding of the issue, but they
better because they would have a
itionale for their respective perspec-

Defaul

The five modes (
sory, and invitational
Any time we interac
tions and practices o
are available to us, w
the conquest and co
have little choice ab(
demand that we op
exclusively. We tend
topic is trivial, whe
about, and when ai
impact on our own
tion with someone
to try to get that pe
adversarial position
tion is turned into
goals might be accc
ing, we have a tend
most situations.

Because we m(
default modes of c
kind of world. Cor

Communication

quest, conversion, benevolent, advi-
erent approaches to communication.
cation is framed within the assump-
odes. Although all five of the modes
use and often are rewarded for using
. In fact, you may feel as though you
s to use because our culture seems to
quest and conversion modes almost
nning and convincing even when the
ally care about what we are arguing
cence to our perspective has no real
When we find ourselves in a conversa-
ith us, our automatic reaction often is
ith us. The other person is put in an
she does not agree, and the conversa-
of right and wrong. Even when our
through other modes of communicat-
o conquest and conversion options for

conquest and conversion rhetoric as
we create and experience a particular
't just words and sounds and gestures

that reflect our world. It is the means through which we create that world. By the choices we make in our use of communication, we create our reality. This relationship may sound backwards from how you think of the relationship between communication and reality. You may assume that reality is outside of you in the external world, and you use communication to name and talk about that reality. But reality or knowledge is the *result* of the process of communication. Reality is not fixed; it changes according to the symbols or the communication we use to talk about it. As linguist Deborah Tannen explains, "When we think we are using language, language is using us. . . . The terms in which we talk about something shape the way we think about it—and even what we see. . . . This is how language works. It invisibly molds our way of thinking about people, actions, and the world around us."[8]

Some examples will clarify the relationship between the symbols we choose and the reality we experience. How we choose to name or label a situation determines how we respond to it. If you call a person a *friend*, for example, that is different from calling the person an *acquaintance* or a *lover*. Each label orients you in a different way to that person, and you treat him accordingly. You experience and treat a rambunctious child differently depending on whether you call her *gifted*, *spoiled*, or *obnoxious*, for example. Similarly, you experience a colleague differently if you describe him as *ambitious* and *motivated* or *pushy* and *aggressive*. You've also probably had the experience of deciding you were not going to have a good time at a party and then having exactly the lousy time you predicted through your self-talk.

The way you label something, then, determines your experience of it and the kinds of responses available to you. The corollary to this notion, of course, is that because you can change your choices about symbols, you can create a different reality from the one you are now experiencing. By changing your thoughts and thus your labels, you can manifest a reality that you like better than your current one. By choosing to see a colleague as ambitious rather than pushy, you can experience and interact with him in a very different—and probably more productive—way.

The world that is created through conquest and conversion rhetorics generally is an adversarial and contentious one. Tannen uses the term *argument culture* to describe this world and suggests that it is marked by "a pervasive warlike atmosphere that makes us approach public dialogue, and just about anything we need to accomplish, as if it were a fight."[9]

Examples of the adversarial world that conquest and conversion rhetorics have created are readily apparent. Negative political advertisements distort candidates' records and predict catastrophic consequences if the opposing candidate is elected. Road rage consumes drivers as they try to keep others from passing them and try to get revenge—through words, gestures, or worse—on those who do. Children experience the harassing behavior of bullies in their schools, and at the college level, the bullying

becomes hazing. Peop
idating, insulting, and
who hold perspectives
we often show less co
ing our own dominar
Haden Elgin describe:
ated in this way: "E\
each other down; eve
and carping and belly;

Several features d
and conversion rheto
because conquest and
equacy, pain, humilia
some and feelings of s
ial world also suits so
pation by everyone.
"those who feel com
participate, and thos
elsewhere."[11] When
spectives and insigh
understanding of isst
it continually creates
are polarized and er
munication continue
Most important, hov
conversion rhetorics
In this world, diffe
growth but as irregu

Conquest and c
and their place. The
best ways—for enga
rhetoric—benevolen
to talk with one ano
to create different ki
to our changing wor
tive rhetorical mo
speaking framed wit

n the radio or on television, intim-
rs who are different from them or
heirs. Even in casual conversation,
ging information than with assert-
tion is harsh, but linguist Suzette
conquest and conversion have cre-
ng and badmouthing and putting
and griping and sneering, whining

ersarial world created by conquest
be a world of negative emotions
rics often produce feelings of inad-
rrassment, or angry submission for
omination for others. The adversar-
r than others, discouraging partici-
ial communication is the norm,
t type of interaction are drawn to
l comfortable with it recoil and go
pate, the result is a loss of the per-
als might have contributed to an
ome of an adversarial world is that
r the next conflict. When positions
est and conversion modes of com-
conflict is the inevitable outcome.
rial world created by conquest and
n opportunities for transformation.
are not seen as opportunities for
shed and squelched.
of communication have their uses
r, the only ways—and often not the
cation. The other available modes of
invitational—offer additional ways
alternative realities. They allow us
offer more flexible ways to respond
this book is on one of these alterna-
rhetoric—and on presentational
f invitational rhetoric.

Core Assu

Invitational rhe
genuine understanc
tives. Invitational r

Invitational Rhetoric

communication designed to generate
viduals who hold different perspec-
erized by five core assumptions: (1)

the purpose of communicating is to gain understanding; (2) the speaker and the audience are equal; (3) different perspectives constitute valuable resources; (4) change happens when people choose to change themselves; and (5) all participants are willing to be changed by the interaction.

Understanding as the Purpose of Communication

The purpose of invitational rhetoric is understanding. Both you and your audience enter the interaction seeking to understand the ideas and attitudes of the other from the other's point of view. You adopt the frame of reference of the other concerning the issue under discussion. As psychotherapist Carl R. Rogers explains this idea, "To be with another in this way means that for the time being, you lay aside your own views and values in order to enter another's world without prejudice."[12] The goal of understanding in invitational rhetoric encourages both the speaker and the audience to "venture outside the walls that normally protect them from hearing things that don't fit their worldview. . . . [T]hey feel a new curiosity about the words and beliefs of people who see things differently. . . . It is more than hearing another's point of view—it is making room for that point of view."[13]

A number of terms have been suggested for the focus on understanding that characterizes invitational rhetoric. Philosopher Martha Nussbaum uses the term *narrative imagination* to characterize the communicator's stance in this kind of interaction. Narrative imagination involves the "ability to think what it might be like to be in the shoes of a person different from oneself, to be an intelligent reader of that person's story, and to understand the emotions and wishes and desires that someone so placed might have."[14] Other terms that have been suggested for this kind of understanding are *trial empathy*, *trial identification*, and *transient identification*.[15] In invitational rhetoric, you try on another person's perspective to experience how it feels and to discover how it makes sense to that person.

Equality of Speaker and Audience

In traditional models of speaking, you as the speaker take center stage, all eyes are on you, and you generally are assumed to be all knowing about your topic. Such a privileged stance typically characterizes speaking in the conquest and conversion and sometimes the benevolent and advisory modes of communicating. In these modes, you as the speaker are viewed as superior to the audience because you are seen as having more knowledge, experience, or resources than others do. In short, you are the expert.

In traditional models of speaking, audience members often are viewed as if they are uninformed, misguided, or naive. The belief systems and behaviors they have created for living in the world are devalued and considered to be inadequate or inappropriate simply because their views

differ from yours. Th
me show you the way
ence member is some
unintentionally reduc
not able to make an ir

The relationship l
ferent in invitational
peers. In invitational
knowing expert. You
to the interaction whi
access to knowledge c
ing do not and that th
experiences or your p
marized by writer Urs
"experience deny, neg
lot more of it, *your e*
another being wrong?
my being is my truth.'

In invitational rhe
experiences and hold
You conceptualize at
who hold the beliefs
good sense to them.
worldview. Grounded
individuals to make th
lives. As former activi
trust that others are d
simply need "to be ui
lives."[18] You approac
to discover what your

The power emplo
ability to affect what
others. In other word:
in invitational rhetori
and make decisions i
Power is not a qualit
employed by all mer
tates, and enables all
the interaction.

Diverse Perspectiv

A third assumptic
tives different from yc
ideas, beliefs, and ph

elp you, let me enlighten you, let
·d the audience.[16] Even if an audi-
respect, in traditional models, you
>meone who is inferior and who is

nunicator and the audience is dif-
:aker and the audience are equal
e a facilitator rather than an all-
; to make their own contributions
making your own. You may have
hose with whom you are interact-
ul, but you do not claim that your
perior to theirs. This view is sum-
hen she asks how can one person's
ther experience? Even if I've had a
truth. How can one being prove
lot younger and smarter than me,

sees audience members as having
that are valuable and legitimate.
as authorities on their own lives
as they do for reasons that make
1, then, is part of an invitational
others, self-determination allows
; about how they wish to live their
explains, this principle involves a
can at the moment and that they
epted as the experts on their own
·ith respect and openness, seeking
·s know and understand.
· in invitational rhetoric is not the
one else or the ability to control
·ver. Instead, the power you enact
·here power to create knowledge
the speaker and the audience.[19]
others but something that can be
action so that it energizes, facili-
:d to contribute to and learn from

·vitational rhetoric is that perspec-
as valuable resources. Numerous
: potential to influence and shape

us, but we generally listen only to people who hold the same perspectives we do. Invitational rhetoric involves a deliberate exposure to and consideration of diverse voices as beneficial rather than detrimental to your thinking. Those who disagree with you are seen as resources for exposure to a variety of diverse experiences, thoughts, perceptions, and feelings. The more diverse voices that are added to the conversation, the more opportunities you have for understanding.

Because every perspective—including your own—is necessarily partial, alternative viewpoints enhance your understanding because they represent other sides of the story. Thus, you depend on others for the fullest understanding of an issue. As communication theorist Stanley A. Deetz suggests, through "otherness,"

> the self is productively transformed. The very capacity to escape the fixity of one's own views and homogeneous community is through seeking the other—that which is different and cannot be denied. Without that, communication is reduced to the reproduction of already possessed meanings. . . . The notion of communication as "to make common" has all too often been read as to make alike, rather than to understand the productivity of mutually holding our differences in relation to each other.[20]

The resources you gain when you are open to and actively seek diverse perspectives are suggested in the story of the blind men trying to understand an elephant by feeling different parts of the animal. One man decides an elephant is long, slim, and flexible because he feels the trunk. Another thinks an elephant is flat and wide because he feels an ear. Another concludes that an elephant is a round and stout creature because he feels a leg. An openness to diverse perspectives allows you to connect your pieces of reality with others who see things differently: "Instead of labeling 'us' as right and 'them' as crazy, blind to the obvious, or refusing to see, we find out that they know something we don't. When we collaborate, we can see the whole elephant."[21]

The assumption that diverse perspectives represent resources for your own understanding means that invitational rhetoric goes beyond tolerance. The connotations of *tolerance* convey a judgmental attitude toward difference. It suggests that you are willing to put up with individuals who hold views different from yours, but you still disapprove of them and wish they held different perspectives. In contrast, at the heart of invitational rhetoric is joyful allowing.[22] From this standpoint, you joyfully allow another person to be different from you, celebrating and appreciating those differences because of the richness they bring to your world. You are delighted with those who hold different perspectives because those differences provide you with new ways of looking at the world. The differences of others constitute an invitation for you to reconsider and expand your perspectives in the face of something different.

Change as Self-Ch

A particular vie
openness to and ap
not try to change th
ric, you do not wan
effort, you miss the
tives can help you g
the world. Changing
fourth assumption c
when people choose

Many approach
another person is po
the target of the pers
individuals gladly en
are presented with,
metaphors, or dynam
outcome of the use o

Our experience of
theories describe, and
that changing someo
which they care deep
how you should think
you get defensive and
you are doing or think
heels" and maintain y
ment than before. Myl
community-based org
try to change others: "
argue them into chang

The view of chan
when people choose t
life experiences throug
get to choose what ou
like our current life ex
the result of our own
theorist Sally Miller G

> No one can chang
> potential in the e
> change"—then the
> (moisture, tempera
> will hatch. A ston
> hatching into a chic
> tions of moisture ar
> mation into a chick

cterizes invitational rhetoric. An
perspectives means that you do
ers. In fact, in invitational rheto-
because when you make such an
lore how their different perspec-
anding of an issue, yourself, and
difficult to accomplish. Thus, a
ric is that change happens only
es.

mplicitly suggest that changing
sy, even when the beliefs that are
eld. According to these theories,
of believing or acting when they
l or emotional appeals, vibrant
y. Persuasion is seen as a natural
eals.

others is different from what these
s, too. You probably have found
icult, especially on issues about
tells you what you should do or
nse? If you are like most people,
gest all sorts of reasons why what
for you. You usually "dig in your
greater enthusiasm and commit-
of the Highlander Folk School for
what often happens when people
tion on something and you try to
to strengthen that position."[23]

rhetoric is that change happens
es. Because we create our own
nunication, we are the ones who
our worlds are like. If we do not
change them, but this change is
diness to change. As rhetorical
e process,

ken. If, however, there is the
. . . the "internal basis for
hat in the right environment
nditions for change") the egg
d, has no internal basis for
of sitting in the proper condi-
ot make possible its transfor-

Change happens, then, when an environment is created in which individuals choose to change themselves. At most, as a speaker, you are going to be able to create an environment in which audience members are willing to consider changing. You plant an idea in someone's mind, and that person continues to think about the idea after your presentation is over in a process not unlike incubation. Ultimately, that individual may decide to make a change.

Willingness to Yield

Participants in invitational rhetoric enter communication situations willing to be changed. In contrast to conquest or conversion rhetoric, the risk involved in invitational rhetoric "is not that you may lose but rather that you may change."[25] As Rogers notes, "if you are willing to enter [another's] private world and see the way life appears to him . . . you run the risk of being changed yourself."[26] Because you anticipate or are open to new ways of understanding, you are willing to yield your perspective or to change your mind about what you believe. Willingness to yield is not compromising your beliefs or surrendering your values. Instead, it is a genuine shift in perspective that results from a consideration of another's views.

To be willing to change violates a very strong tenet of human nature: "Human beings like to be right. It is programmed into us as a survival mechanism. If we were to question everything, we wouldn't survive."[27] When the things you know to be true and right are challenged, you often find that you are very uncomfortable. In an invitational interaction, you may be asked to call into question even the things that are most inviolate to you, which can be a frightening process. As Simmons points out: "There is always a risk when you engage in the process of learning. Even though you can be assured that this mental redesign will incorporate a higher level of understanding than you have right now, the potential disruption is daunting. Like renovating a house, it can be inconvenient to add that new wing."[28]

Invitational rhetoric, however, involves such a process. Not unlike philosopher Martin Buber's notion of the "I-Thou" relationship, the basic movement of a willingness to yield is a turning toward the other. It involves meeting another's position "in its uniqueness, letting it have its impact."[29] You enter the communication situation willing to deconstruct and dismantle your point of view, willing to revise yourself. Gearhart offers an example of this willingness in her life. She is strongly opposed to the hunting of animals, but she deliberately leaves open the possibility that hunting is acceptable: "And that means that I've got to risk believing that hunting . . . may be in some cases a viable thing for human beings to do. And that's scary."[30]

To summarize, invitational rhetoric is a mode of communicating in which your goal is to invite others to understand your perspective just as

you try to understand | ?ctives of others are not seen as
impediments or obstac͏ /our goals but as resources that
encourage you to move͏ perspective to gain a more comprehensive view of an i͏: You and the audience are equal
as you each explore th͏ ͏ive. You issue an invitation for
others to participate in͏ ͏:r than seeking to change those
with whom you come i͏ ͏ılso are aware that the only way
change happens is whe͏ ͏o change themselves. Both you
and your audience mem͏ ͏ımunication situation willing to
be changed by what hap͏

Invitational Rhe   oninvitational World

A description of i͏ ͏ric usually provokes concerns
about how it can or shoͱ ͏ıoninvitational world—a world
where conquest and conͷ ͏ıre the norm. If you are typical,
your concerns about inͮ ͏: are likely to fall into one or
more of three categories:͏ ͏n whether invitational rhetoric
will allow you to succeeͺ ͏2) you enjoy the experience of
using conquest and conversͺ ͏ıd are reluctant to give them up
in favor of invitational rhetoric, ͏ ͏/itational rhetoric seems to suggest that you must ignore the proͱ ͏you see in the world. We will
address each of these concerns in turn ͏ ͏ınd hope we can allay some of
your uneasiness about the invitational rhetoric you will be learning about
in the rest of this book.

Invitational Rhetoric and Success

You may be thinking that an invitational mode of communication is
not practical if you wish to be successful in your personal and professional life. You may believe, because conquest and conversion rhetorics
are prominent features of our contemporary world, that you need to
employ these kinds of communication to accomplish your goals. Furthermore, you may believe that if everyone else is engaging in conquest or
conversion rhetoric, you will be left behind if you are using invitational
rhetoric. Others will take advantage of you, you won't earn promotions,
and you won't get ahead.

In responding to these concerns, we first want to make clear that invitational rhetoric cannot and should not be used in all situations. We are
not asking you to forego the other modes of rhetoric and to use invitational rhetoric exclusively. Conquest, conversion, benevolent, and advisory rhetorics have their place, and when situations require their use, they
are the appropriate modes to use. In systems based on modes of rhetoric
such as conquest and conversion, you must operate according to the con-

ventions of those systems. In the legal context, for example, argumentative rather than invitational methods are necessary for pleading criminal and civil cases. On the job, you will encounter situations where you need to use persuasion and convince someone to adopt your proposal to be effective. In situations of crisis, when time is short and decisions must be made quickly, conquest rhetoric also may be your only feasible choice. There also are times when you must argue against offensive or dangerous ideas, as Yugoslavian poet Charles Simic suggests: "There are moments in life when true invective is called for, when it becomes an absolute necessity, out of a deep sense of justice, to denounce, mock, vituperate, lash out, in the strongest possible language."[31] Conquest and conversion rhetorics are legitimate and valuable options that help achieve particular communication goals in many situations.

You also may discover, however, that there are more opportunities than you originally had believed for employing invitational rhetoric in contexts that are predominately conquest or conversion in nature. You may find, even when conquest and conversion rhetorics are being used around you, that invitational rhetoric can be used for some kinds of communication. You are likely to be more successful in all aspects of your life if you are able to take in new information and seriously consider its application and relevance to an issue, recognize that others may believe differently from you, and genuinely try to understand others' positions. The invitational mode also enables you to secure important information, build community rather than competition, and create a safe environment for the sharing of ideas. A presentation focused on winning at the expense of someone else creates division among competitors, while the invitational mode is likely to create a more beneficial professional environment—one of safety, respect, and affirmation. As philosopher Janice Moulton notes, "A friendly, warm, nonadversarial manner surely does not interfere with persuading customers to buy, getting employees to carry out directions conscientiously, convincing juries, teaching students, getting help and cooperation from coworkers, and promotions from the boss."[32]

Even in environments that are predominantly conquest and conversion in nature, such as the legal context, opportunities for using invitational rhetoric exist. Speakers engage in pretrial conferences and bargaining, and there are increasing opportunities to resolve disputes by mediation in cases involving personal relations and labor relations. One example of invitational rhetoric used within the legal system is the approach used by family court judge Anne Kass in Albuquerque, New Mexico. She holds settlement conferences with divorcing couples to help them collaborate on workable solutions to the issues involved in divorce. She is interested in having the couples take a collaborative rather than an adversarial approach to divorce.[33]

Invitational Rhetoric and the Excitement of Adversarial Communication

Perhaps your uneasiness about invitational rhetoric has to do with the excitement and energy that can come from participating in the conquest and conversion modes of rhetoric. You might be the kind of person who enjoys the competitive, adversarial world. Perhaps you love a heated debate and find the experience of trying to get your viewpoint to prevail to be an energizing and exhilarating experience. You may see this kind of communication as a kind of sport or game that you enjoy playing. You have well-developed skills in crafting good arguments, speaking on your feet, and responding with well-timed comebacks and witty responses. In another version of this concern, you may feel that invitational rhetoric is a weak way of presenting ideas and communicates a lack of confidence. Invitational rhetoric would require that you change in significant ways, you might believe, and would significantly decrease your enjoyment of many communication interactions.

An energetic and spirited exchange of ideas can be fun, and we are not suggesting that such exchanges are not appropriate. These kinds of exchanges, however, are not appropriate for all situations. If the only way you know how to communicate with others is through conquest and conversion rhetorics, the results you are able to achieve will be limited. Learning how to employ other options can provide you with a communication repertoire that will allow you to enjoy a range of communication modes. Finally, there are ways to engage in energetic and spirited exchanges in which ideas truly are being discussed and worked through together that do not involve trying to win others over to your view. Lively discussions of ideas done for the purpose of expanding everyone's perspectives are almost always appropriate.

Addressing World Problems with Invitational Rhetoric

You may be feeling uncomfortable with invitational rhetoric because it implicitly suggests that you should not use communication to try to solve problems such as poverty, injustice, homelessness, war, or oppression. The assumptions that underlie invitational rhetoric suggest that you are to try to understand diverse perspectives, to welcome them as resources for your own thinking, to be willing to be changed by them, and not to try to change those who hold them, all of which seem to require a hands-off approach to problems you see in the world.

Does invitational rhetoric require that you consider being changed, for example, by the perspectives of neo-Nazis? How about the perspectives of corporate executives who cash out their stock options without informing their employees and investors that the company is about to fold? Are you to welcome the perspectives of those who crash planes into buildings to express their hatred of the United States? Are you to stand by when you see people being discriminated against because of their race or sex? Does invitational rhetoric require that every position go unchallenged and not be subjected to scrutiny? Are you to be so open minded that you simply shrug your shoulders when you encounter a condition in the world that you do not like?

Invitational rhetoric does not mean simply responding uncritically to problems you see. At least five options are available to you for engaging the problems of the world from an invitational perspective: (1) direct your communication to those who are seeking information on an issue; (2) use an understanding of distasteful perspectives to create conditions in which those perspectives are less likely to flourish; (3) create the conditions you want in the world instead of resisting the conditions you do not want; (4) enact the changes you would like to see in the world; and (5) reframe your understanding of the problem.

Targeting messages to uninformed audiences.   One option you can use to address a problem is to direct your communication to those individuals who are uninformed about it—those who are seeking information because they have not made up their minds. These are the people who are most likely to be interested in hearing from you. Focus your efforts on them instead of on those who already have clearly developed perspectives to which they are committed. You also can make sure, in situations where divergent opinions arise, that you give the fullest possible expression to your perspective and encourage others to do the same. In this way, those who are uninformed and undecided have the full benefit of multiple views on the problem.

Creation of conditions for potential change.   Another option available to you for engaging the larger world is to make an extra effort to understand those perspectives that are repugnant or distasteful and to use that understanding to address problems creatively. If you can come to an understanding of why a neo-Nazi perspective might make sense to someone, you are more likely to understand the conditions that are likely to produce such a perspective. You then can help to create different kinds of environments in which that viewpoint has less opportunity to flourish. By understanding how perspectives that are abhorrent to you make sense and are attractive to someone else, you can set about creating an environment in which individuals are likely to make other choices.

Exploring perspectives that are distasteful to you also generates new ideas. You cannot know where these explorations will take you. They might suggest solutions to problems or compromises among positions, they might set off chains of events you never would have expected, or they might create openings for new possibilities. Exploring others' ideas—no matter how distasteful—might provide the fresh thinking that will allow you to tackle and solve a problem successfully that you had not been able to solve from your own perspective. Engaging in the process of invitational rhetoric means that you do not know, at the start of the process, where you will end up. You enter a situation, seeking to address a problem, staying open to various possibilities, and trying not to close off any fruitful avenues for the further generation of ideas. As a result, this deliberate openness to transformation will bring you to places, thoughts, and solutions you could not have envisioned at the start of the process.

Creation of what is desired. Invitational speakers who seek to address problems also can focus on creating what they do want rather than resisting what they do not want. This act is one of moving toward something, not away from something. In this option, you focus on or pay attention to those things that you choose for your world—those aspects of the world that you see as positive. If you want the world to be an environmentally sound place, for example, you seek out, appreciate, and encourage instances where you see sound environmental practices going on around you. If you want a world where workers are paid equitable wages, you look around and find examples where workers are being paid fairly. You applaud and affirm these cases when you find them. You use these examples to try to recreate favorable conditions when you have opportunities in other places.

A number of scholars and activists from different fields suggest that creating what you want is much more effective than resisting what you do not want. They explain that resistance and opposition are ineffective options for creating change because what we resist persists.[34] To resist something grants it life and establishes it more firmly in place. Whatever you give your attention and energy to in the form of communication thrives and grows. Communication is creative—it generates or produces the nature of the reality in which we live. When you talk about what you do not want, you create more of it in your reality. By communicating about it and bestowing your belief on it, you reinforce it as reality, you strengthen it, you become its accomplice, and it remains a part of your life experience.

Two metaphors for the option of focusing on what you want rather than resisting what you do not want may help clarify the stance being suggested here. When you go through a buffet line in a cafeteria, you choose the foods you want to eat, but you do not ask the manager of the cafeteria to remove the foods you do not like. You let them stay on the buffet table and allow those who want to eat them to choose them. Similarly, when you walk through a clothing store, looking at all the clothes that are available, you do not petition against the ones you think are ugly. You simply seek out and pay attention to the ones that are attractive and interesting to you and let the others stay on the racks.[35] The same holds true for communication. You can choose to communicate about and focus on what you want in the world instead of demanding that the things you do not want be banished or removed.

As an invitational communicator, then, you understand that you do not need to make others' views line up with yours in order for you to be happy. To spend time in such a pursuit limits the information you have available for knowing and understanding. When you force your viewpoint on others, you already have decided that their perspectives offer nothing of value to you.

The war on drugs is an example of the benefits of creating a desired condition instead of resisting what is opposed. Widespread agreement exists that the war on drugs has not ended drug use but actually has increased it. The DARE [Drug Abuse Resistance Education] program, for example, based largely on messages of resistance to drugs, has been shown to be largely ineffective. The program's effects are diminished by the senior year of high school and, in fact, drug use by suburban high school students who have completed the program tends to increase. A 10-year study on DARE's impact found that the program has no effect on students by the time they are 20 years old.[36]

In contrast to DARE is a drug-prevention program implemented by the National Center on Addiction and Substance Abuse (CASA) called CASASTART [Striving Together to Achieve Rewarding Tomorrows]. Instead of sending broad anti-drug messages to entire student bodies, CASASTART workers focus on individual students, asking them about and then trying to eliminate the problems they are facing in their lives: "It works one-on-one to lead them in a different direction." After two years of CASASTART pilot projects, researchers found students using and selling fewer drugs, participating in less violent crime, and developing closer friendships. They also were more likely to pass to the next grade level, compared with youth outside the program.[37] The focus in the program is on creating the desired conditions instead of resisting unwanted ones.

Enactment.   If you seek to address the problems in the world, you can do so and still remain in the invitational mode by making the choice to engage in enactment—displaying in your own life the changes you desire. In this option, you embody the world as you would like it to be, enacting your commitments in your daily life. Sonia Johnson recommends that we begin living the desired life fully in the present: "Live today as you want the world to be."[38] She gives as an example how peace can be created in the world through this option of enactment: People often "say that, their goal being peace, naturally they are going to have to bomb and bomb and massacre and rape and pillage and torture and lay waste and then—this is the place at which I used to feel as if I were the only person on earth who hadn't caught on—suddenly, miraculously, there will come a magical moment, a moment when some sort of alchemy takes place, and—*voila!*—peace!" She suggests instead "that there is only one way to have peace and that is to be peaceful right now.

We have understood that, because the means are the ends, *how* we behave is *what* we get."[39] Cultural critic bell hooks[40] suggests a similar approach to change with her concept of enactment, which she defines as the lived practice of interaction so that your life is "a living example" of your commitments and beliefs.[41] Writer Gloria Anzaldúa echoes these notions of enactment when she suggests, "I change myself, I change the world."[42]

Reframing of perspective.   Another way in which you can create change is to focus your change efforts on your own communication choices. The option of reframing suggests that you have a choice about how you label and view conditions in the world. You create your world through your communication choices, and what you see in the world can be changed with a shift in those choices. Because you can reframe what you see by choosing a different label, you may discover that what you once labeled a *problem*, for example, can be viewed as an *opportunity*. To label and view an administrator as *stupid* and *insensitive*, for example, makes railing against him an easy and appropriate response to his behavior. A change in the labels for his behavior to *overworked* and *lacking the resources he needs to do his job well*, in contrast, suggests responses to him that were not available to you before.

You also can choose to see an issue or situation from the other's perspective rather than only from your perspective. You may believe, for example, that a group of people in another country should enjoy the same living conditions you do. You may feel that you should work to change their lives so that they have washing machines, television sets, and automobiles. If you reframe your observation from their point of view, however, you may discover that they have effective ways of washing clothes that produce clean clothes, that they enjoy the company of friends and are part of caring and stimulating communities because of the absence of television, and that a lack of cars contributes to a peaceful pace of life. You may discover, in this kind of reframing, that there is no problem where you once perceived one.

The option of reframing may strike you as denying reality. Recall, however, that you get to choose the labels for your perceptions, and these labels are interpretations that create your reality. If you change your labels, you create a different reality, so you are always denying some potential realities through your communication choices in the very act of choosing your labels. There is nothing inherently superior about choosing the labels that require that you see conditions in the world as problems. A shift in your chosen terms may enable you to see solutions you did not see before or help you understand the different perspectives of those around you.

Invitational rhetoric, then, is one mode of interacting in the world but not the only one. We suggest that its addition to your communication repertoire may enable you to accomplish your communication goals more effectively in both personal and professional situations. As you explore invitational rhetoric in the remainder of this book and as you practice it in your presentations, we hope you will discover the positive benefits of inviting, facilitating, and deliberately seeking out opportunities for transformation in your interactions with others.

Choosing
Interactional Goals

When you make the decision to enter a communication situation, you have a reason for doing so. This is your interactional goal—what you hope to accomplish by initiating or joining an interaction. It is what you want to have happen as a result of your decision to speak. The idea of invitation introduced in the last chapter is a good starting place for understanding how interactional goals function. When you host a party, you generally have a reason for doing so. Maybe you want to celebrate a birthday or have friends in to watch the Super Bowl or play Cranium. When you invite friends to come over, you let them know the purpose behind the invitation. An interactional goal functions the same way. It provides you and your audience with a clear sense of why you are choosing to speak.

The interactional goal you select depends on the context or situation in which you are speaking. Rhetorical theorist Lloyd Bitzer labels this context the *rhetorical situation*, in which "speakers or writers create . . . discourse" to respond to an exigence—a need, problem, or defect in a situation.[1] When we speak, our discourse comes into existence because of some "specific condition or situation which invites utterance."[2] Another rhetorical theorist, Kenneth Burke, adds to our understanding of how we respond to situations in his discussion of rhetoric as "a *strategy for encompassing a situation*."[3] Rhetoric or communication is an answer to the question "posed by the situation."[4] Your presentations are examples of rhetorical strategies designed to address or encompass situations that you believe require a response. When you give a presentation, you are labeling a situation in a particular way and choosing a response on the basis of that definition. Your interactional goal is the strategy you choose for responding to that situation.

There are five interactional goals or purposes for speaking: (1) to assert individuality; (2) to articulate a perspective; (3) to build community; (4) to seek adherence; and (5) to discover knowledge and belief.

To Assert Individuality

All speakers continuously engage in communication that reveals who they are as individuals. You reveal your identity and your uniqueness, for example, through your clothing, where you live, the friends you have, your major in school, your favorite kind of music, and your choice of occupation. In some instances, however, the assertion of individuality is the main purpose of your communication, so this interactional goal becomes the focus of a presentation. In a presentation designed to assert individuality, projection of your personality and assertion of who you are as a unique individual receive primary emphasis. You reveal something about your values, beliefs, attributes, roles, and/or experiences to help your audience members come to a better understanding of who you are.

Presentations to assert individuality are used in a variety of situations. The workplace is one of the most common contexts for presentations focused on asserting individuality. In a job interview, for example, asserting individuality is your primary goal. You want the interviewer to recognize your abilities and fit with the organization, and you want to make such a good impression that you stand out from the other candidates for the position. Every aspect of your presentation is geared toward achieving this end, including how you answer questions, the questions you ask, how you dress, and the attitude you convey. Once hired, the process of asserting individuality continues. When you introduce yourself to your new coworkers, you are asserting individuality. Every day on the job, you have opportunities to let others learn more about you through your interpersonal communication, formal presentations, reports, memos, and e-mail messages.

Although the workplace is a common place where asserting individuality occurs, interactions as a part of conversations with acquaintances, friends, and family members also can be presentations of self-assertion. When you are introduced to someone you do not know, you are asserting individuality as you engage in small talk with the new acquaintance. When you want to impress your mother-in-law, make a good impression on the faculty of the department where you hope to attend graduate school, or be noticed by the cute guy on the floor above you in your dorm, asserting individuality is your goal.

You cannot possibly communicate every facet of yourself to everyone you encounter and probably would not want to if you could. The process of asserting individuality, then, involves a selection process. When this is your interactional goal, you continuously make choices about what to reveal about yourself. You disclose different kinds of information to someone on a first date than you do in a medical school interview, for example. The choices you make about how to assert your individuality depend on your expectations for the interaction, your audience, and the setting in which the interaction takes place.

Your choices in a presentation on asserting individuality also occur within a larger context, which has an impact on the nature of such a presentation. Asserting individuality is a very Western notion grounded in individualism—the privileging of the self over the collective or the group. In the United States, where autonomy and independence are highly valued, presentations to assert individuality are common. In cultures in which the collective is valued over the individual self, however, efforts to preserve consensus and harmony far outweigh the assertion of individuality. You would be much less likely to engage in presentations designed to assert individuality in these cultures, and if you did, the strategies available to you for revealing information about yourself would be much more limited. In Japan, for instance, communicators tend to seek unanimous agreement or consensus on an issue, and preservation of the collective harmony of the group is privileged over individual expressions of difference or individuality.

The goal of asserting individuality also must be balanced against the interests and needs of others. Individuals who talk only about themselves or who believe that everything they have to say is so important that they must share their perspectives on every subject are examples of the excessive assertion of individuality. Similarly, the speaker who is asked to speak to an organization for half an hour but goes on and on, convinced that what she has to say is more important than what anyone else might contribute, is engaging in assertion of individuality at the expense of the contributions of others. All of these examples serve as reminders that, to be most effective, the goal of asserting individuality must reflect a balance between the assertion of self and concern for and interest in others. Individuality is a value but not at the expense of everyone else and their interests.

The goal of asserting individuality, then, is centered on the act of self-expression. In presentations designed to assert individuality, you attempt to reveal aspects of your identity and your uniqueness. The cultural context in which you are speaking and a concern for the interests and contributions of others in the interaction mitigate the choices you make in constructing these kinds of presentations.

To Articulate a Perspective

A second interactional goal for presentations is articulating a perspective. When this is your goal, you share information or present your viewpoint on a subject so that all participants in the interaction have a better understanding of that subject. Articulating a perspective requires that you share information or express a perspective as fully and carefully as possible.

Articulating a perspective is different from advocating for a position. When you articulate a perspective, you may believe strongly in your perspective and may hope that your audience members find it attractive enough to consider adopting. But your goal is not to persuade them to adopt it. Your interest is in explaining the perspective, developing it in all of its richness and complexity, and giving it the best opportunity to be understood. Presentations focused on articulating a perspective are designed to offer, not to advocate, a perspective.

Presentations in which your goal is to articulate a perspective range from simply sharing information—sharing perspectives developed by others—to offering your own opinion. When an airlines agent provides information about flight times and fares to a potential traveler, a supervisor explains to a new employee the correct way to fill out his timesheet, or a teacher explains to her first-grade class how to write the letters of the alphabet, information is being shared. In other instances, you may have a perspective but make an effort to present a balanced view. In a professional situation, for example, you may be asked to present a report on your findings about the advantages and disadvantages of moving the organization for which you work to a new location. You advocate neither for nor against such a move in a presentation in which you articulate a perspective but lay out the relevant information for making the decision. At other times, you hold a particular perspective and offer it to others. In a discussion with friends about the movie you just saw, for example, you might offer your opinion about how good the movie was. You are not interested in getting others to accept your views but in explaining why you feel as you do about the movie. All of these are examples of presentations to articulate a perspective.

Articulating a perspective is used more than any other interactional goal because it is the foundation of any presentation. You must give your audience some information as the starting point upon which you will build the rest of your presentation. For example, when you give a presentation in which you assert individuality, you also are articulating a perspective. The nature of your unique perspective is the starting point for asserting your individuality. Virtually every presentation, then, has some element devoted to articulating a perspective. You need to make choices about how much and what information to include and how you want to present it to an audience so that the information provides the necessary foundation for your other interactional goal(s).

You may be wondering why the goal of articulating a perspective is not labeled *presenting information* or *informing*. Although presenting information certainly is part of the process, the idea of informing does not adequately convey that the presentation of information necessarily involves the presentation of a perspective. This is because language is always a "carrier of tendency."[5] Rhetorical theorist Richard M. Weaver describes this characteristic of language by suggesting that all rhetoric is sermonic: As communicators, we are "preachers in private or public capacities. We have no sooner uttered words than we have given impulse to other people to look at the world, or some small part of it, in our way."[6]

A second reason why the act of informing conveys a perspective is that you cannot discuss everything there is to know about a subject, so presenting information is always subjective as you select what you will talk about from all of the possibilities available. Your choices of what to discuss make your process of informing different from someone else's and constitute your perspective. The notion of articulating a perspective, then, is meant to convey that the process involves a particular and unique perspective—it is not an objective process.

If you are a travel agent booking a cruise for a client, for example, you might begin by discussing how fun a cruise can be, by noting how inexpensive cruises are for the money, or by describing a favorite cruise that you took to Mexico. Each of these introductions carries with it the suggestion that the client look at the world as you do and focuses the audience's attention in a particular direction. Each subsequent decision you make in your presentation does the same—your choice of organizational pattern, the ways in which you elaborate ideas, or your manner of delivery. Every decision you make about the presentation contributes to the creation of a particular perspective on the information you are offering.

The term *articulating a perspective* captures the idea that even when you are not advocating on behalf of a viewpoint, that viewpoint is a perspective. You cannot ever offer information in a neutral manner, and the interactional goal of articulating a perspective acknowledges this fact and reminds you that every statement you make, no matter how objective or factual it may seem, communicates something about your worldview.

To Build Community

At times, the interactional goal you choose is designed to build community. This may involve creating a sense of community where there is none, maintaining an existing sense of community, or restoring community when it has been disrupted. *Community* describes a group of individuals who share core values, ideas, interests, beliefs, or practices and feel connected to one another as a result of what they share. When community is a value, qualities such as connection and shared interests are privileged over individual interests. When you make the interactional goal of creating community primary, you are concerned about and committed to the stability and preservation of the knowledge, themes, beliefs, values, and practices that form the core allegiances of the community you are addressing.

Presentations designed to build community function differently in collectivist and individualistic cultures.[7] Presentations in collectivist cultures tend to incorporate reminders of the community that already exists because there is less need to build community. In individualistic cultures, however, there are many occasions on which you want or need to bring people together in ways that encourage them to recognize themselves as a community so that they can work together in productive ways.

Presentations to build community are of three main types: (1) to reinforce a sense of community when it already exists; (2) to create community when it does not exist; and (3) to create community when it has been disrupted. In a presentation designed to reinforce community, your primary task is to remind audience members about what they already share with one another. You want to reiterate and reemphasize the core commitments that are central to the group, which you can do in a number of ways. Asking the group to engage in a shared ritual—reciting the Pledge of Allegiance, singing "We Shall Overcome," or marching together in an annual parade, for example—can remind them of the community they share and reinvigorate their commitment to that community. Telling stories of important shared events or repeating an event that created group cohesiveness are other ways in which community can be recreated. Holiday parties in organizations or celebrations such as Fourth of July picnics are designed to reaffirm community when it already exists. To maintain the harmony already present in a community, your focus is on strengthening the social bond, calling the audience to a collective experience, and reinforcing and validating the common worldview.

A second type of presentation in which building community is the goal is when a sense of community does not exist and you want to create it. You might want to try to create community, for example, among new team members in an organization or among neighbors in a newly formed neighborhood association. In these instances, you would want to focus on creating identification among the individuals in the group so that they are able to work together effectively. Your efforts would be directed at creating knowledge and common perspectives, encouraging members of the nascent community to get to know and trust one another, and creating connections of various kinds among the group members.

You also might want to create community when an already existing community has been disrupted. In such cases, you attempt to recreate order and shared meaning, to energize the group around the common perspectives the group members once shared, and to neutralize obstacles to harmony. Focusing on past shared experiences, the successes they have had, the sorrows they have shared, and the commitments they hold in common are your primary efforts in this situation. The most common situation in which restoration of community is the subject of presentations is when conflict has disrupted a community. Perhaps a faction of a church has split from the main congregation, a strike has disrupted a community divided along the lines of labor and management, or a conflict between two coworkers is harming the collegial atmosphere of a work environment. Other examples are when a new manager has been brought into a work group or a divorce has disrupted a group of friends. Abraham Lincoln's Gettysburg Address, in which he sought to unify the North and the South, is an example of this kind of presentation. In these situations, a community that once existed and was valued has split apart. When communities are disrupted and you are trying to restore community, your focus is on asking the members to recall and remember what they once had together.

To Seek Adherence

In some instances, you direct your efforts toward asking others to consider accepting your way of thinking or acting in ways that you advocate. You encourage others to make a change in a particular direction that you suggest. In these cases, you are seeking adherence. You are seeking to persuade your audience by influencing their attitudes and/or their behaviors.

You may choose to seek adherence as your interactional goal in a variety of situations. Sales and marketing are primary contexts for this goal. Selling shoes, houses, cellular phones, or advertising constitute presentations in which you seek adherence. At other times, you want to sell proposals or ideas. In these cases, you advocate a particular option because you believe it will work best for an organization or individual. Each of these situations involves seeking adherence. You believe strongly in a product or plan and its benefits and would like your audience members to choose it over others available to realize those benefits for themselves.

Another common situation in which your interactional goal is to seek adherence is when you are in a supervisory role. You may be responsible for producing particular results within an organization, and, as a supervisor, you want to persuade your employees to produce the kind of work required to create the desired results. As a parent, you also sometimes seek adherence as you guide your child in particular directions. A mother might ask her son to consider carefully the consequences of dropping a particular class or to consider certain factors when selecting a college to attend.

The goal of seeking adherence may seem antithetical to invitational rhetoric. After all, many of the assumptions of invitational rhetoric (understanding rather than persuasion as the purpose of communication, equality of the speaker and audience, diverse perspectives as resources to be welcomed rather than changed, change as self-chosen, and the requirement of willingness to yield your own perspective) seem to contradict the effort to seek adherence. There are ways to engage in seeking adherence, though, that do not violate the principles of invitational rhetoric.

One way in which seeking adherence can be invitational is when you choose the full articulation of your perspective as your primary strategy. You offer your audience members as complete a picture as you can of your perspective, giving the clearest, most comprehensive, and most respectful articulation of your beliefs that you know how to do. If the audience members have the opportunity to see a situation clearly for themselves because you are offering as full a picture as you can of a subject without manipulation or deception, they may choose to change. Burke suggests the importance of offering a complete perspective when he asks communicators to "advocate their choice by *filling it out!* That is: let each say all he can by way of giving body to the perspective inherent in his choice. Let each show the scope, range, relevancy, accuracy, applicability of the perspective. . . . And only after each has been so filled out, can we evaluate among them."[8] Offering your perspective as carefully, thoughtfully, and completely as possible is one way in which seeking adherence can be accomplished invitationally. A presentation to seek adherence would look very much like a presentation to articulate a perspective when this particular strategy is used.

A second way in which you can create a presentation designed to seek adherence and still remain invitational is by including in your presentation opportunities for you to learn about and understand the audience's perspective. One common way for doing this is to ask for questions at the end of your presentation. Instead of assuming that you have the superior perspective that you want to impose on your audience, you enter the interaction believing that you hold the best perspective but are willing to alter that perspective once you hear from your audience members. The perspectives audience members share with you may provide you with information that you can use to suggest an idea from which they can benefit. More important, however, listening to their perspectives also may encourage you to change your mind on the subject.

Seeking adherence can be done invitationally as well by making very clear to your audience members that they have freedom of choice. A speaker who communicates to audience members that they have choices and have the right to exercise them creates a very different atmosphere for an audience than a speaker who argues for a point of view as if it were the only reasonable view to hold. When you speak to your audience members in a way that not only acknowledges but values their perspectives and ability to make their own choices about their lives, they will be more willing to listen, knowing that they can choose whether or not to change.

The interactional goal of seeking adherence can be enacted in ways that honor the integrity of others and their viewpoints. Such an approach to persuasion is more respectful of the range of perspectives on any given issue. Individuals are more willing to change when they do not feel coerced, and the changes that do occur typically are more thoughtful, better integrated, and longer lasting than ones produced in more manipulative ways.

To Discover Knowledge and Belief

In some interactions, the speaker and audience are unsure of their views on a situation or uncertain about how to handle something. They come together to sort out the information, experiences, and possible actions available to them. The interactional goal in this situation is to discover knowledge and belief. Together, the speaker and audience members explore a subject to discover what they know and believe about it and how best to respond on the basis of that information. To discover knowledge and belief, then, is substantially different from the other four interactional goals in that you do not enter the interaction with an idea or a proposal you already have developed or that you already know you believe. Instead, you genuinely do not know what you think or believe or how to handle a situation. You hold no perspective yet or, at best, have a sketchy, tentative one and allow the discussion to direct the development of your perspective.

If the interactional goal of discovering knowledge and belief is to be successful, it must take place in a context in which talk is valued as a means of coming to know and making decisions. Everyone involved must share a belief in the possibility of arriving at an acceptable solution or decision by talking it through. This kind of talk is valued in the U.S. educational system, where many classes incorporate some kind of sharing of opinions beginning with show and tell in kindergarten and progressing to more formalized discussions and debates in high school and college.

In many cultures within and outside of the United States, joint talk to discover or create ideas is not seen as appropriate or useful. In a situation with a highly authoritarian parent, for example, the goal of discovering knowledge and belief between parent and child is very unlikely. A father who "knows best" and does not tolerate challenges to his authority probably will not be willing to hear the opinions of his daughter about when she is old enough to date. In China, with its tradition of authoritarian government, discussions are not seen as a legitimate way to develop ideas. Instead, ideas are supposed to come from experts and authorities, not through a discussion among a group of non-experts.

In presentations to discover knowledge and belief, participants must be committed to the use of questions as a way to learn and understand. By their very nature, questions invite levels of reflection on both content and process. Questions also can produce a collective energy and commitment among participants that is highly motivating and satisfying. When a questioning framework rather than one of assertion is used, participants can be more creative and collaborative, and the answers generated "can serve to open up conversation for deeper discovery."[9]

The interactional goal of discovering knowledge and belief is selected most often in two situations: (1) When you want to generate new ideas or find solutions to a problem that take advantage of all of the expertise in a group; and (2) When you are unsure or unclear about what you know or believe and use talk with others to articulate your knowledge or beliefs.

The most common situation in which you construct presentations to discover knowledge and belief is when you want help solving a problem or generating ideas. You understand that by involving the input of many others, you are likely to come up with better solutions or richer ideas. The group you engage may be a work group or an ad hoc group that you bring together for the sole purpose of helping you think. For example, let's assume that you are a member of a university department faced with how to distribute merit pay. The chair of the department has asked you to serve as chair of the merit committee. Numerous mechanisms exist for determining merit pay, and you do not want to make the decision about what method to select without having the input of the entire faculty. You call a meeting and facilitate a discussion that allows multiple proposals to be voiced and discussed. After all views have been considered, the group selects the one with the most potential. Similarly, perhaps you are the advisor to a school newspaper and are trying to decide what kinds of changes in format would be beneficial. You realize that you do not know what students think of the newspaper, and you call a meeting at which students can express their views.

The examples discussed above involve workplace situations. This is not the only context, however, in which the interactional goal of discovering knowledge and belief comes into play. When a friend talks to you about the difficulties he is having in an intimate relationship and you help him figure out what to do, you are using this interactional goal. When your daughter comes home from junior high, discouraged by always being picked last for teams in her P. E. class, you help her see what her options are. Perhaps your partner is trying to decide whether to change careers, and together you brainstorm other career possibilities. All of these are examples of discovering knowledge and belief in action.

A second situation for which presentations to discover knowledge and belief are needed is when members of a group are unsure or unclear about what they know or believe on a subject. They talk through their ideas to express what previously was unstated or even unconscious. A group that gathers to develop its mission statement, for example, may have a vague idea that there are some principles and commitments that unite all of the group members. As they think together about their mission, these principles are voiced and language is selected to communicate the group's commitment. Theologian Nelle Morton has labeled this phenomenon *hearing into speech*,[10] a process whereby hearing someone generates new insights that the speakers themselves did not know they had.

Through the discovery process, you not only arrive at an opinion or decision, but you learn how productive different opinions and ideas can be in helping frame an issue more fully. In the end, you often have a more creative and comprehensive understanding than you would have developed by tackling an issue on your own. Furthermore, the process of discovering knowledge and belief itself may strengthen group solidarity and foster a greater commitment to the ideas or solution the group has generated simply because the group members themselves came up with the ideas.

When you choose the interactional goal of discovering knowledge and belief, you are assuming the role of a facilitator. When you adopt this position in a formal presentational situation, you have primary responsibility for initiating and guiding a group discussion. You are not there to control what others say but to ensure that participants feel comfortable sharing their opinions, thoughts, and feelings about an issue. You are responsible for framing the subject for discussion, guiding those present through an analysis and investigation of the subject, and summarizing the insights produced by the discussion. Even in informal situations—talking with a child or a roommate, for instance—you assume the role of facilitator, although the steps in the process are not as obvious as in a formal meeting. Regardless of the degree of formality, however, the essence of your role is the same: You act much like a midwife, coaching and assisting the group to share, think through, and talk over various perspectives with a goal of coming to a better understanding of issues, generating new ideas, and perhaps reaching a decision.

Because the interactional goal of discovering knowledge and belief involves a group in the decision-making process, to attempt to complete this process in a short classroom presentation is unrealistic. If you do want to try out this goal in a presentational speaking course, devote your presentation to just one step of the process—generating ideas, for example. Another option is to engage in the process of discovering knowledge and belief in only a small segment of a presentation in which another interactional goal is primary. You may ask your audience to generate definitions of something—the word *friend*, for example—that you then use in the body of your speech. Or you may ask audience members to offer a few examples of their expectations about something, which you later incorporate into your presentation. You cannot expect to resolve complicated issues in the course of a 5- or even a 10-minute presentation. Limit this goal in classroom situations to smaller, more manageable segments that are possible within the amount of time that you have.

Multiple Interactional Goals

We have been talking about interactional goals as if you will select only one for any given presentation. Although you are likely to have a primary goal, most presentations have multiple goals. You may have as your goal seeking adherence, for example, as when you want the approval of your manager to change the accounting process for a project. As part of that presentation, you need to explain why the proposed change makes sense in light of the overall project, which requires you to articulate a perspective or put together information about the nature and status of the project. At the same time, you are seeking to present yourself in a positive light to your manager—to have her see you as a creative individual—so the goal of asserting individuality also is operating.

Not only are you faced with multiple interactional goals, but you may need to decide which goal is most important for what you want to accomplish and make it your primary focus. A teacher in a classroom, for example, might be presented with a group of disruptive students. He could respond with the goal of asserting individuality by focusing on how he is personally insulted by the students' behavior and their lack of respect for what he is trying to do in the classroom. He could adopt the interactional goal of creating community, choosing to engage in a series of activities designed to create cohesiveness among the students. Yet another way he could approach the situation is by engaging in a discussion designed to discover why the class is choosing to behave so disruptively, structuring his interaction with them around the goal of discovering knowledge and belief. Although all of these goals might be at the heart of the teacher's presentation, the teacher would want to decide which goal is most important to him and design a presentation that features that goal.

Interactional goals, then, are the core of a presentation. The goal you select names a rhetorical situation in some way and encompasses your response to it. It becomes your chosen strategy for addressing the need you have defined as operating in this situation. The five interactional goals—to assert individuality, to articulate a perspective, to create community, to seek adherence, and to discover knowledge and belief—encompass most of the speaking situations you are likely to encounter. The goal you choose for your presentation serves as your guide for the other decisions you will make about your presentation.

3

CREATING
ENVIRONMENT

With the identification or selection of your interactional goal or goals for your presentation, you are ready to begin thinking about your specific speaking context. You want to consider how, through your presentation, you can create an environment that will facilitate possibilities for growth and change. As the speaker, you want to do what you can to encourage audience members to consider your perspective carefully as well as to share their perspectives with you.

Creating External Conditions for Transformation

To create an environment that allows audience members to be receptive to transformation, you want to create particular external conditions in the speaking situation. When these conditions are present in an interaction, the possibilities for transformation on the part of the speaker and the audience increase, and audience members feel free to contribute to the interaction. Both you and the audience are encouraged to consider new perspectives, and the opportunity to understand one another is enhanced. As you prepare and deliver your presentation, the communication options you select either will facilitate or impede the development of these conditions in your particular speaking situation.

The four external conditions you want to create in the speaking environment are freedom, safety, value, and openness.[1] Freedom allows your audience to choose what to believe and how to act, safety creates an environment in which audience members feel they are able to share ideas without retribution, value is appreciation of the contributions that audience members make to the interaction, and openness is an eagerness to explore and understand diverse perspectives.

Freedom

Freedom is the power to choose or decide and involves providing your audience with more than one option. It allows each participant in the interaction to make decisions about what to believe and how to act. When freedom is present in a speaking situation, there is no pressure on audience members to make the same choices as the speaker.

You can develop freedom in a speaking situation in a number of ways. Freedom is created when you do not place restrictions on the nature of the exchange. Participants feel free to bring any topic into the interaction, and all assumptions are open to questioning and rethinking. If audience members challenge assumptions you consider sacred or bring up topics you would rather not talk about, you do not exclude them from participating in the interaction or discontinue your interaction with them.[2]

Probably the most important way by which you can create the external condition of freedom is to convey to your audience members that they do not have to adopt your perspective. If your audience members are truly free, they can choose not to accept your viewpoint without fear of reprisal, ridicule, punishment, or humiliation. You communicate to them that your relationship with them does not depend on their sharing your views.

The condition of freedom is at the heart of an invitation to transformation because whether to change or not is a choice. If your interactional goal is seeking adherence, for example, you help create the condition of freedom by conveying that changing the minds or behavior of audience members is not the most important thing for you in your interaction with them. You are more interested in maintaining your connection with the audience members, understanding them, learning from them, and enjoying the process of interaction.

A commitment to the condition of freedom means, then, that you cannot control the end result of the process of presentational speaking. You enter the situation, inviting others to explore a subject with you, and you trust that what you create together will be beneficial for everyone involved. You are willing to live with and even to appreciate the "creative, messy, unfolding"[3] of perspectives that your presentation engenders because you are committed to the freedom of the others with whom you are interacting.

⸮ Safety

Safety is the condition of feeling free from danger and feeling secure physically, emotionally, and intellectually. Safety includes the experience of well-being at a physical level as well as confidence that when individuals express their feelings and ideas, they will be treated with respect and care. When you create safety in a speaking situation, audience members trust you, are not fearful of interacting with you, and feel you are working with and not against them. Safety is a prerequisite for transformation because if participants in an interaction do not feel safe, they are reluctant to share ideas, which are the stimuli for the emergence of new perspectives.

To ensure safety for your audience members is difficult because safety does not have the same meaning for everyone. What feels safe to one audience member may make another feel very uncomfortable. Just as some individuals "feel safe in a small town, surrounded by friends and family in a wood-frame house with the screen door unlocked and windows wide open," others "feel safer surrounded by expensive security alarms, gates, and impenetrable walls."[4] In a speaking situation, some participants may feel safest in an intimate circle, engaging in high self-disclosure. Others feel safest sitting in rows of chairs in a large lecture hall, where there is no expectation for them to reveal personal information. Similarly, safety for some might mean energetic participation in heated debate, while for others, such participation feels unsafe. In some situations, safety is less a matter of personal preference and more an issue of potentially severe consequences. Certain audiences do not feel safe expressing perspectives that are different from those of their supervisors, church officials, or governments. You want to discover, then, how your audience members define safety and how safe they feel in the environment in which you are going to speak.

If your decisions about how to create safety depend on your audience's perspective on safety, you want to find ways to gather this information from your audience members. One way to discover their views is to ask audience members to construct their own communication guidelines for the interaction. Typically, the guidelines that groups generate cover some topics explicitly related to safety. They might develop ground rules such as "speak only for yourself, not others"; "listen carefully to the perspectives of others"; "treat others respectfully"; and "speak briefly and share speaking time." If the group creates its own guidelines, you will learn how the audience views safety. You then can use this information to create an environment that is likely to feel safe for most participants. You also want to work with your audience members to be sure that the guidelines the group develops are followed.

Another way in which you can help create the condition of safety for your audience members is by modeling how to respond to others in ways that facilitate a feeling of safety. If you listen to the ideas and feelings of others with respect and care and do not hurt, degrade, or belittle them or their beliefs, you will show that you truly value all opinions and perspectives. If an audience member challenges you, demonstrate openness and make a real effort to understand the perspective of the challenger. You also want to model that you feel safe yourself, perhaps by taking some risks. If self-disclosure is a feature that means safety for your audience, you might want to talk about your children or tell a story in which you demonstrate that you made a mistake. Such disclosures can communicate to audience members that they also can feel free to take risks. Use yourself as "'exhibit A' to prove this is a safe place."[5] As management consultant Annette Simmons suggests: "If you feel safe, you communicate that to everyone. If you don't, you can't. A relaxed, confident, peaceful composure tells the group that you, at least, believe in this process and believe in them."[6]

人 Value

Value is a belief in the intrinsic or inherent worth of each individual. It is a condition that suggests that each participant is a significant and critical part of the interaction because each individual's perspective is unique. To gain a full understanding of an issue, everyone's perspective must be heard and appreciated. If some perspectives are privileged and others are ignored or devalued, new understandings cannot emerge. When value is created in a speaking situation, audience members feel that they have something important to contribute to the interaction and that the speaker cares about and appreciates their contributions.

One way in which you can convey that you value your listeners is by inviting and encouraging all participants in the interaction to be heard. By structuring opportunities for discussion into your presentation and using question-and-answer sessions, for example, you invite audience members' perspectives. You may want to encourage shy members in your audience to have their perspectives heard if you can find ways to do this without violating their feelings of safety. You might ask them, for example, to write down questions or comments, which you then collect.

If you truly value your audience members, you must listen carefully to them. By taking their ideas and feelings seriously, you suggest that what they have to say matters. You respect them enough "to view them as subjects, worthy of a hearing, not just objects"[7] to be used to accomplish your goals or meet your needs. As psychologist Michael P. Nichols suggests, "To listen is to pay attention, take an interest, care about, take to heart, validate, acknowledge, be moved . . . appreciate."[8]

Sonja recently attended a colloquium of faculty members at her university, where the speaker presented a paper and asked the audience for ideas about how to revise it to give it a stronger conceptual framework. Sonja took the speaker's request seriously and offered a suggestion for such a framework. The speaker nodded and went on talking about her experience of writing the paper. Sonja and the other audience members got the message very clearly that the speaker really did not want suggestions for revision and did not value those that were offered. The colloquium ended soon after.

Listening in a way that communicates value is different from how we usually listen. Often, we listen to develop comebacks to the other speaker. In these situations, we often are not really listening because we are busy formulating our own responses. Your task when you want to create the condition of value is to listen so that you really do understand—to the fullest degree possible—the perspective being articulated. When audience members' perspectives vary widely from yours, try to learn more about the individuals in your audience to discover why they might have developed the perspectives they hold. Make the effort to think from the standpoint of your audience members, and try to make their perspectives vivid in your own mind. These kinds of listening go a long way toward the creation of the condition of value in the speaking situation.

Openness

If communication is to create an environment in which transformation may occur, no perspectives can be deliberately excluded. Both speaker and audience must seek out and consider as many perspectives as possible. The condition of openness, then, is a fourth characteristic required for a potentially transformative environment. An attitude of openness involves genuine curiosity about perspectives different from yours.

Openness is the operationalization of the assumption of invitational rhetoric that diverse perspectives are resources. Both you and your audience members acknowledge that the greater the diversity of the perspectives you encounter, the greater the understanding you can have of a subject. Diverse perspectives, then, increase opportunities for transformation, so they are approached thoughtfully and respectfully with an attitude of appreciation and delight.

Analyzing the Speaking Environment

In the ideal speaking situation, you want the conditions of freedom, safety, value, and openness to be present. To create such conditions, you must assess your speaking environment to discover the elements that are available to you to assist you in this process. If your analysis of the speaking environment reveals that certain factors are likely to facilitate a transformative environment, you know these are factors to emphasize as you begin to form your ideas into a presentation. If other factors in the situation appear likely to be obstacles to transformation, you want to adjust them or neutralize their impact so that they do not hinder the creation of the conditions of freedom, safety, value, and openness.

The four primary components of the speaking environment to consider when creating the four conditions for transformation are: (1) setting; (2) audience; (3) speaker; and (4) subject. Below are lists of questions to stimulate your thinking about each of these components. Your goal is to discover the factors that are likely to foster or prevent your creation of the conditions of freedom, safety, value, and openness. These questions are only starting points. The details of your particular speaking situation undoubtedly will suggest other environmental factors that you will want to consider. At the end of the lists of questions are some examples of how you might use these questions to discover the factors in the speaking environment that contribute to or detract from the creation of freedom, safety, value, and openness.

Setting

Date. What is the date on which you are speaking? Is there anything unusual or significant about it for either you or your audience?

Hour. At what time of day are you speaking? Is it early? Late? At a time when you and your audience members are functioning at peak levels?

Meeting place. What are the characteristics of the place in which you are speaking? Is it indoors or outdoors? What is the shape and size of the space? Are there acoustical problems? What is the temperature? What kinds of lights are available in the room? What is the noise level in the room? Are there features of the room that might function as distractions for the audience? Will the audience be standing, sitting on chairs, or sitting on the floor? How are the chairs arranged? In rows? In a circle?

Size of audience. How large is your audience? Are you speaking to one person? To a small group? To a large group? Can the space accommodate your audience comfortably? _why?_

Purpose for gathering. What is the purpose of the event, meeting, or interaction at which your presentation will be given? To conduct business? To socialize? To solve a problem? To reinforce community ties?

Order of events. What or who precedes and follows your presentation? Are other presentations planned? On what subjects? How long has your audience been listening to presentations before yours? Are food and refreshments to be served and, if so, when?

Time constraints. How much time do you have for your presentation?

Presence of an interpreter. Will someone be translating your presentation into another language? Will someone be signing your presentation for deaf members of your audience? If so, do you need to adjust your presentation so that audience members relying on the interpretation feel safe, comfortable, and able to contribute? Do you need to make adjustments so that the presence of the interpreter does not distract other audience members?

Time Your Speech.

Audience

Knowledge of subject. How much do your audience members know about the subject of your presentation?

Interest in subject. Do your audience members care about your subject? To what degree?

Perspective on subject. What are the perspectives of your audience members on your subject? If the subject is controversial, what positions do your audience members hold on it? What experiences of audience members are likely to influence the perspectives they hold? What demographic variables of the audience—age, sex, economic status, religious affiliation, political affiliation, or cultural identity, for example—are likely to influence the audience's perspectives? Topic

Receptivity to change. How committed are your audience members to their perspectives? To what degree are your audience members willing to yield their perspectives?

Homogeneity. To what degree are your audience members homogeneous? Are they the same age, for example? The same sex? Members of the same political party?

Speaker

Position. What is your position, title, or rank? How is it likely to be perceived in this situation?

Attitude toward self. How do you feel about yourself in this speaking situation? Confident? Excited? Tentative? Intimidated? Scared?

Cultural identities. Which of your cultural identities are evident to your audience? Race? Ethnicity? Sex? Sexual orientation? Will you choose to reveal some aspects of your identity that are not readily available? How will these identities affect the audience's perceptions of you and your presentation?

Speaking competencies. What kinds of communication competencies are required in this situation? The ability to explain clearly? To lead a discussion? To generate excitement? How confident are you about your ability to demonstrate these skills? Do you experience communication anxiety that may interfere with your communication competence?

Vulnerabilities. Are there aspects of the speaking situation that make you feel vulnerable? Are they related to your subject? Communication ability? Relationship with your audience?

Attitude toward audience. What is the nature of your relationship with your audience? Affection? Respect? Compassion? Irritation? Frustration? Do you have prejudices that may affect your attitude toward your audience?

Previous experience with audience. Are your audience members acquainted with you? From what context? What experiences, if any, have you had with your audience previously that might affect this situation?

Knowledge of subject. How much do you know about the subject of the interaction? Research

Comfort with subject. How comfortable are you talking about this subject?

Perspective on subject. What is your initial viewpoint on the subject?

Receptivity to change. How committed are you to your perspective? To what degree are you willing to yield your perspective?

Subject

Comfort level. Is the subject a comfortable and easy one for your audience members to listen to and discuss?

Complexity. How complex is the subject?

Nature of evidence. What sources of information or evidence about the subject are allowed or privileged? Library research? Personal experience? Testimonials from others?

Controversial nature. How controversial is the subject? Are there likely to be opposing perspectives on it?

Interactional goal. What is the interactional goal guiding your presentation? Will your effort to invite transformation assume the form of asserting individuality? Building community? Articulating a perspective? Seeking adherence? Discovering knowledge and belief? What expectations and constraints are generated by your goal?

Creating a Transformative Environment

Each of the questions concerning setting, audience, speaker, and subject from the lists above should be used to help you discover how the elements discussed contribute to or detract from your ability to create the conditions of freedom, safety, value, and openness. Some examples will suggest how you might want to make use of these questions for this purpose.

If an analysis of your **setting**, for example, tells you that you will be speaking following dinner at a conference that has been going on all day, you can assume that your audience members probably will be tired of sitting, tired of listening to speakers, and tired of thinking. Consequently, they are not likely to be as interested in engaging in the sustained listening necessary to follow a presentation and to allow it to serve as a catalyst for self-change. Instead, they are likely to stick with their current ways of thinking because they are interested in other things—perhaps joining friends for after-conference partying or going home to bed. To convert this obstacle into a dimension that facilitates transformation, develop your topic in ways that will connect particularly strongly with your audience. Think about ways to involve your listeners in a discussion of the subject rather than simply presenting your ideas to them. Keep your presentation short. In general, select as communication options those that prevent the setting from becoming an obstacle to the presentation of your perspective.

To give you an idea of how your analysis based on **audience** factors might proceed, suppose you have been asked to give a toast at a wedding. You know, from your analysis of the audience, that you will be speaking to a highly homogeneous group in terms of education. In your toast, you probably would not want to use specialized jargon from your field that others in the audience are not likely to understand. Such talk may intimidate and silence others at the wedding who may feel they cannot speak because they do not have the same level of education that you have. The choices you make in terms of the subject on which to focus, your language, and your style of delivery should make your audience members feel safe and free to share their own experiences about the couple following your toast.

In your analysis of the factors that you as the **speaker** bring to the speaking situation, you reflect on your own strengths, weaknesses, and degree of comfort as a speaker. You may find that you are less comfortable with particular forms of communication. If this is the case, see how you can reduce your uneasiness in the speaking situation. If you feel removed and distant from your audience when you stand behind a lectern, walk around the room as you speak and encourage your audience members to voice their impressions and opinions. Conversely, if you feel you lack the skills to lead a discussion well, you probably will not be comfortable incorporating a great deal of discussion into your presentation because you would not be able to model a feeling of safety for your audience.

Your analysis of **subject** dimensions may suggest that the subject you will be discussing has the potential to be a highly controversial one. Such a topic may act as a barrier to the creation of a transformative environment simply because it encourages participants to defend their own positions instead of trying to understand the perspectives of the others. To encourage the creation of the conditions of freedom, safety, value, and openness when a subject generates controversy is difficult, but by selecting communication options that encourage receptivity, you can move closer to creating these conditions. For example, select as your interactional goal articulating a perspective rather than seeking adherence. This goal will allow full presentation of multiple views and convey to participants that they are being heard. Incorporate into your presentation self-disclosure about your background and the influences that led you to adopt the perspective you hold, helping other participants understand the context for your perspective. Be careful, as you lead the discussion or answer questions, not to belittle or devalue any opinions that others contribute.

Re-sourcement

The creation of the conditions of freedom, safety, value, and openness is not always easy, even if the members of your audience are inclined to communicate in invitational ways. The process is made much more difficult when you find yourself involved in interactions framed in the conquest or conversion modes of rhetoric. In instances in which you are confronted with conquest or conversion rhetoric and want to create the conditions of freedom, safety, value, and openness, you might want to engage in re-sourcement.

Re-sourcement is a term coined by rhetorical theorist Sally Miller Gearhart that means "going to a new place" for energy and inspiration: "To re-source is to find another source, an entirely different . . . one."[9] Re-sourcement involves choosing not to interact within the frame in which the interaction has been developed and using a source other than the original frame in the development of a response. Re-sourcement involves two processes: (1) disengaging from the conquest or conversion frame of the precipitating message; and (2) formulating a response within a new frame.

Draw energy

Disengagement

If the message to which you are responding occurs in the context of a frame such as conquest (in which the speaker is trying to dominate you or bully you into acquiescence), the first step in the process of re-sourcement involves stepping away from that frame. Disengagement means simply that you recognize that you have an option of how to respond, and your response does not have to be in that same conquest mode. You recognize that if the interaction continues within the original framework, nothing will be gained and, in fact, the relationship and future interactions may be jeopardized.

Sometimes, disengagement itself constitutes the entire process of re-sourcement. You literally might choose to walk away from an encounter rather than continue a negative interaction. Karen's grandson talked to her about having to fight the school bully. He acted very surprised when she suggested he just walk away without fighting. Such responses tend not be valued in our culture because they are interpreted to mean that the person is spineless or is being a *wuss*, a *sissy*, or a *wimp*. The tendency not even to see disengagement as an option is illustrated in an episode of the comic strip *FoxTrot*, in which Jason Fox, a video-game fanatic, spent a month trying to kill off a particular enemy to get to the next level of the game. When his sister quickly made it to the next level simply by walking past the enemy, Jason responded: "I spent an entire month trying to kill this one video game foe, and it turns out all I had to do was walk past him! Who knew you weren't supposed to club him or kick him or lob fireballs at his head, just because he's huge and fierce and can squash you at will!"[10]

Disengagement can occur in the daily interactions that mark our professional and personal lives. Sonja once received an e-mail message from a colleague who viciously attacked her for a position she held on a department issue. After working very hard to formulate an effective response to the message, Sonja figured out that she had the option of simply deleting the e-mail message and not responding, which she did. She heard no more from her colleague on the issue. When you do not participate in conquest or conversion rhetoric, it cannot continue. When someone throws a pillow at you, hoping to engage you in a pillow fight, and you let the pillow fall to your feet and don't pick it up, there can be no fight. Not responding to the message by not taking the bait offered by the speaker can change the dynamics of the interaction and open up a space in which freedom, safety, value, and openness can begin to develop.

Formulating a Response within a New Frame

The second step in re-sourcement is the creative development of an invitational response to the conquest or conversion message being offered. This response is communication that aims to foster understanding, conveys that the speaker and audience are equal, does not denigrate the other's perspective or suggest that it is wrong, and suggests an interest in continuing to interact with the other. Often, this second step involves engaging in communication that does not directly argue against or even address the message being offered. It presents a response addressed to a different exigence from the one implicit in the conquest and conversion rhetoric. This step consists of offering some kind of communication that is different from the initial message that helps shift the nature of the interaction and enables the conditions of freedom, safety, value, and openness to begin to develop. At the very least, it makes future interactions possible by preserving enough of the relationship that the parties are willing to try again.

Author and activist Starhawk describes an incident that followed a protest against nuclear weapons at the Livermore Weapons Lab in California, providing an example of re-sourcement. She and other activists were arrested and held in a school gym. During their confinement, a woman ran into the gym, chased by six guards. She dove into a cluster of women, and they held onto her as the guards pulled at her legs, trying to extract her from the group. The guards were on the verge of beating the women when one woman in the group sat down and began to chant, and the other women did the same. Starhawk describes the reaction of the guards: "They look bewildered. Something they are unprepared for, unprepared even to name, has arisen in our moment of common action. They do not know what to do. And so, after a moment, they withdraw. . . . In that moment in the jail, the power of domination and control met something outside its comprehension, a power rooted in another source."[7]

Another example of the use of re-sourcement as a response to conquest or conversion rhetoric is found in the movie *The Long Walk Home*. The movie recreates the boycott by African Americans of buses in Montgomery, Alabama, in 1955–1956. The protest was aimed at securing seats on buses on a first-come-first-served basis instead of on the basis of race. As the boycott continued, white women began to drive their black maids to and from their homes, often in defiance of their husbands. In one scene, men surround a group of white women and their black maids, jeering and taunting them. The men appear ready to beat them. The women respond by joining hands and singing a gospel song, and the men back away without harming them. The men's message was one of anger and conquest, and the women's message in response communicated their intent to act in ways that would foster freedom, safety, value, and openness. They acknowledged the perspective of the men, did not try to change it, and enacted a feeling of safety.

Re-sourcement is not limited to creating the external conditions of invitational rhetoric in protest situations. Poet Adrienne Rich demonstrated re-sourcement when she was awarded the National Book Award's prize for poetry in 1974. When she accepted the award, she read a statement she had coauthored with Audre Lorde and Alice Walker, both of whom also had been nominated for the prize. In the statement, the three women announced that they were accepting the award together and would share the prize: "We believe that we can enrich ourselves more in supporting and giving to each other than by competing against each other; and that poetry—if it *is* poetry—exists in a realm beyond ranking and comparison."[8] The message of the award was framed within a context of competition and thus conquest rhetoric. Rich, Lorde, and Walker chose not to respond with a message congruent to that frame, which would have supported the competitive, hierarchical system in which one person wins and the others lose. They responded instead with a message of cooperation, creating a collaborative rather than a competitive frame for the poetry competition with their statement. (Their complete statement is one of the sample presentations included at the end of this book.)

Linguist Suzette Haden Elgin provides an example of re-sourcement in everyday situations when she suggests a tactic by which individuals can respond to instances of sexual harassment. If a colleague, customer, or supervisor makes a sexual proposal or sexually suggestive remark, Elgin suggests, the Boring Baroque Response can be used to reply. This response involves ignoring the content of the message and responding by telling a long story with many tedious details that does not address the unwanted message.[11] Because this story can be made up as the speaker tells it, no special training, talent, or skill are required. A Boring Baroque Response to an unwanted sexual comment might be something like this:

I'm reminded of when I was growing up on a farm in South Dakota. I remember sitting on the swing on summer evenings, looking at the sky, watching the wheat—you could almost see it growing—and realizing how much I like summers. I associate summers with wheat, grasshoppers, blue sky, and swing sets, and even today, I can't wait for summer to arrive. I know a lot of people can't stand heat and would much prefer spring or fall or even winter, but not me. Winters are too cold for my taste. I might enjoy one snowy evening, but the rest is just a pain—shoveling snow, frozen pipes, cars that won't start. I'm just a summer person!

This is an example of re-sourcement in action because the speaker refuses to participate in the frame established by the harasser—a frame of conquest—and creatively devises a response that is outside of that frame. The conversation moves to another frame without pronouncing judgment, causing the instigator to lose face or become defensive, or escalating the interaction, all of which would destroy the conditions or any fragments of conditions of freedom, safety, value, and openness that might have existed in the environment.

Re-sourcement is useful in a variety of other situations in which a communicator tries to goad you into participating in conquest rhetoric. Kathy, a friend of Karen's who is a facilitator and trainer, is the daughter-in-law of a prominent politician. In the middle of a training, one of the participants asked her about her name and whether she was related to the politician. When she learned that they were related, the participant said, "That's interesting because the work you do and the perspectives you hold seem so at odds with the approaches he takes." Rather than denigrate or defend her father-in-law—the options offered in the framing of the original message as conquest rhetoric—Kathy responded from an invitational frame: "Yes, the work I do is very interesting; it allows me to work with diverse issues and to meet lots of people. I like it very much." By using the participant's own term, *interesting*, differently from how it was intended, she contributed to the creation of the conditions that are the mark of invitational rhetoric.

Another form re-sourcement can take is appreciation. Frequently, our response mode is criticism when others attack us or do things we perceive as harmful to us. In response, they defend themselves and often launch new attacks, creating an exchange that tends to destroy any feelings of freedom, safety, value, and openness that might have existed. Appreciating instead of criticizing sometimes can change the entire nature of the interaction because it deliberately reintroduces and focuses on the conditions desired. At Sonja's university, there was a period when the mailroom was not operating well because of high turnover in staff positions and lack of training of new staff members. As a result, her department consistently received the mail of other departments, and the mail the department sent out was very late in reaching its destination. Sonja's program assistant repeatedly complained to the mailroom supervisors about the problems, with no noticeable impact. Sonja and her program assistant then decided to try appreciation. They brought boxes of chocolates to the mailroom employees with a note acknowledging how hard the employees worked, how difficult their jobs were, and how much the department appreciated what they did. Mail service to the department improved dramatically. The environment in which the initial interaction was framed was one of opposition and defensiveness, but Sonja and her assistant chose to communicate instead within a frame of appreciation, thus generating feelings of freedom, safety, value, and openness in their interaction with the mailroom employees.

Re-sourcement, then, is a response you can use to communicate invitationally and to create freedom, safety, value, and openness when those around you are communicating noninvitationally. It consists of disengaging from the frame of conquest or conversion in which the message to which you are responding is framed and constructing a response from within a different frame—an invitational one. Re-sourcement enables you to continue to value others because you do not engage them in negative confrontation, and you are able to offer your perspective while remaining invitational. Re-sourcement also opens up possibilities for a greater array of options for communication in the future. Because you have not cut off other communication options for interacting with someone, you may go on to articulate your perspective in more traditional ways, using any of the five interactional goals.

In the ideal environment for invitational rhetoric, the conditions of freedom, safety, value, and openness are present and increase the possibilities that a mutual understanding of perspectives will be achieved and that participants will choose to grow and change. An analysis of the dimensions of the speaking environment—setting, audience, speaker, and subject—reveals which factors are likely to facilitate the creation of this transformative environment and which are likely to obstruct it. If you determine that the creation of these conditions will be very difficult because the interaction is framed as conquest or conversion rhetoric, re-sourcement may create a space in which a wider variety of communication options remain possible. Through the use of re-sourcement, opportunities for transformation may emerge that may have seemed virtually impossible to create at the start of an interaction.

FOCUSING

Following an analysis of environmental factors relevant to your speaking situation and the formulation of ideas about how you plan to use them to create freedom, safety, value, and openness, you are ready to begin developing your presentation. Five processes are involved: (1) focusing; (2) framing; (3) elaborating; (4) beginning and ending; (5) connecting ideas; and (6) delivering. Although the various processes involved in developing your presentation are treated here as a series of discrete steps, in fact they overlap considerably. You will find that although your focus at a particular time in the development of your presentation is on elaborating your ideas, you simultaneously are working on how you are going to connect those ideas to one another and how you are going to express them through your delivery. Each of the next six chapters deals with one of these processes.

Three preliminary processes that help you begin to focus your presentation are the subject of this chapter: (1) selecting a commitment statement; (2) generating the main ideas for your presentation; and (3) making use of speaking resources. The processes involved in focusing are those that get you started on a presentation—clarifying where your initial commitments lie, selecting the main ideas by which to develop your ideas, and seeking out resources that will help you throughout the preparation process. By the time you have completed these steps, you will have a good sense of the basic elements of your presentation and will be ready to shape and refine it.

Commitment Statement

The first decision you make in the course of focusing your presentation is to develop a commitment statement. This is a statement that (1) summarizes the subject matter or gist of your presentation; (2) offers your initial commitment to a position; and (3) suggests your interactional goal. A commitment statement guides you in developing your major ideas, organizing the ideas you generate, and omitting irrelevant information.

A commitment statement is not the same as a subject or topic. A subject simply names a field, a body of knowledge, or a situation. A commitment statement incorporates your position toward the subject you intend to explore, explain, or support. For example, if the subject is *accounting*, a commitment statement on the subject could be, "I believe accounting currently offers excellent employment opportunities." This commitment statement signals that you have a perspective regarding the accounting field and that you will be articulating that perspective for your audience. In your commitment statement, then, you should be able to locate the subject of your presentation, your particular perspective on it, and your interactional goal.

The commitment statement represents only an initial or tentative commitment to a perspective. If you think of your commitment statement as tentative, it serves as a reminder that your position is evolving and that you are willing to be changed as a result of the interaction, just as you hope your audience will be. As a result of interacting with your audience in the course of your presentation, you may change your perspective about something, and the next time you address that issue—whether formally or informally—you then will have a different commitment statement. Implicit in the commitment statement, then, is the recognition that the interaction is not complete without the incorporation of the audience's perspective. The audience has a central role to play in the further development of your thinking on this subject.

The function of a commitment statement is not unlike the planning you do when you host a party. The commitment statement is the equivalent of a commitment by the host to have done some initial thinking, planning, and preparation for the gathering—cleaning the house or apartment, decorating, and providing refreshments. Your commitment statement communicates to the audience that you have done some initial thinking about the subject and some preparation concerning how to present the results of that initial thinking. You do not know how the party or the presentation will go, however, and the outcome may be different from what you expect.

If the commitment statement is tentative, you might be wondering why we use the term *commitment* to describe it. Commitments like marriage, for example, tend to have connotations of permanence associated with them. We are defining the term *commitment* here not in the sense of a pledge or a promise but in the sense of making known an opinion or view—sharing your commitments or taking a stand. When you select a commitment statement, you are declaring where you stand on a subject as you enter an interaction.

The commitment statement is very much like what many people call a *thesis statement*, but we use the term *commitment statement* because it better captures the declaration of or adherence to an initial idea that is central to the statement. *Commitment statement* suggests that you have made a carefully considered choice in regard to something, and you are declaring your commitment to it. In all other ways, however, a commitment statement functions as a thesis statement. It states your subject matter and indicates the particular stance or perspective you have chosen to take regarding it.

In most presentations, you will find yourself incorporating your commitment statement—or a slight rephrasing of it—directly into your presentation. You will find that how you word your commitment statement varies depending on your interactional goal. Commitment statements usually can be identified by certain words or phrases that indicate to your audience which goal is guiding your presentation.

Commitment statements for the interactional goal of articulating a perspective often begin with or imply phrases such as *I believe, my view is, I think,* or *my current understanding is.* Your commitment statement makes clear that your belief or position is of primary importance in this presentation. Commitment statements for articulating a perspective are statements such as:

- My opinion is that our school system needs to implement a foreign language requirement.
- I believe that moving to a voucher system in our schools would improve educational opportunities for our children.
- I have a particular perspective on ethics concerning artificial intelligence that I would like to share with you.

When your interactional goal is asserting individuality, phrases such as *I am, I have certain qualities, I want to,* and *I want to communicate* are included or implied. With this goal, your focus is on certain aspects of self that you want to highlight for your audience. Commitment statements for presentations to assert individuality might look as follows:

- I am a bilingual speaker and personally understand how valuable knowing more than one language is.
- Because of my extensive experience implementing voucher systems in schools, I am an excellent choice for the position you have open.
- I am delighted to be joining this company and would like to share some of my background in the area of artificial intelligence with you.

When your interactional goal is creating, maintaining, or restoring community, your commitment statement is likely to begin with phrases such as *we can, we share,* and *we value.* Your focus is directed collectively rather than individually, and your language is similarly inclusive. Commitment statements that have building community as an interactional goal might take the following form:

- As bilingual speakers ourselves, I know we all share the value of speaking more than one language.
- All of us want the best possible education for our children, and a voucher system is the best route to take to improve education in this community.
- All of us here appreciate the critical importance of artificial intelligence to this line of work, and I hope that, after we've talked, the ways that each of us can contribute will be clear.

Commitment statements for the interactional goal of seeking adherence often use phrases such as *should, would, could, benefit, best,* or *desirable.* With such commitment statements, you are seeking the assent of the audience members to something or asking them to adopt a particular idea or plan. The following commitment statements are examples of statements appropriate for presentations centered around this goal:

- We should seriously consider adopting a foreign-language requirement for students in our school.
- Our educational system would benefit from the introduction of vouchers, and I urge us to vote to implement the proposed voucher system at this meeting.
- Our organization should develop our resources in artificial intelligence so that we can distinguish ourselves from others in the field.

Discovering knowledge and belief is the fifth interactional goal, and commitment statements associated with it often incorporate words such as *explore, determine,* and *decide* and phrases such as *how can we solve . . .?, I'd like you to help me with . . ., I could use some help with . . .,* or *what ideas do we have for . . .?* The focus in these commitment statements is on the exploration process central to this interactional goal. Commitment statements for discovering knowledge and belief assume forms such as these:

- I need your help to figure out when a student is exempt from our foreign-language requirement.
- I would like to explore how a system of educational vouchers might benefit our school district.
- How can we use artificial intelligence to benefit the company?

The commitment statement is central to your presentation. It communicates your general subject matter and reveals your commitments around that subject. Although you may find that you often are asked to speak on the same subject matter—the area of your expertise—your choice of interactional goal affects how you word your commitment statement.

Main Ideas

Once you have developed your interactional goal and your commitment statement, you are ready to move to thinking about the main ideas of your presentation. The main ideas should be ones that clearly relate to and develop your commitment statement and that are consistent with the interactional goal you have selected. Often, the main ideas emerge naturally from the commitment statement. Once you have done the thinking and research necessary to formulate your commitment statement, the main ideas often are obvious. Some sample interactional goals, commitment statements, and main ideas are listed below to show the connections among these components.

Scenario 1

Audience. Manager
Setting. Job interview
Interactional goal. To assert individuality
Commitment statement. I am well prepared for this position
Main ideas.

- Emphasize educational background

- Emphasize experience in similar positions

- Emphasize dependability and creativity

Scenario 2

Audience. City council members
Setting. City council meeting
Interactional goal. To articulate a perspective; to seek adherence
Commitment statement. The noise problem downtown needs to be taken seriously, and I urge the city council to pass a noise ordinance.
Main ideas.

- Noise from downtown bars is excessive and disruptive.

- Passage of a noise ordinance will manage this problem.

Scenario 3

Audience. Web designer
Setting. Meeting to revamp company's Web site
Interactional goal. To discover knowledge and belief

Commitment statement. I want to explore ways to improve our Web site.

Main ideas.

- What is effective and less effective about the current Web site?
- How can the Web site be improved?
- Which of the proposed changes are cost effective for the company?

Scenario 4

Audience. State legislators
Setting. Legislative hearing
Interactional goal. To seek adherence
Commitment statement. I believe the budget for alcohol-education programs directed at under-age drinkers should be increased.

Main ideas.

- A majority of alcohol-related traffic fatalities involve under-age drinkers.
- This state traditionally has devoted funds to prosecution rather than to the prevention of alcohol-related traffic accidents.
- Education programs have been found to be effective in reducing traffic accidents involving alcohol in other states.

In all of these scenarios, notice how closely tied the main ideas are to the commitment statement. Once you have your commitment statement, you are likely to have a good idea of some of the major ideas to develop in your presentation. Locating some sources to help you develop your ideas is useful at this stage in the process of creating your presentation.

9/14 lecture

Speaking Resources

Some common speaking resources for developing the ideas in your presentation are print sources, electronic sources, interviews, and personal experience. When you are asked to speak because you have developed a particular perspective on a subject, you probably will rely on speaking resources already at your command such as your current knowledge and personal experience. If you are developing a new perspective on a subject or developing a presentation with a new interactional goal or commitment statement, you probably will want to turn to various resources to assist you in this process. Regardless of how extensive your knowledge of a subject matter is, you undoubtedly will want to update your knowledge so that you can present the most current information in the course of your presentation, take into account how your perspective is evolving, and analyze alternative viewpoints. Searching out new perspectives, materials, and viewpoints enables you to rethink your perspective and to update how you think about it.

In suggesting some of the speaking resources available to you, our intention is not to instruct you in how to do research. As a college student, you undoubtedly are familiar with how to search the Internet, how your library works, and how to access other useful sources on your campus. If you are a first-term freshman, you still may be learning about these resources, but your campus, if it is typical, offers workshops, tours, and programs for new students to become acquainted with the library and its services. Our intent here, then, is simply to remind you of some of the major speaking resources available to you when preparing a presentation.

Print Sources

Traditional sources for finding the materials you need for your presentation are printed ones—books, newspapers, journals, and magazines. Each of these sources is valuable for different reasons. Although books are the least current source of information due to the extensive time required to write and publish a book, they provide historical information and more in-depth analyses than publications devoted to current events can offer. Newspapers and magazines provide up-to-date information, with magazines usually providing more in-depth coverage than newspapers simply because their deadlines are not as immediate. A newspaper story reports daily information about an incident, while a weekly news magazine can provide an overview of the story from start to finish.

Journals or scholarly periodicals are another useful print source. The journals published by academic disciplines provide current research findings on various topics. In the discipline of communication, there are journals specializing in areas such as mass communication, communication theory, applied communication, women's studies in communication, and intercultural communication, as well as many journals that are not topic specific and that publish articles about all aspects of the communication field. You can find research in these journals on such diverse topics as the process of compliance gaining in interpersonal communication, religious communication, public relations campaigns, organizational communication, and analyses of television programs and films.

Internet Sources

The Internet has changed how research is conducted, and you are now able to find massive amounts of material on virtually every subject through Internet searches. When you use the Internet as a source for your presentations, you must deal with two primary problems: (1) how to find relevant information; and (2) how to find reliable information. Deciding which Internet sources are most valuable for your project requires

.org

patience and practice, and you may find that a search on a particular subject produces many screens and includes hundreds or thousands of items. Search engines vary in the ways to broaden or narrow searches, but the Help command in a particular search engine will give you the search strategies specific to that engine.

Although you may be able to find much of what you need by searching various Web sites on your own, numerous databases exist that can assist you with specialized information. The Lexis/Nexus database, for instance, catalogs legal material, newspapers, and public records and may provide you with more detailed information than you might find in a more random search. Other databases allow you to access the tables of contents of certain bodies of material such as journals in the social sciences, for instance. Reference librarians can help you find the most efficient databases for a search on your subject.

A second problem you face in using Internet sources is how to evaluate the quality and legitimacy of the information you find. Because of the democratic nature of the Web, there is no oversight body or organization that evaluates the credibility, trustworthiness, and reliability of Internet publications. Anyone can put anything on the Internet, whether it is true or false, accurate or inaccurate. In addition, earlier databases on the Internet were constructed by scanning articles, often leading to imperfect renditions of the documents. Thus, if you are using a document—an article, poem, or essay—from several years ago, there may be typographical errors or other problems with the document in terms of accuracy.

A number of documents are available on the Web to help you evaluate your sources. If you type in +Internet AND "source credibility," you will find several Web sites devoted to information reliability and credibility on the Web. Elizabeth Kirk identifies five major criteria for evaluating information found on the Web:

- **Authorship**. To find out more about the author of an Internet document, search for the author's name on the Web or in Usenet. If the author maintains a homepage, it will be listed. If biographical links are available, follow them. Also seek out comments from others about the author's work. Your goal is to establish the author's qualifications for making the claims you want to use.

- **Publishing body**. This criterion deals with the credibility of the publishing source. The publishing body for an Internet document is the server on which the file is stored, but there is no way for the server to guarantee the reliability of the information it stores. More important than the server's name are any names or logos appearing within the document that represent organizations that may stand behind the document. For example, Leslie Harris's essay "Writing Spaces: Using MOOs to Teach Composition and Literature," which appeared in *Kairos: A Journal for Teaching Writing in*

Webbed Environments (Summer 1996), lists *Kairos* on the document. *Kairos* is an electronic journal sponsored by the Alliance for Computers and Writing, and it has a reputation for publishing articles of high quality.

- **Referral to and/or knowledge of other sources**. This criterion has to do with how the document in question treats other sources. You can use two approaches to help you make this judgment: (1) examine the content of the document to see whether it represents other sources fairly; and (2) seek out other sources to see if the author has considered enough alternative views.

- **Accuracy or verifiability**. How you establish the accuracy of data you find on the Internet is not very different from how you establish the accuracy of print data, but the special features of hypertext may make your task easier. You often will find a direct link in a document to a source cited in a document. You then can go to that document to see if the author of the document you are reviewing has cited from it accurately.

- **Currency**. The currency of an Internet document is the history of its publication and any revisions. A document with no dating at all is less reliable in terms of currency than one that lists numerous revisions.[1]

Interviews

Another valuable source of information is personal interviews. If you are working in a particular field, you undoubtedly have or can gain access to a variety of individuals with expertise in that field. Interviewing individuals who are working directly in your area of concern provides you with current information about the issue. It also gives you the opportunity to understand diverse perspectives on an issue and to begin to see how different people can hold different perspectives on it. In addition, interviewing individuals gives you an opportunity to obtain brochures, reports, and other documents from the organizations with which they are associated, which may be useful sources for your presentation.

Personal Experience

A final resource for your presentation is your own experience. Thinking through the process of how you came to hold a belief about something can help you articulate the various facets of your perspective and make decisions about how to present it to your audience. Realizing how your own perspective developed also makes you more sensitive to similar evolutions in the perspectives held by members of your audience. You can be more appreciative of the variety of perspectives your audience members hold when you understand the role personal experiences have played in your own thinking about an issue. Finally, thinking about the experiences responsible for your perspective can be a source of stories and other forms of elaboration that you can incorporate into your speech.

You will make use of print resources, Internet sources, interviews, and personal experience at a number of places in the process of creating your presentation. Such sources are critical in the early stages of your thinking about your presentation as you select your topic and begin to develop your commitment statement and the main ideas of your presentation. You will continue to make use of these sources in other parts of the process as well. When you develop your introduction and conclusion, for example, you may find that some of these sources are useful for providing a beginning or ending to your presentation. When you refine the specific ideas of your presentation, you also will draw on these sources for the forms of elaboration for the main ideas in your presentation.

The processes involved in focusing the presentation—clarifying where your initial commitments lie and pointing you in particular directions for the development of your main ideas—are those that get you started. Formulation of your commitment statement and major ideas leads to a consideration of the frame or structure you will create for your presentation.

FRAMING = 10 on Test
Know @ lest 10 y ao.

Framing is the process by which you structure the main ideas of your presentation by means of an organizational pattern. Because a frame increases the ease with which your audience members can understand your ideas and allows them to retain information more easily, it communicates to your audience members that you value them. There is no one right way to frame a presentation on a particular subject. To make the decision about which frame works best to construct relationships among your ideas, you want to take into account the preferences and expectations of your audience, the cultural context in which you are speaking, your subject, your interactional goal, and your own personal style.

You do not have to begin from scratch to come up with an organizational pattern for your presentation. Ideas for any presentation tend to sort out into some basic or conventional organizational patterns that speakers and writers have found useful for framing ideas. You probably will discover that many of these frames already are familiar to you and that you automatically use some of them to organize your ideas, even though you may not have known their formal labels.

Following is a list of conventional organizational patterns with a description and example of each. The patterns are arranged in alphabetical order rather than in terms of frequency of use, linkage to particular interactional goals, or most effective or most creative because we do not want to privilege some over others. We want to encourage you to consider all possible organizational formats for a presentation rather than selecting one that is familiar or formulaic. In the few cases where a specific pattern is appropriate for only one interactional goal, that goal is noted in the description of the pattern.

Alphabet. The alphabet pattern involves arranging ideas in alphabetical order. You can organize a presentation on the importance of the arts, for example, around three values that you link to letters of the alphabet: A is for awareness, B is for balance, and C is for creativity. A variation of this pattern is the structuring of a presentation around an acronym that uses letters of the alphabet such as *SAFE* to discuss earthquake preparedness. *S* might stand for securing the environment, *A* for advance planning, *F* for family meeting place, and *E* for emergency supplies.

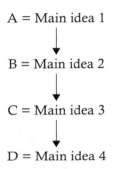

$$A = \text{Main idea 1}$$
$$\downarrow$$
$$B = \text{Main idea 2}$$
$$\downarrow$$
$$C = \text{Main idea 3}$$
$$\downarrow$$
$$D = \text{Main idea 4}$$

Category. You can organize ideas around the categories that naturally arise from your subject matter. The major components, types, questions, functions, or qualities of a subject can be used as the categories in this organizational frame. Because almost any subject can be divided into categories, this is a very common organizational pattern. Christine Todd Whitman, administrator of the U. S. Environmental Protection Agency (EPA), used a category pattern, for example, when she testified before a Congressional subcommittee about what the EPA was doing to combat bioterrorism. She discussed four categories of actions in which the EPA was involved: undertaking the cleanup of buildings contaminated by anthrax, developing collaborative relationships with other agencies to develop health and safety standards for cleanup efforts, developing a counter-terrorism program, and ensuring that the chemicals used to treat anthrax spores are effective and safe.[1]

Category 1
↓
Category 2
↓
Category 3
↓
Category 4

Causal. A causal organizational pattern is structured around a cause or series of causes that account for an effect or effects. You can organize ideas according to this pattern by beginning either with cause or with effect. You can discuss how certain causal factors produce a particular effect, or you can suggest that a particular set of conditions has been produced by a certain cause or causes. In a presentation on the condition of the U.S. school system, for example, educational consultant David Boaz spent the first part of his presentation establishing that schools do not work (the effect). In the second part of his presentation, he established that there is no competition and thus no incentive to improve the school system (the cause).[2]

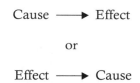

Cause ⟶ Effect

or

Effect ⟶ Cause

Circle. In this organizational pattern, ideas are structured in a circular progression. You develop one idea, which leads to another, which leads to another, which leads to another, which then leads back to the original idea. You might suggest to your coworkers, for example, that greater cooperation is needed to accomplish your unit's goals. To achieve this cooperation, you propose that the members of the unit establish a goal of being honest with one another. You then discuss how honesty can contribute to a greater feeling of trust, and trust, in turn, contributes to an environment in which team members are more likely to cooperate.

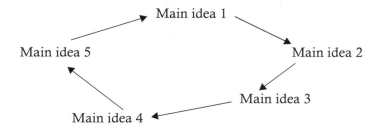

Continuum. Ideas can be organized along a continuum, spectrum, or range. All of the ideas on the continuum share some common quality or substance, but they differ in the degree or level to which they contain that quality. Using this pattern, you move from one end of the continuum to the other to discuss your ideas. You might organize a presentation using a continuum pattern by discussing ideas from small to large, familiar to unfamiliar, simple to complex, or least expensive to most expensive.

Chapter one of this book contains an example of a continuum organizational pattern. In the discussion of different modes of rhetoric, five kinds of rhetoric are organized and discussed in turn along a continuum that moves from conquest rhetoric to conversion rhetoric to benevolent rhetoric to advisory rhetoric to invitational rhetoric. All of the points along the continuum—the different modes of rhetoric—share the quality or substance of being rhetorical modes, but they differ in the degree to which the speaker seeks to change the perspectives of audience members.

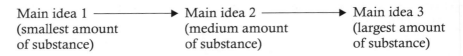

Main idea 1 ——————▶ Main idea 2 ——————▶ Main idea 3
(smallest amount   (medium amount   (largest amount
of substance)   of substance)   of substance)

Elimination. An organizational pattern of elimination begins with a discussion of a problem, followed by a discussion of several possible solutions to that problem. You examine the solutions in turn and eliminate them one by one until the one you prefer remains. In a presentation on the state's budget deficit, for example, you might suggest solutions such as imposing an additional tax on cigarettes, implementing a sales tax, cutting state programs, and raising property taxes. You dismiss the first three solutions for various reasons and focus in your presentation on advocating an increase in property taxes.

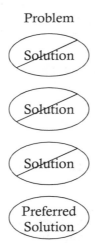

Facilitation. The facilitation pattern is always used for presentations in which discovering knowledge and belief is the interactional goal, but it can be used for presentations with other interactional goals as well. It is a pattern designed to enable the speaker to work with a group to generate ideas. The pattern involves two and possibly three steps: (1) definition of the problem; (2) joint search for ideas; and, in some cases, (3) evaluation or decision.

- **Definition of the problem**. In the first step of the facilitation pattern, you state the problem or issue for the group as clearly, concisely, and comprehensively as you can. You want to make sure all of the participants in the interaction have a clear understanding of the subject or issue about which they will generate ideas. For example, if you are a member of the Parent Teacher Association at your child's school and have been asked to facilitate a discussion on the best way to decrease violence in the schools, you need to be sure the group members agree on what they mean by *violence*. Otherwise, there will be ongoing confusion about exactly what is under discussion: Is the issue bullying, students carrying weapons, hate speech, or something else? If the group is not aware of the problem, you need to spend more time on this step. In such a case, you might want to prepare a visual aid that summarizes the background and basic facts involved.

- **Joint search for ideas**. The second step in the facilitation pattern is a joint search for ideas. You and your audience members talk together either to discover what you know or believe about a subject or to generate ideas that might solve a problem. This step largely consists of questions you ask the audience to stimulate discussion. You might ask such questions as: "What can you tell us about yourself and your life that would help us understand your commitments in terms of this issue?" "What do we stand for as a group?" "What could we do better to improve how we function?" "What are different ways that we might solve this problem?" "What are the advantages and disadvantages of adopting this proposal?"

You may want to use formal brainstorming techniques at this stage of the facilitation. In brainstorming, you ask participants to generate as many solutions as they can to a problem while someone records all of the ideas suggested on a blackboard, overhead, flipchart, or computer screen so that everyone can see them. What is important in the brainstorming process is that there be no judgment or even commentary on the ideas generated. Any idea, no matter how silly or unworkable it seems, is recorded because even those ideas that appear to be unusable may stimulate further thinking on the part of group members.

You may discover, in your search for alternatives, that the group needs more information. Perhaps some creative solutions have been offered to a problem, but you don't know, for example, if they violate company policies or can be implemented in the time available. When this is the case, you can give individuals particular assignments such as making calls to the appropriate people or looking up relevant reports to get the information you need. You set another meeting time when participants report on what they have found and, at that time, the idea-generation process will begin again, taking into account the new information that has been brought to the group. The facilitation pattern may conclude with participants free to make use of any of the ideas generated however they choose. In such cases, the facilitation pattern ends with the joint search for ideas.

- **Evaluation/decision**. In most cases, the group comes to a decision about which of the ideas or solutions generated is the best— which solution to the problem will be implemented, for example. In these cases, there is a third step to the facilitation pattern—evaluation/decision.

The evaluation/decision step begins with reaching agreement on the criteria group members will use to evaluate the ideas generated. Criteria might include workability of the solution, simplicity of the solution, lowest cost, or whether the solution meets everyone's needs. As the facilitator, you lead the participants through the suggested ideas or solutions one by one, helping them apply the criteria they have developed. Frame the evaluation process positively so that those whose ideas are being evaluated do not feel hurt or dismissed by the process. Instead of asking which ideas are unacceptable or bad, ask which appear to be the most promising and should be given the most serious consideration. The discussion at this stage is a process of clarification. As each idea or proposal is discussed, group members become increasingly clear about what they want, and often the best solution becomes obvious.

The chair of a university department might use the facilitation pattern to brainstorm with her faculty members about how the department can save money on copying costs. In the first stage, definition of the problem, she would share with the faculty how high the copying bill for the department is each month.

In the second step of the process, the joint search for ideas, she would ask the faculty members to brainstorm ways in which they can reduce the number of copies they make. They might generate ideas such as developing individual Web sites on which they could post their syllabi, e-mailing handouts to their students instead of copying and distributing them, making double-sided copies, and putting course materials on reserve in the library. In this case, the consensus or evaluation step probably would not be necessary because there is no need to come to consensus on which option the faculty members are to use. All ideas can be used by faculty members to reduce copying costs. The presentation would end with the chair encouraging the faculty members to use all of the options they can

and to think carefully about those options before they head to the department's copy machine.

If the faculty members wanted to develop a departmental policy to
follow concerning copying, they would have to come to consensus on the
option or options they would be required to follow. They might use criteria such as amount of money saved and amount of additional work for
faculty as criteria by which to evaluate the various options.

Statement of problem or issue by speaker/facilitator

↓

Generation of ideas by group

↓

Evaluation and consensus

Location. In an organizational pattern of location, ideas are assem-
bled in terms of their spatial or geographic relationships. This pattern
only works when you have ideas that can be discussed according to places
or locations. In a presentation on the closing of military bases in the
United States, for example, you could discuss the bases to be closed in
geographical order, beginning with the Midwest and moving to the
Northeast, the Southeast, the Southwest, and the Northwest.

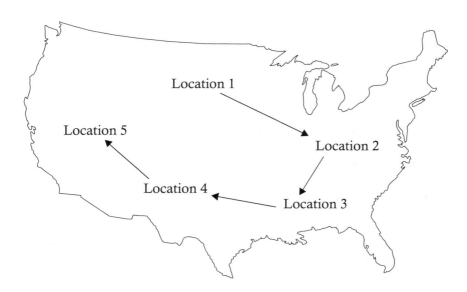

Metaphor. Metaphor, a comparison between two items, ideas, or experiences, can be used as an organizational pattern that structures a presentation. Usually, with this pattern, you compare an item, idea, or experience that is familiar to audience members with one that is less familiar to help them understand the less familiar subject. One example of this use of metaphor as an organizational pattern was a presentation by Richard R. Kelley, the CEO of Outrigger Hotels Hawaii. He used the metaphor of a cold to organize his ideas on how the company could survive in recessionary times in a presentation titled, in part, "How to Avoid a Cold When the World is Sneezing."[3]

Familiar item, idea, or experience		Less familiar item, idea, or experience
Characteristic 1	=	Characteristic 1
Characteristic 2	=	Characteristic 2
Characteristic 3	=	Characteristic 3
Characteristic 4	=	Characteristic 4

Motivated sequence. The motivated sequence is a five-step organizational pattern designed to encourage an audience to move from consideration of a problem to adoption of a possible solution. This pattern is appropriate only for the interactional goal of seeking adherence, although it is not the only pattern that can be used for this goal. The steps are:

- **Attention.** The introduction of the presentation is designed to capture the attention of audience members. In a presentation to high-school students on the sexual transmission of AIDS, for example, you might begin by citing statistics on the number of high-school students who are HIV positive.

- **Need.** In the need step, a problem is described so that the speaker and audience share an understanding of the problem. At this point, you describe the transmission of AIDS through sexual intercourse and suggest there is a need for young people to engage in honest, explicit discussion about sexual practices with their partners.

- **Satisfaction.** A plan is presented to satisfy the need created. You might suggest various ways in which young people can initiate talk about sex with their partners.

- **Visualization.** In visualization, the conditions that will prevail once the plan is implemented are described. Here, you encourage the audience to visualize the results of the proposed plan—perhaps the reduced risk of AIDS and more open communication in relationships.

- **Action.** The audience is asked to take action or approve the proposed plan. In this case, you ask audience members to use the techniques you have offered to discuss sex more explicitly and openly with their partners.[4]

Attention

Need

Satisfaction

Visualization

Action

Multiple perspectives. An organizational pattern created around multiple perspectives is one in which an idea or problem is analyzed from several different viewpoints. This pattern is designed to generate a full understanding of a subject. There are two forms this pattern can assume:

- **Non-oppositional perspectives**. In this version of the multiple-perspectives pattern, you summarize different perspectives that can be taken on an issue. These perspectives are different lenses through which the issue can be viewed. They are not oppositional perspectives, where some perspectives are opposed to and some are in favor of a particular position. Instead, they are different ways of looking at the problem as a result of different areas of specialty, interest, or expertise. In a presentation at a meeting on how to deal with the drug problem in the schools, for example, you might examine the problem from several different perspectives—medical, social, legal, and educational—to enable you and your audience to understand it fully.

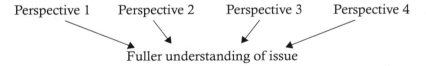

Perspective 1   Perspective 2   Perspective 3   Perspective 4

Fuller understanding of issue

- **Common ground**. Common ground is an organizational pattern in which you present opposing viewpoints on an issue with a goal of highlighting the common ground that exists between the perspectives. This pattern has three primary components. In the first, you discuss the subject from one perspective (it might be yours or that of someone else). In the second, you present the perspective of another person or group (again, this second perspective might or might not represent your own view). Following this dialogue between the two perspectives, you suggest the ideas that unify them or what they have in common, focusing on similarities and looking beyond the obvious differences between them. Instead of foregrounding the conflict between oppositional perspectives, you highlight the common ground or potential points of unity between the two conflicting viewpoints.

If you are a supervisor who is meeting with your work group to try to resolve a conflict among group members about how to determine salary increases, you might use this organizational pattern to begin the meeting. You would summarize the perspective of those members who believe that the supervisor should determine the pay increases, then summarize the perspective of those who believe that a committee should make the decision, and conclude with a discussion of what the two perspectives have in common. Both perspectives, you might suggest, are designed to make sure salaries are determined fairly, both would use the same evaluation forms on which group members would report their accomplishments, and both focus on quality of work rather than length of time employed. You then would want to ask your colleagues to join you in trying to resolve the conflict.

Perspective 1

↓

Perspective 2

↓

Common ground between perspective 1 and perspective 2

↓

Discussion with Audience

Narrative. In a narrative organizational pattern, ideas are structured in the form of a story using characters, settings, and plots. The story may be a true story or one you invent, but it usually is connected to the larger world, helping the speaker and audience understand a subject beyond the simple facts of the story. Rhetorical theorist Sally Miller Gearhart's presentation, "Whose Woods These Are," for example, consisted of a story about a man named Ivan who is trying to prevent the nuclear annihilation of the planet. The narrative was used to convey Gearhart's ideas about the violence implicit in many forms of communication.[5] (This is one of the sample presentations included at the end of this book.)

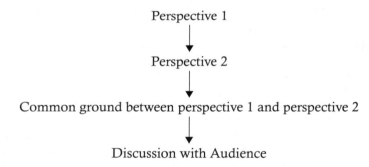

Narrative progression. A variation of the narrative pattern is the use of narrative progression, where you tell several stories, one after another, following the leads or implications of one story into the next. President Jimmy Carter gave a speech in 1977 to benefit the Hubert Humphrey Institute in Minnesota that was organized by narrative progression. The speech consisted of one story after another about Carter's various encounters with Humphrey throughout his life. The progression began when Carter was in the Navy and heard about Humphrey for the first time; it ended with a narrative about Carter's daughter and Humphrey when Carter was governor of Georgia.[6]

Story 1

Story 2

Story 3

Story 4

Problem/solution. A problem/solution organizational pattern begins with a discussion of a problem and concludes with your suggestion for a solution or solutions. If you are asking your city council representative to get the large potholes fixed on your street, for example, you could use this organizational pattern and begin by describing the problem. You would describe how tires and rims are damaged by the holes. You then would suggest the solution—that your city council representative intervene with the appropriate agency to get the potholes fixed quickly.

Problem

Solution

Spiral. A spiral pattern is an organization of ideas that begins at a broad level and moves to an in-depth explanation of those ideas. You begin by talking about something at a general level and wind down into the particular, focusing in greater detail on the subject. You move or proceed toward greater specificity as you develop your ideas.

In your self-presentation on a first date, for example, you tend to use a spiral pattern to organize your ideas. You reveal something about yourself in broad, general terms—perhaps that you enjoy music. If your date is interested in this topic and asks you to tell more about your interest in music, you go into more depth. You might explain that you like many different kinds of music, that you particularly like alternative country, that you have a CD collection of many alternative country musicians, and that you would like to play in a band someday.

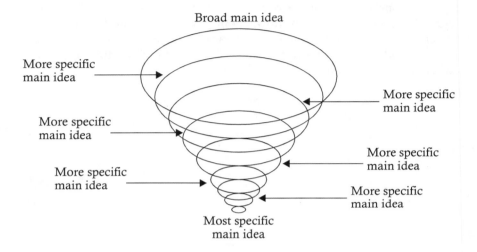

Broad main idea

More specific
main idea

More specific
main idea

More specific
main idea

More specific
main idea

More specific
main idea

More specific
main idea

More specific
main idea

Most specific
main idea

Thinking things through. In this pattern, you lay out the actual thought processes you followed while trying to answer a question or solve a problem. You take your audience on the journey you took in thinking something through, helping the audience understand how you came to the point at which you are now in your thinking. You end the presentation with a tentative decision, but this does not have to be a specific decision or acceptance of a "pro" or "con" position. You can reach the decision that the issue is not easily resolved for anyone. This is a good organizational pattern to use for the interactional goals of discovering knowledge and belief and articulating a perspective because it enables others in the interaction to see how you are thinking about an issue under discussion.

Let's assume that you are on a search committee to hire someone for a position that is open in your organization. At the meeting to select the person for the job, you can use the thinking-things-through pattern to explain why you are leaning toward one candidate over the others. You might tell the other committee members, for example, that you began by thinking about the position and the skills it requires, which led you to think about the differences in skills among the candidates interviewed. You decided that the skills of candidate A are adequate for the organization's needs, though perhaps not as strong as those of candidate B. But then you thought about how each candidate would fit into the organization, and you sense that candidate A, who seems very community oriented, would work hard to fit into the organization. Continuing to show your train of thought, you then explain that you next remembered experiences you've had with people who didn't fit into the organization and how they tend to leave the organization fairly quickly after they are hired. That's why you have ended up concluding that you probably favor candidate A, who fits in, even though she doesn't have the same level of skill as candidate B. You might conclude your presentation by saying that this is where you are in your thinking right now, but you certainly are open to hearing others' thoughts on the candidates.

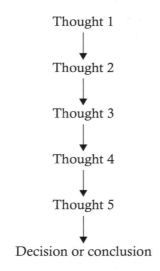

Thought 1

Thought 2

Thought 3

Thought 4

Thought 5

Decision or conclusion

Time. When you organize the ideas of a presentation according to their temporal relationships, you are using an organizational pattern of time. Ideas presented in this form are organized chronologically from past to present or from present to past. The units of time can be time periods or steps in a process. If you are orienting a new employee, you might use a time pattern when you explain to him how to secure his ID card. You would explain the first step, which is to bring his driver's license, Social Security card, and contract in to the organization's fiscal officer. The second step is to have the fiscal officer make copies of these documents and complete an ID form. He then must take all of the documents to Human Resources, where he gets his picture taken. You would conclude by explaining that he will have to wait just a few minutes for his ID card to be issued after his picture is taken.

Time period 1/Step 1

Time period 2/Step 2

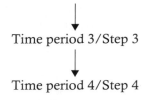

Time period 3/Step 3

Time period 4/Step 4

Web. A web organizational pattern revolves around a central or core idea. Other ideas branch out from the core, with each branching idea a reflection and elaboration of the core. In the web form, you begin with the central idea and then explore each idea in turn, returning to the core idea and going out from it and returning to the core again until all of the ideas have been covered. This pattern is very close to a category organizational pattern in that both address different aspects or categories of a subject. In a web pattern, you return to the core idea and explicitly reference it between your discussions of each of the ideas, but in the category pattern, various ideas are explored in turn, without explicit reference to the core idea. The web structure is especially useful when you really want to emphasize a core or primary idea in your presentation.

A web structure could be used by a manager to explain to her new program assistant how she will be evaluated each year. The core of the job, she might emphasize, is customer service—treating the clients with respect and helping them solve their problems. She discusses the other aspects on which the program assistant will be evaluated—managing the budget, providing support to the team members, completing the paperwork when new employees are hired, processing the mail, and maintaining the organization's Web site. The primary function of the job, though, is customer service, and the manager would keep coming back to that and its importance to the job between her discussions of each of these other duties.

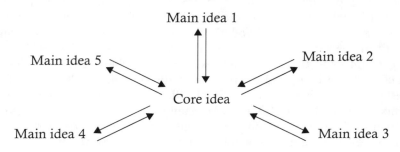

In the framing step of your presentation, you construct the relationships among your major ideas, resulting in an organizational pattern in which to present the ideas you are generating. Your next task is to develop the main ideas of your presentation through various forms of elaboration.

6

Read.

ELABORATING

Elaborating is the development of the ideas that have emerged in the process of creating your presentation. In the process of elaboration, you work out the specific details that will support, expand on, and give presence to the main ideas that comprise your presentation. Because of their specificity, forms of elaboration help an audience fully understand your perspective. You make a presentation come alive for your audience through examples, figures of speech, statistics, or some other form of elaboration.

Many different forms of elaboration are available, and you probably will want to choose different forms to develop each of your main ideas. The particular combination of forms you select for a presentation depends on your interactional goal; your personal and cultural preferences; and the nature of the audience, setting, and subject. As is the case with all communication options, you naturally will prefer some over others. If you are uncomfortable sharing highly personal information with a particular audience, you probably will not choose to use personal narrative in a presentation. Similarly, an audience not used to discourse with a strong pattern of rhythm and rhyme might be baffled or even irritated if you incorporate it into a presentation. If you are attempting to build community, you probably do not want to use forms of elaboration that are highly individualistic. Instead, you would choose forms such as myths, participation, and proverbs that bring audience members together.

What follows is a list of possible forms of elaboration or ways to extend your main ideas. These forms are designed to serve as starting points for thinking about how to develop your ideas for your specific audience. As with the organizational patterns in chapter 5, the forms of elaboration are arranged in alphabetic order rather than in terms of frequency of use, linkage to particular interactional goals, or most effective or most creative. We want to encourage you to consider all possible forms of elaboration for a presentation rather than simply selecting those that are most familiar.

Audiovisual aids. Audiovisual aids are materials that supplement spoken words by providing visual or audio elaborations. Charts, graphs, photographs, sketches, and cartoons are visual and can be presented via media such as slides, videotapes, overhead projectors, and blackboards. Audio aids include audiotapes, music, and other sounds that elaborate your ideas. Audiovisual aids are dealt with more extensively in chapter 9.

Comparison and contrast. In comparison and contrast, you develop an idea by discussing something unfamiliar through the lens of a concept or experience that is familiar to your audience.

- **Comparison**. Comparison is the process of showing the similarities between the familiar and the unfamiliar. In a presentation about fashion, for example, you might suggest that the 1920s and the 1970s were similar in how fashion functioned as rebellion.

- **Contrast.** Contrast links items to show their differences. President George W. Bush used contrast in his 2002 State of the Union address: "As we gather tonight, our nation is at war, our economy is in recession, and the civilized world faces unprecedented dangers. Yet the state of our union has never been stronger."[1]

Credentials. Providing evidence of your background and experience with a subject shows your audience that you have some expertise and resources upon which to base your ideas. Credentials may include a discussion of your cultural background, years of relevant work experience, or other factors that suggest a personal knowledge of or connection to your topic. Harvey Milk, the first openly gay supervisor in San Francisco, presented his credentials in his campaign for the office by contrasting himself with his opponent: "He's been an observer, not a participant, and has never really experienced the daily fight for survival that most of us have to face. I'm not being accusatory here—in some respects, I may be envious. I'm a small businessman and I'm well aware of the uncertainties of the economy, exactly what the 'inflationary spiral' means when I'm forced to raise prices to my customers, and how taxes can eat into your earnings."[2]

Definition. With definition, you elaborate by providing the meaning of a word or concept in terms the audience will understand. Lawyer Patricia Roberts Harris used a definition of law, for example, to develop her perspective on the relationship between law and morality: "By law, I mean that body of rules and regulations established by official governmental units to control public and private behavior, the observance of which is secured by the threat of the imposition of penalties in the nature of fine, imprisonment, or withdrawal of a government granted benefit."[3] Various kinds of definition are available:

- **Authority**. Definition by authority is a definition offered by an expert on a subject. In the following example, Microsoft CEO Bill Gates offered his definition of the phrase *trustworthy computing*:

  Another key element and probably the top priority at Microsoft, even beyond the key stuff we're doing around usability and new capabilities, is what we call trustworthy computing. This is the idea of taking the need for extreme reliability, knowing that when you install a new application that it won't disturb other things, knowing that your privacy and your security settings will be appropriate without your having to become an expert or your having to go out and get the new software updates manually going across the network.[4]

  As an expert on computing matters, Gates provides his own example of this phrase. You also could use definition by authority if you quoted Gates and his definition of trustworthy computing.

- **Display**. In definition by display, a word or idea is explained by pointing to something visible. A lawyer might use definition by display when showing a jury the position of stab wounds in the clothing of a crime victim to help define the act of self-defense. An architect who shows a sketch of a proposed building remodel also would be using definition by display.

- **Etymology**. An etymological definition explains the history, origin, or derivation of a word. In a presentation supporting a boycott of a company, you might begin by referring to the original meaning of *boycott*. The term developed following an incident in Ireland in 1880 in which a land agent named Captain Boycott was ostracized for refusing to reduce rents.[5]

- **Operational**. An operational definition explains how something works. A dietician talking to a group of hospital patients might define a low-fat diet operationally by saying it is one in which the average adult consumes fewer than 25 grams of fat per day.

Dreams and visions. Dreams are thoughts, images, or emotions that occur during sleep or that are constructed to convey an ideal future. A vision, on the other hand, is an imaginary, supernatural, or prophetic sight derived from a revelatory dream, trance, or ecstatic state. Dreams and visions are considered by many audiences to be powerful sources from which to learn about and understand experience.

- **Dreams.** In some cultures, dreams are considered qualitatively more vital than waking experiences because they provide the opportunity to communicate with nonhuman and superhuman forms and thus to experience alternative levels of reality. Individuals unfamiliar with such a perspective on dreams still can appreciate the fact that dreams—whether those that occur during sleep, in daydreaming, or as conscious efforts to envision a different future—

can shape experiences in significant ways. In his remarks upon re-
tiring from baseball, Orioles player Cal Ripken, Jr. used a dream as
a form of elaboration:

> As a kid I had this dream. And I had the parents that helped me
> shape that dream. Then, I became part of an organization, the Balti-
> more Orioles, to help me grow that dream. Imagine, playing for my
> hometown team for my whole career. And I have a wife and children
> to help me share and savor the fruits of that dream. . . . To be
> remembered at all is pretty special. I might also add that if, if I am
> remembered, I hope it's because by living my dream, I was able to
> make a difference.[6]

Sleeping dreams are also possible forms of elaboration. Activist
Sonia Johnson recounted a dream to illustrate the notion of trust:

> A woman in Missouri told me this dream. She was in a city, stand-
> ing on top of a tall building, looking out upon other buildings as far
> as she could see. She was a country woman, uneasy amid all the
> concrete and steel, and longing for home.
>
> Gradually she became aware that to get home she would have to
> leap off the edge of the building. Looking down at the miniature cars
> creeping along the miniature street far, far below, she said to herself,
> "But that's ridiculous! I'll kill myself if I jump off here!" Still, the
> feeling persisted that if she didn't jump, she would never get home
> again. And the grief that overwhelmed her at the thought of being
> exiled forever from the grass and trees and fields of home became so
> much stronger than her fear of dying that she leapt.
>
> As she began to fall, a rope appeared before her; she reached out,
> grabbed it, and swung way out over the street. At the end of its arc,
> she knew that if she didn't let go, she would swing back to where she
> had been before and not be any closer to home. So she let go. As she
> began to fall again, another rope appeared. Grabbing it, she swung
> out to the end of its arc, and let go again.
>
> Trusting herself, letting go, reaching out, swinging out over the
> abyss, trusting, letting go, reaching out, she found her way home.[7]

- **Visions.** Similarly, visions are valuable sources of power, energy,
  and insight that may be used to elaborate ideas. Visions may be the
  inspirations and intuitions of artists or scientists, the vision quests
  of Native Americans, those that occur within conventional religious contexts, or the visionary statements of organizations. In spiritual contexts, visions function as vehicles through which special
  powers or insights are made available to those who experience
  them. In secular contexts, visions capture or summarize the ideals
  of a group. Professor Mary Catherine Bateson, for example, envisioned a particular kind of future in the following excerpt:

The visions we construct will not be classic pioneer visions of struggle and self-reliance. Rather, they will involve an intricate elaboration of themes of complementarity—forms of mutual completion and enhancement and themes of recognition achieved through loving attention. All the forms of life we encounter—not only colleagues and neighbors, but other species, other cultures, the planet itself—are similar to us and similarly in need of nurture, but there is also a larger whole to which all belong. The health of that larger whole is essential to the health of the parts. . . . The visions will be both like and unlike familiar religious visions: like, in that they involve the hesitation of reverence before acting to change, the attentive appreciation of the sacredness of what is; unlike, in that they are open. Instead of worshipping ancestors or deities conceived as parents, we must celebrate the mysterious sacredness of that which is still to be born.[8]

Emotions. Although the emphasis on logic in contemporary Western culture often discourages speakers from considering emotions as a possible form of elaboration, they can be a powerful way to develop ideas. Human beings respond emotionally—with their feelings—as well as logically to what happens in their lives. Emotions are aroused indirectly through means such as narration, vivid description, and display. Telling a story, describing something in great detail, and displaying an emotion yourself all invite identification with the emotion you want your audience to experience. Mountain climber Gwen Moffat invoked the emotion of fear in the following story:

Once I was climbing with my partner on the summit of an ice and rock ridge 10,000 feet up. Suddenly I heard a sound like singing. It was the metal head of my ice axe humming with electricity. My hair began to rise and I realized we were in the middle of the storm. It became absolutely still and we were surrounded by black clouds. In the next moment we heard a series of strikes of simultaneous thunder and lightning like one enormous explosion, which lasted several hours. There was absolutely nothing we could do, except either stand there and literally wait to be struck or keep on moving. We went on moving.[9]

Exaggeration. Overstating a point can serve to elaborate an idea by making it striking and memorable. Exaggeration often is used in humorous presentations, after-dinner speeches, or other ceremonial occasions. Exaggeration, as it is used in these settings, is not to be confused with the deliberate distortion of information or evidence. Exaggeration as a form of elaboration does not deal with actual facts as much as with the interpretation of ideas in a light-hearted way. In a commencement address at Drew University, actor Alan Alda used exaggeration as one way to develop his idea that contemporary leaders are unprincipled and unethical: "All across the country this month, commencement speakers are saying to graduating classes, we look to you for tomorrow's leaders. That's because today's leaders are all in jail."[10]

Examples. The example is a short illustration that usually is no longer than a sentence or two. It is a specific illustration of a category of people, places, objects, actions, experiences, or conditions that shows the nature or character of that category. Charlton Heston, an actor and the president of the National Rifle Association, used a series of examples to illustrate his thesis that "a cultural war is raging across our land":

> For example, I marched for civil rights with Dr. King in 1963—long before Hollywood found it fashionable. But when I told an audience last year that white pride is just as valid as black pride or red pride or anyone else's pride, they called me a racist.
>
> I've worked with brilliantly talented homosexuals all my life. But when I told an audience that gay rights should extend no further than your rights or my rights, I was called a homophobe.
>
> I served in World War II against the Axis powers. But during a speech, when I drew an analogy between singling out innocent Jews and singling out innocent gun owners, I was called an anti-Semite.[11]

Explanation. An explanation is a description of a term, concept, process, or proposal to make it clear and understandable. When you describe the requirements for graduation from your university, you are using one type of explanation. A general who explains to the news media how a scud missile works is offering a functional explanation. As the director of an agency, you could explain why a certain condition exists—why layoffs are necessary, for example.

Facts. Facts are statements that generally are agreed upon as true by a culture. They are pieces of information that are verifiable by direct observation, by reference to scientific findings, or because they are offered by individuals who are granted expert status on an issue. If you state in a presentation that the use of condoms substantially decreases the sexual transmission of the HIV virus, you are using a fact derived from scientific findings.

Figures of speech. Figures of speech are unusual turns of language that can elaborate ideas in particularly vivid ways. Some frequently used figures of speech include:

- **Alliteration**. Initial or middle consonants are repeated in two or more   adjacent words. Vice president of the United States Spiro T. Agnew provided an example of alliteration in a speech on television news coverage when he asserted, "Normality has become the nemesis of the network news."[12]

- **Antithesis**. Antithesis involves the juxtaposition of opposing concepts or the contrast or opposition of ideas. John F. Kennedy's admonition in his inaugural address, "Ask not what your country can do for you, but what you can do for your country," demonstrates antithesis.[13]

- **Metaphor**. A metaphor is a comparison in which something is spoken about in terms of something else. President George W. Bush used a metaphor of freedom as a beacon of light in a presentation following the September 11, 2001, terrorist attacks: "America was targeted for attack because we're the brightest beacon for freedom and opportunity in the world. And no one will keep that light from shining."[14]
- **Oxymoron**. An oxymoron is a form of antithesis in which opposite words are placed back to back or the pairing of words that normally do not belong together. B. B. King's Blues Club in Memphis uses the oxymoron "famous unknowns" as a label for the musicians who appear in the club. Walt Bresette used an oxymoron to close his speech to Green Party members, suggesting that to secure their rights, Native Americans must engage in "non-violent ass kickin'."[15]
- **Personification**. In personification, the speaker attributes human qualities to nonhuman objects or concepts. Annie Dillard discussed how a book can take over its author, using the figure of personification to give the book agency: "Sometimes part of a book simply gets up and walks away. The writer cannot force it back in place. It wanders off to die."[16]
- **Simile**. A simile involves a comparison introduced by either *like* or *as*. In a speech presented at an arts conference, writer Andrei Codrescu used a simile to compare art to a river: "Trying to restrict its liberty is like damming the Mississippi River. Sooner or later Old Man River gets what it wants by the sheer force of its desire."[17]

Humor. Humor can function not just to entertain and amuse but also to develop and extend ideas. Humor is appropriate as a form of elaboration only when it is relevant to the idea you are developing. Writer and radio-show host Garrison Keillor used wry humor to describe the inhabitants of his imaginary hometown of Lake Wobegon:

> Since arriving in the New World, the good people of Lake Wobegon have been skeptical of progress. When the first automobile chugged into town, driven by the Ingqvist twins, the crowd's interest was muted, less whole-hearted than if there had been a good fire. When the first strains of music wafted from a radio, people said, "I don't know." Of course, the skeptics gave in and got one themselves. But the truth is, we still don't know.[18]

Myths. Myths are stories—either real or fictitious—that explain the origins of practices, beliefs, institutions, or natural phenomena. They express fundamental social, cultural, and religious values important to a community. In testimony before the Supreme Court in 1915, Chief Weninock of the Yakimas told the story of the origins of Native Americans as a way of developing the idea that Native Americans have legitimate claims to their traditional fishing places:

God created the Indian Country and it was like he spread out a big
blanket. He put the Indians on it. They were created here in this
Country, truly honest, and that was the time the river started to run.
Then God created fish in this river and put deer in the mountains and
made laws through which has come the increase of fish and game.
Then the Creator gave us Indians Life; we walked, and as soon as we
saw the game and fish we knew they were made for us.[19]

Narratives. Stories as elaboration involve telling real or fictional narratives, usually complete with characters, settings, plots, and dialogue. You may use stories told by others or personal narratives, where you recount your own experiences. This is the kind of narrative Professor Patti P. Gillespie told in a presentation she gave as president of the Speech Communication Association:

As some of you know, I try to spend part of every other summer
camping in Kenya. During my last trip in Amboseli, I was awakened
just before daybreak by the sound of furiously pounding hooves that
grew closer and closer to my tent. There was a horrible cry that inter-
mingled with growls until both seemed within a few feet of where I
was lying. Suddenly the cries and growls stopped, and all I heard was
a very deep vibrating sound. . . .

Gradually, as I thought about it, the sequence became clear to me.
A zebra had been fleeing a lion, who had caught it just outside my
tent and was now feasting on it. The five of us in the camp would
remain hostage inside our tents until the heat of the day when the
lion, satisfied and sleepy, would move away from us. Very well, I
thought, I will try to calm down and wait. I waited. I had only begun
to regret my last night's beer when I heard what sounded like human
footsteps—yes, they were human because I next heard the unmistak-
able sound of pots and pans. The cook was out of his tent. Thinking
him slightly mad, I dressed hastily, looked out carefully, and then
joined him hurriedly at the fire. "Where was the lion kill?" I asked in
butchered Swahili. "No lion," he said, "hyena fight."[20]

She continued the story, making the point that, just as with the hyena
fight, things in higher education may not be as they seem.

Participation. Audience participation is an invitation to the audience
to respond verbally during the course of the presentation. This form of elaboration allows you to use the ideas, comments, or responses of the audience
to develop your ideas. Audience participation assumes a variety of forms:

- **Call/response** is a pattern of spontaneous vocal and nonverbal
  responses from listeners in reply to a speaker's statements or questions that testify to the impact of the message. Call/response functions much as applause does—as a form of affirmation and support.
  It tells you when the audience is with you and when you can move
  to a discussion of your next idea. Call/response patterns may be

formulaic, or they can rely on innovation and improvisation, with each exchange generating new meanings, creating an ever-evolving context and story that shift to fit "individual and group needs as they present themselves at the specific moment of the telling."[21] Football fans engage in call and response when cheerleaders call out the letters *D, E, F, E, N, S, E* and the audience repeats each letter in turn. Denver Broncos fans use call and response when one group in the stadium yells *Go!* and another group answers *Broncos!*

- **Discussion**. Discussion is the consideration of a question through informal exploration by at least two individuals. This is a necessary form of elaboration with the goal of discovering knowledge and belief, although it can be part of any presentation. Most interviews and informal conversations naturally take the form of a discussion, with all participants sharing ideas and responding to the thoughts of others.

- **Encouragement**. In encouragement, the audience simply offers encouraging remarks to a speaker without the speaker's initiation of the call/response pattern. Participants at a campaign rally, for example, might call out "I hear you" to signal their agreement with the candidate. They might urge a speaker to continue in a particular direction by shouting "take your time," "speak on it," "work it," "amen," "hallelujah," or "right on!" Nonverbally, audience members might offer encouragement by waving their hands in the air, whistling, jumping up and down, or clapping their hands.

- **Testimonials**. Asking the audience to offer examples from their own lives to support an idea is a testimonial, another form of audience response that may serve to develop ideas. The stories told by participants in meetings of Alcoholics Anonymous or other support groups, for example, constitute testimonials. Religious revivals sometimes make use of testimonials to help secure new converts, and the testimony of witnesses in courts of law is another example.

Poetry. Poetry is the use of meaning, sound, and rhythm in language, chosen and arranged to create a concentrated image of a particular condition or experience. You could use William Shakespeare's poetry about the world as theater to elaborate on the idea that we all live in dramas of our own making:

> All the world's a stage,
> And all the men and women merely players:
> They have their exits and their entrances;
> And one man in his time plays many parts.[22]

Prayers. Prayers are entreaties, supplications, or requests, usually directed at a force the audience acknowledges as a supreme being. The speaker who prays for wisdom for those about to make an important decision, for example, is using prayer as a form of elaboration. Religious leader and humanitarian Mother Teresa used prayer as a form of elaboration in a speech to the National Prayer Breakfast:

> As we have gathered here to pray together, I think it will be beautiful if we begin with a prayer that expresses very well what Jesus wants us to do for the least. St. Francis of Assisi understood very well these words of Jesus and His life is very well expressed by a prayer.
>
> And this prayer, which we say every day after Holy Communion, always surprises me very much, because it is very fitting for each one of us. . . .
>
> . . . "My peace I leave with you, My peace I give unto you." He came not to give the peace of the world which is only that we don't bother each other. He came to give the peace of heart which comes from loving—from doing good to others.[23]

Proverbs. Proverbs are succinct cultural sayings that express obvious truths and capture audience members' experiences. In a sermon, Barbara Brown Zikmund cited a Yoruba proverb to develop her idea that each person is an important part of God's creation: "There is an old Yoruba proverb told among the indigenous tribes of Nigeria in West Africa that expresses the same message: 'The hand of a child cannot reach the ledge; the hand of the elder cannot enter the gourd: both the young and the old have what each can do for the other.' "[24]

Puns. Puns are plays on words based either on different words that sound alike or on various meanings of the same word. In a presentation about her work, visual artist Janet Hughes used puns to describe what her selection for inclusion in an art exhibition meant to her. One portion of her presentation included puns on the word *read*:

> She was well read.
> She became widely read.
> She painted the town
> the picture
> and her lips.
> Her lips were read.
> Her lips were red.[25]

Questions. Questions can be used to develop an idea by encouraging listeners to think about the idea and to become mentally engaged in the subject matter. Three common kinds of questions are rhetorical questions, substantive questions, and questions of facilitation.

- **Rhetorical questions**. Journalist Ted Koppel's commencement speech at Duke University included several questions designed to develop his idea that television packages people and ideas. He labeled this phenomenon the *Vanna factor*, referring to Vanna White, the woman who turns the letters on Wheel of Fortune: "We have no idea what, or even if, Vanna thinks. Is she a feminist, or every male chauvinist's dream?"[26]

- **Substantive questions**. Substantive questions are those that you as speaker both ask and answer or ones you expect your audience to answer. Ted Koppel used this kind of question later in his Duke commencement address when he asked, "What then should we, or must we conclude?" He answered his own question by responding, "Whatever your merchandise, if you want to move it in bulk, you flog it on TV."[27]

- **Questions of facilitation**. Questions of facilitation help manage a group interaction. As a facilitator, you use questions to ensure that all perspectives are offered, to prevent any individual from monopolizing the discussion, and to keep the discussion on track. The examples below suggest some questions you can use to handle these situations.

  - To ensure full representation of all perspectives:
    - To draw out a silent member:
      - "Does anyone who hasn't spoken care to comment?"
      - "Roger, what is your opinion of . . ."
      - "Cecilia, from your experiences in local government, would you comment on that?"
    - To suggest the need for sharing personal experiences:
      - "Does anyone know of instances where this has worked?"
      - "How has this affected each of you personally?"
      - "Will each of you be thinking about your own experiences in this matter so that I can ask each of you for your reactions later?"
      - "Have any of you had experiences with this in another company that you would be willing to share with us?"
      - "What is at the heart of the matter for you?"
      - "How did you get involved with this issue? What is your personal relationship to or personal history with it?"
    - To call attention to points that have not been considered:
      - "Does anyone have any information on this point?"
      - "What has been your thinking on this issue?"
      - "Before we continue, would it be profitable to explore this angle more fully?"

- "Whose lives are affected by the issue? In what ways are they affected?"
- "Whose perspectives are not represented in our discussion?"

- To suggest the need for additional information:
  - "Do we have enough information to decide now?"
  - "Should we form a subcommittee to research and bring back the information we need on this issue?"

- To prevent a few from monopolizing the discussion:
  - "Excuse me, Sally. Before you continue, may I ask if anyone has a comment on the point you've just made?"
  - "Thank you, Anthony. May we hear from someone else who hasn't expressed an opinion?"

- To keep the group on track and on task:
  - "That's interesting—and how does this point fit in with the issue being considered?"
  - "I might have missed something you said. Will you please explain the connection between your suggestion and the main issue?"
  - "Does the group feel that this point bears directly on the issue at hand?"
  - "Would we make more progress if we confined our discussion to the facts of the case rather than to the people involved?"
  - "Since we don't seem to be able to resolve this difference now, could we move on to the next point? Perhaps further discussion will reveal additional information that will help us resolve this issue."
  - "What are we up to in this conversation? What do we want to see happen here?"
  - "Shall we go back and revisit our purpose to see if we're still working toward that end?"

Quotations. With quotations, you use the words of others to develop and extend an idea. A quotation may draw its effectiveness from the content of the quotation or from the reputation or expertise of the person who is quoted. Charlton Heston used a quotation to introduce his concept of a civil war: "Dedicating the memorial at Gettysburg, Abraham Lincoln said of America, 'We are now engaged in a great Civil War, testing whether this nation or any nation so conceived and so dedicated can long endure.' Those words are true again. I believe that we are again engaged in a great civil war, a cultural war that's about to hijack your birthright to think and say what resides in your heart."[28]

Repetition and restatement. In repetition, words or phrases are repeated exactly. In restatement, an idea is repeated using different words. Both forms of elaboration function to reinforce an idea. A Yoruba masquerade chant uses repetition to convey the idea of the supreme power of death:

> On the day death would kill the rich man
> Money would be of no avail
> On the day death would kill the medicine man
> The charm that locks up man's intentions,
> The one that stupefies one
> The one that makes one look like a fool
> The one that arrests one's movements,
> Indeed, everything will perish.
> On the day death will kill the great priest,
> Gentle winds will carry off all his papers.[29]

Rhythm and rhyme. In rhythm and rhyme, words and phrases are chosen for their sound effects. In this form of elaboration, the sounds of the words develop the idea the speaker wants to convey. Many forms of elaboration, such as alliteration and repetition, rely to some degree on the sounds of words, but in rhythm and rhyme, the sounds of the words are emphasized more than the content.

- **Rhythm**. Rhythm is the arrangement of words to achieve a regular recurrence of beat or accent. Jesse Jackson used rhythm in his speech to the Democratic national convention in 1984:

  > I told them in every slum, there are two sides. When I see a broken window, that's the slummy side. Train that youth to be glazier, that's the sunny side. When I see a missing brick, that's the slummy side. Let that child in the union, and become a brick mason, and build, that's the sunny side. When I see a missing door, that's the slummy side. When I see the vulgar words and hieroglyphics of destitution on the walls, that's the slummy side. Train some youth to be a painter, an artist—that's the sunny side.[30]

- **Rhyme**. Rhyme involves words that correspond with one another in terms of ending sounds. Jesse Jackson used rhyme in his "Rainbow Coalition" speech when he said, "Jesus said that we should not be judged by the bark we wear but by the fruit that we bear."[31]

Rituals. Rituals are set forms or systems of rites in which members of a community participate. Often handed down from generation to generation, rituals and ceremonies function to connect community members to their heritage, their community, their country, or the cosmos. Through that connection, they generate feelings of power and wholeness. Author Diane Stein often uses rituals in her workshops designed to create changes in consciousness. In her "Croning" ritual, for example, a woman who is undergoing a transition—menopause, retirement, or her last child's departure from home, for example—is given tangible or verbal gifts by each of those present.[32] In the African-American community, men sometimes engage in communication rituals such as jiving and boasting that demonstrate allegiance to the group and its identity.[33] A speaker who asks listeners to join her in reciting a credo or a pledge they all know also is using ritual as a form of elaboration.

Sensory images. Sensory images are words or phrases that communicate feelings and perceptions through one or more of the five senses—sight, smell, sound, taste, and touch. Author Barbara Kingsolver used olfactory images to help capture the idea of a rainstorm: "That was when we smelled the rain. It was so strong it seemed like more than just a smell. . . . I don't know how a person could ever describe that scent. It certainly wasn't sour, but it wasn't sweet either, not like a flower. . . . To my mind it was like nothing so much as a wonderfully clean, scrubbed pine floor."[34]

Songs. When a speaker sings a song or asks the audience to join in the singing of a song, an idea can be elaborated in a particularly vivid and powerful way. A speaker might ask an audience of union members to join in the singing of "Joe Hill" to remind them of the strength and tenacity of labor, for example. Likewise, "We Shall Overcome" often is sung at civil-rights events to suggest the perseverance and determination of those involved in the struggle. The singing of "Amazing Grace" at funerals and the singing of the "Star-Spangled Banner" to kick off baseball games are other examples of songs as forms of elaboration.

Statistics. Statistics are numerical data designed to show relationships between or among phenomena. The relationship expressed can emphasize size or magnitude, establish trends such as increases or decreases in a particular population, or make comparisons. In a presentation about homelessness, a statistic might be used to show a change in the configuration of the homeless population: "In contrast to the usual conception of the homeless as hardcore unemployed, 1 in 5 residents of shelters now holds a full- or part-time job."[35]

Understatement. In understatement, the speaker states an important point in a restrained style. The low-key nature of the understatement highlights its importance. Holden Caufield, the protagonist in the novel *The Catcher in the Rye*, uses understatement in his announcement, "It isn't very serious. I have this tiny little tumor on the brain."[36]

This list provides some suggestions for ways in which the ideas of your presentation may be elaborated. Your own inventive processes will generate others as you work to develop the main ideas of your presentation. Your next task is to develop an introduction and a conclusion that complete the frame of your presentation.

7

BEGINNING AND ENDING

Now that you have selected the basic structure of your presentation and the forms of elaboration by which to develop your main ideas, your next step is to develop an introduction and a conclusion. Because your ideas often change extensively as you work to put them into an organizational structure, you want to wait until after the body and main ideas of your speech are prepared to decide how you want to introduce and end your presentation. Furthermore, the organizational format and the forms of elaboration you choose for the presentation may suggest possible directions for your introduction and conclusion.

The Introduction

The introduction is a critical part of your presentation because it is where you have your first opportunity to invite your audience to see the world as you see it. You offer your audience a glimpse of your perspective and your framing of that perspective. By the end of your introduction, your audience should know the subject of your presentation and your interactional goal(s). Your audience also will have begun making assessments about you as a speaker, and you want them to see you as someone with whom they want to continue to interact.

The introduction not only gives the audience information about you and your topic but also begins the process of establishing the conditions of freedom, safety, value, and openness for your audience. Everything you do in your introduction should communicate your desire that your audience members feel free to choose whether and how to incorporate new ideas that emerge from their interaction with you. Communicating genuine warmth as part of an introduction is likely to put your audience members at ease and encourage them to continue listening. When you are energetic about different ideas, you communicate that you value diverse perspectives. If the four speaking conditions are met, your audience will want to continue to be part of the interaction that you have initiated with your introduction. Carefully considering how you introduce your presentation is important, then, because it makes a difference in how the entire presentation is received.

You may have been told that introductions should be dramatic and exciting or that you should tell a joke to get the attention of audience members. Such openings generally are unnecessary because your audience has come to listen to you and already is interested in what you have to say. Startling introductions also tend to irritate audiences rather than put them in the frame of mind to listen to a presentation. A joke, especially if it is unrelated to your topic, takes audience members' attention away from the subject of your presentation. Both the startling introduction and the joke violate the condition of value. By using such openings, you signal to your audience that you do not believe they are interested in your topic or are able to be attentive listeners and thus need to be startled or cajoled into listening to you.

Even interested audience members, however, may not be fully present mentally for a variety of reasons as you begin your presentation. There also will be times when you must speak to a captive audience—one that is required to be there for some reason. A supervisor may have asked the members of your audience to attend a seminar in which they personally are not very interested, or your audience members may be attending a conference and discover that a particular presentation is not what they thought it would be. In these instances, we still do not recommend a startling opening statement or joke for your introduction. The most effective introduction in this situation is one that connects the topic to the audience in an engaging, specific, and perhaps personal way. Telling a story in some detail, for example, about something that happened to you that is directly relevant to audience members might be a good way to begin in these instances.

There are many different ways to begin a presentation. Below are descriptions of some commonly used types of introductions. You do not need to select your introduction only from this list. Often, your subject matter will suggest an introduction unique to your presentation. You also might find that there are times when you want to combine some of the suggested introductions to use as the opening for your presentation.

Narrative. In a narrative or story that functions as an introduction, you describe a particular incident, furnishing specific details about the characters, actions, and settings involved. For example, Peggy Dersch, a student at Southeast Missouri State University, began a presentation on misconceptions about rape with the following story:

> It was winter, 1976. A news item concerning the attempted rape of an eight-year-old child was reported on WABC-TV in New York City. Following the news, the station's weather announcer, Tex Antoine, began his report by reminding viewers of what he called an ancient proverb: "Confucius once say: If rape is inevitable, relax and enjoy it!" After enough protest calls, station officials required Antoine to offer a public apology. He said simply, "I regret making the statement." And then he added, "I didn't realize the victim was a child."[1]

Poem. Poetry can be used to introduce a presentation. When you use a poem, the concentrated imagery and rhythmic use of language combine to evoke a powerful introduction to the main idea of the presentation. A poem from *The Prophet* by Kahlil Gibran frequently is used as the introduction for presentations of various kinds at wedding ceremonies:

> Love one another, but make not a bond of love:
> Let it rather be a moving sea between the shores of your souls.
> Fill each other's cup but drink not from one cup.
> Give one another of your bread but eat not from the same loaf.
> Sing and dance together and be joyous, but let each one of you
> be alone,
> Even as the strings of a lute are alone though they quiver with the
> same music.
> Give your hearts, but not into each other's keeping.
> For only the hand of Life can contain your hearts.
> And stand together yet not too near together:
> For the pillars of the temple stand apart,
> And the oak tree and the cypress grow not in each other's shadow.[2]

Question. Questions can function as introductions, just as they can serve as forms of elaboration. An introduction can consist of a rhetorical question, a substantive question, or a series of questions of either kind.

- **Rhetorical question.** Rhetorical questions are ones you expect your audience to answer mentally. Such questions require audience members to engage the material by answering the questions for themselves. A welcoming presentation to camp counselors, for example, could begin with this series of rhetorical questions:

  > So why do we do it?
  > What *good* is it?
  > Does it teach you anything
  > Like determination? Invention? Improvisation?
  > Foresight? Hindsight?
  > Love?

Art? Music? Religion?
Strength or patience or accuracy or quickness or tolerance or
Which wood will burn and how long is a day and how far is a mile
And how delicious is water and smoky green pea soup?
And how to rely
On your
Self?[3]

- **Substantive question**. Your presentation can begin with an actual question you expect the audience to answer. In a presentation about the drawbacks of technology, you might ask your audience members to raise their hands if they upgraded a computer within the last year, purchased a cell phone, or bought a flat-screen TV. By answering your questions, they become involved in your subject and begin to anticipate your presentation.

[handwritten margin note: give ✓ Wait for answer]

Quotation. When a quotation is used to start a presentation, you use a statement made by someone who has addressed your topic in a particularly eloquent way. Business consultant Melodie Lancaster, speaking to a meeting of the American Business Women's Association in Houston, Texas, started with such a quotation: "I'd like to begin with a quote from Charles Handy's book, *The Age of Unreason*, which strikes at the heart of what I'd like you to remember today, 'The future we predict today isn't inevitable,' he writes. 'We can influence it if we know what we want it to be. . . . We can take charge of our own destinies in a time of change.'"[4]

Reference to speaking situation. Remarks that mention or allude to any of the components of the speaking situation—the audience, occasion, place, the speaker, or a previous speaker—are frequent introductory forms.

- **Reference to audience**. When beginning with a reference to your audience, you focus on special attributes that characterize your audience. Father Theodore Hesburgh, president of the University of Notre Dame, used a reference to his audience in the introduction of an address to Notre Dame alumni: "What I am celebrating tonight is your personal lives, your married lives, your children, your business and professional lives, the kind of ideals you attained here in one way or another. I am celebrating the kind of spirit and faith you left here with, the high enthusiasm and all that has been accomplished since then."[5]

- **Reference to occasion.** A reference to the occasion makes use of the reason for gathering as a shared starting point. Kim Woo Choong, chair of the Daewoo Group, chose a reference to the occasion as the opening for a presentation: "Let me extend to you all my heartfelt congratulations in establishing the Southern California Chapter of the Korea-America Friendship Society. And I am deeply honored to have been invited to speak today at this, the inaugural meeting of the Chapter. I sincerely hope that the Chapter will make tremendous contributions to cooperation and friendship between the United States and Korea, and I look forward to your efforts in this quest."[6]

- **Reference to place.** The setting where the presentation takes place is mentioned when reference to place is used as a form of introduction. President George W. Bush's introduction to his 2002 State of the Union address included a reference to place: "The last time we met in this chamber, the mothers and daughters of Afghanistan were captives in their own homes, forbidden from working or going to school. Today women are free and are part of Afghanistan's new government."[7]

- **Reference to self**. A reference to you as the speaker is another way to begin a presentation. In this case, you may serve as a representative of a particular category of individuals that you will discuss in your speech, or you highlight a quality or experience you bring to the speaking situation. English professor Karen Carlton used a reference to herself to begin a commencement address at Humboldt State University: "Exactly 30 years ago, I graduated from a small, liberal arts college in southwest Texas and prepared to live in a world I knew and understood. Roles were defined for me: I was engaged to be married; I would teach school so that my young husband could proceed with his studies; we would have children and live happily, safely ever after."[8]

- **Reference to previous speaker**. In an introduction that refers to the previous speaker, you recall a major idea developed by someone else earlier in the interaction and relate it to your presentation. You might use this type of introduction in a speech about smoking by beginning, "We haven't really come a long way, baby," referring to the previous speaker's main idea that more women than men are taking up smoking. *W*

The introduction to your presentation is critical because it not only introduces your audience to your topic and your perspective on it, but it establishes the tone of the entire presentation. As a result of what you say in the introduction, your audience members will decide whether to continue listening, whether they want to continue interacting with you, and whether they feel safe and valued and able to discuss and consider a variety of perspectives. *what type of introduction*

The Conclusion

The conclusion of your presentation provides a final opportunity to leave your audience members with your perspective clearly in mind. This is one last place in which to communicate the overall vision of your presentation. The primary function of the conclusion, then, is to reemphasize the main idea or gist of your presentation. To accomplish this function, your conclusion needs to be consistent with the tenor of the rest of the presentation. You want to continue to enact in tone the qualities and conditions you have been seeking to create in the content of your presentation. Changing tone drastically at this point is jarring for the audience because it is unexpected. For the same reason, the conclusion is not the place to introduce new ideas. Doing so can detract from audience members' understanding and retention of your central idea. Think of the conclusion as a place for summarizing, emphasizing, and highlighting the main ideas you've offered in the body of your presentation.

A second function of the conclusion is to convey to the audience what you would like to have happen next in the interaction. If you are not planning any kind of question-and-answer session with your audience, conclude in a way that signals the definite end of the interaction. For example, you would not call for questions if time is limited, if the group is extremely large, or if a call for questions is inappropriate for the occasion. Delivering a toast at a wedding or a eulogy at a funeral are two situations in which you would not call for questions. Close with a sentence that leaves no doubt that the presentation is finished. Quotations and poems often are used as endings when a speaker wants to conclude with finality.

On the other hand, if you want to encourage the participation of audience members following your presentation, signal that now is the time for them to speak by using a conclusion that is open and tentative. At the end of your prepared remarks, pause briefly and then call for questions. If you want the audience to do something specific—sign a petition or get into small groups, for example—this is the time to make that request or, if already made, to reinforce that request.

Conclusions assume a variety of forms. Some of the most common types are listed below. As with the options for introductions to a presentation, these are only some of the kinds of conclusions possible. We hope they will stimulate your thinking so that you construct a conclusion that effectively meets the needs of your speaking situation.

Call to action. With some interactional goals, a challenge to the audience to take some kind of action is an appropriate conclusion. George C. Fraser, director of marketing and communications for United Way of Cleveland, challenged his audience of teachers as he began to conclude his speech:

> I am throwing the gauntlet down and asking each of you for a *commitment* to do more. Now!
> To become indispensable.
> To vertically network by reaching down and lifting up and
> To reach back and pull forward.[9]

Narrative. Just as a story can serve as an organizational pattern or introduce a presentation, so you can use a narrative as the summary for a presentation. Senator Huey P. Long from Louisiana used a narrative to conclude a speech in 1935 outlining his plan to redistribute the wealth of the United States:

> Well ladies and gentlemen, America, all the people of America, have been invited to a barbecue. God invited us all to come and eat and drink all we wanted. He smiled on our land and we grew crops of plenty to eat and wear. He showed us in the earth the iron and other things to make everything we wanted. He unfolded to us the secrets of science so that our work might be easy. God called, "Come to my feast."
>
> Then what happened? Rockefeller, Morgan, and their crowd stepped up and took enough for 120 million people and left only enough for 5 million for all the other 125 million to eat. And so many millions must go hungry and without these good things God gave us unless we call on them to put some of it back.[10]

Pledge. A pledge is a promise or commitment to undertake certain actions. Ending in this fashion can signal your dedication to a proposal or a cause. Chief Dan George of the Coast Salish tribe ended his presentation commemorating Canada's 100th birthday with a pledge: "Oh, God! Like the Thunderbird of old I shall rise again out of the sea; I shall grab the instruments of the white man's success—his education, his skills— and with these new tools I shall build my race into the proudest segment of your society. Before I follow the great Chiefs who have gone before us, oh Canada, I shall see these things come to pass."[11]

Poem. Just as a poem can be used to begin a presentation, it can be used as a conclusion. In his eulogy for John F. Kennedy, Jr., Senator Edward M. Kennedy included a poem as part of his conclusion:

> The Irish ambassador recited a poem to John's father and mother soon after John was born. I can hear it again now, at this different and difficult moment:
>
> "We wish to the new child,
> A heart that can be beguiled,
> By a flower,
> That the wind lifts,
> As it passes.
> If the storms break for him,
> May the trees shake for him,
> Their blossoms down.
>
> In the night that he is troubled,
> May a friend wake for him,
> So that his time may be doubled,
> And at the end of all loving and love
> May the Man above
> Give him a crown."

We thank the millions who have rained blossoms down on John's memory. He and his bride have gone to be with his mother and father, where there will never be an end to love. He was lost on that troubled night—but we will always wake for him, so that his time, which was not doubled, but cut in half, will live forever in our memory, and in our beguiled and broken hearts.[12]

Quotation. You can use an eloquent statement made by someone else as a conclusion, just as you can use it as an introduction. Congressional Representative Barbara Jordan ended her keynote address to the Democratic national convention in 1976 with a quotation from Abraham Lincoln: "Well I am going to close my speech by quoting a Republican President and I ask you that as you listen to these words of Abraham Lincoln, relate them to the concept of a national community in which every last one of us participates: 'As I would not be a slave, so I would not be a master.' This expresses my idea of Democracy. Whatever differs from this, to the extent of the difference is no Democracy."[13]

Reference to introduction. A reference back to the introduction of your presentation provides a sense of completeness to the main ideas you've developed. Christine D. Keen, issues manager for the Society for Human Resource Management, began a presentation with a reference to a Chinese proverb: "The Chinese have a curse: 'May you live in interesting times.' And these certainly are interesting times. American business and American society are undergoing dramatic changes, and human resources sits right at the crossroads of these changes." To close, she referred back to her opening proverb: "For at least the next decade, then, we will all live in interesting times. And it's up to us to determine if that's a curse or a blessing."[14]

Reference to speaking situation. You can conclude your presentation by commenting on the situation, audience, place, or yourself in ways that remind audience members of the structure and main ideas of your presentation.

- **Reference to audience.** A reference to the audience in a conclusion highlights the importance of the audience to the interaction. In a commencement address to the California Western School of Law, Richard W. Carlson, director of Voice of America, closed with a reference to the audience:

  To you may be given the opportunity either to nurture or snuff out the germinating seed of information accessibility. All of us, in fact, have a role to play in ensuring that decades from now an informed public worldwide will have the opportunity to play an increasingly significant role in world affairs. The legal boundaries that people like you help to establish may make the difference between a world in which democratic principles are held high and one in which exploitation and misery are the norm. I know you are up to the challenge.[15]

- **Reference to occasion.** If the occasion on which you are speaking is significant, referring back to that occasion leaves your audience with a clear sense of the significance of your presentation in relation to that event. In a speech delivered on the anniversary of the Queen of England's coronation, you could use a reference to the occasion to conclude, noting the significance of the day on which you are speaking.

- **Reference to place.** A reference to place is an appropriate ending to a presentation given at a significant location. In a speech at the site where the World Trade Center stood in New York City, a reference to Ground Zero would make a particularly fitting conclusion.

- **Reference to self.** In a case where you were selected as the speaker because of certain accomplishments, a reference to self is an appropriate conclusion. A Nobel prize laureate might end an acceptance presentation with such a reference, acknowledging the theory, novel, or action for which the prize was given.

Summary of basic theme. In a conclusion that summarizes the main idea, you emphasize the primary idea of the presentation. George C. Fraser, whose call to action is cited above, followed that call with a restatement of the theme of his presentation: "In closing, ladies and gentlemen, I say to you once again: We must redefine the meaning of life. Life is about happiness and happiness includes the self-respect that comes from accepting responsibility for one's life and earning one's way in the world. We have all the tools we need, right here, right now."[16]

Summary of main ideas. In this type of conclusion, you reiterate your major ideas rather than restate the overall theme of your presentation. You list the main points of your speech so that your audience members can remember them easily. Communication professor Richard L. Weaver II concluded a presentation on self-motivation with a summary of his main ideas:

> Several things, now, should be clear to you. First, self-motivation is directly related to stress-reduction. Second, stress is not always negative. Third, we are the makers of our own stress; thus, we can control it. Fourth, there are some useful workable techniques for controlling it. . . . Self-motivation is most likely to occur when we can successfully deal with the stresses in our lives. Your personal advance hinges on effort—your willingness to put into practice techniques for activating or freeing the spirit.[17]

The conclusion to your presentation, like the introduction, is crucial to the overall impact of your speech. By means of your conclusion, you provide your audience with a reminder of the gist of your message and its main ideas and have a final opportunity to create an environment of freedom, safety, value, and openness. The conclusion also indicates to your audience that you are closing. It either provides a sense of finality or suggests that now is the time for the audience to assume a larger role in the interaction. You are now ready to develop the transitions that will enable you to move from one part of your presentation to the next and from one idea to another.

8

CONNECTING IDEAS

The process of connecting ideas involves the use of transitions that enable you to communicate to your audience how you see the frame or form of your presentation. The frame you have created is "the organization of an entire personal world,"[1] as literary critic Umberto Eco puts it, and your task now is to communicate that world to the audience by providing guideposts as you move from one idea to the next.

You cannot assume that your listeners will grasp the frame of your presentation that you see so clearly. As your listeners decode your ideas, they are engaged in a number of processes that work against their coming to the same understanding of your frame that you have. They are forgetting much of what you say simply because the short-term memory can handle only a limited number of new inputs at one time. They are consolidating information into manageable and retainable chunks. They are fitting your new information into a context or framework with which they are already familiar, and it may not be the one you envision. They are developing expectations and making predictions about what will come next in your presentation. They are drawing inferences or developing new ideas from the ideas you discuss. In general, then, they are hard at work using your ideas to build an idea structure of their own. If your presentation does not help them build that structure, what they construct may have little resemblance to your own. You can increase the possibility of a common structure by using transitions to provide explicit cues about your frame.

The use of transitions is the process of linking the various parts of your presentation so your audience easily can follow the frame for the perspective you are offering. Just as builders frame a house, providing its broad structure, so you frame your presentation, providing your audience with the general form of your speech. The connections you construct serve as guideposts that direct your audience from one part of the presentation—one area of the house—to another. These internal indicators are structural guideposts that orient listeners to your frame and direct them to the next point or section in your presentation.

Some speakers concentrate so hard on preparing each segment of a presentation—the introduction, the body, and the conclusion—that they forget to think about how they will move from one of these sections to the next. Consequently, their transitions are rough or non-existent. If you haven't made decisions about how to move from one point to the next, you might find yourself saying *uh* and then launching into your next point. You also might end up using the same transition over and over, such as *another point is* or *next*. You want to think deliberately about your transitions—and perhaps even to write them out in your notes—so that they help promote rather than detract from the perspective you are offering in your presentation.

The connections or transitions in a presentation fulfill several functions. Most important, they remind and forecast. They summarize or restate the point you have just discussed and preview what will happen next in the presentation. They let your audience know where you've been and where you're going. Consequently, transitions orient audience members to where you are in your larger organizational structure.

A second function of transitions is to help your audience stay on track. Transitions help reorient audience members who may have become so focused on a specific idea that they've missed part of your presentation. Other listeners might have become distracted by something else happening in the room and stopped listening. Transitions provide a means for all of these audience members to rejoin the presentation and to begin attending to it again.

Transitions serve yet another function. They are a way to communicate freedom, safety, value, and openness, thus helping you create the kind of speaking environment in which everyone can consider all perspectives fully. Transitions help an audience feel safe because you are providing clear signals about the structure of your speech and its progression. Audience members will not be surprised by where you are going if you offer continuous internal indicators of your structure. They also feel valued because you have taken the time to include connections that will make listening easy for them.

The use of transitions enhances the conditions of freedom and openness. Transitions demonstrate to your audience that you truly want them to understand the perspective you are offering and to be able to consider it as a viable option. If audience members are confused about what you are proposing because you have not taken the time to make the connections among the ideas in your presentation clear, they will be unable to give your presentation complete consideration. When you make deliberate choices about your transitions, the audience is more likely to perceive, understand, and appreciate the presentation and the coherence you have given it.

Transitions can assume a variety of forms, including: (1) paragraphs; (2) sentences; and (3) words and phrases. In each case, transitions assist your listeners in following your structure or frame as you move from one idea to the next in your presentation.

Paragraphs

Paragraphs are the longest kind of transition or connection in a presentation. They most often are used: (1) between the introduction and the body and between the body and the conclusion of a presentation; and (2) between main ideas within the body itself. In each case, the paragraph contains some combination of summarizing and forecasting.

At times, your transition paragraph will consist primarily of a summary and a short forecast or preview. This transitional arrangement most often is used when the ideas offered are complicated or new to the audience, and a summary of them is necessary if audience members are going to be able to move with you to the next set of ideas. Perhaps you have been discussing the virtues and limitations of various security systems for the networked computers in your office. Because the systems are complex, a summary of the strengths and weaknesses of each system will be helpful to your audience before moving to a quick preview of the need to make a decision about security quickly, which is your next main idea. A transition that focuses on summary also could be used when the ideas you are offering are novel for an audience. If you are discussing reasons why audience members should consider sending their children to a new charter school—something they have not considered before—reiterating the benefits of this kind of education may be the most helpful transition for your audience of parents.

In other cases, the paragraph of connection consists of a short summary and a much lengthier forecast. This kind of transition paragraph is used when you are most concerned with focusing your audience's attention in a new direction. If you are using the organizational pattern of elimination, for example, you might choose this kind of transition from your introduction to the body of your presentation to alert listeners to the fact that you will be describing various solutions, ending with the one you believe is most desirable. Similarly, if you are describing multiple perspectives in your presentation, you might want to devote the bulk of your transition paragraph to forecasting to ensure that your audience members understand that this is the approach you will be taking.

Sometimes, the transition paragraph is fairly balanced between re-statement and forecasting. You might use a couple of sentences to summarize and a couple of sentences to preview where you are heading next. In a presentation to the 2002 International Consumer Electronics Show, Microsoft CEO Bill Gates used a transition paragraph balanced between summary and forecast to move between the introduction and the body of his presentation: "So what are the fundamental hardware trends? You know, consumer electronics historically have been mostly about hardware. How is that changing? Well, first and foremost we have the continued truth of Moore's Law. It may not last forever, but for the next decade we're certainly going to get this doubling in power every 18 months to two years."[2] He then went on to discuss the impact of Moore's Law on the computer industry.

Sentences

When sentences serve as transitions, they most often are used to move: (1) between major segments of a presentation; and (2) between main ideas. This kind of transition can be a single sentence or one or two sentences. The sentence that moves between segments of a presentation contains both a reference to the previous section and a preview of what will follow in the next section. Senator Edward Kennedy used such a sentence transition in his eulogy for John F. Kennedy, Jr. when he said, "I think now not only of these wonderful adventures, but of the kind of person John was."[3] John Kennedy, Jr.'s adventures were the focus of the previous section, and attributes of him as an individual were the focus of the subsequent section.

A sentence moving between main ideas also contains both restatement and forecast, making clear the connection between the two. In a speech about an upturn in the economy, you could use a sentence transition to move from the main idea that financial indicators point to growth in the nation's economy to the main idea that such growth can be seen in your own city: "But indicators of growth at the national level are impersonal and abstract. We can also see evidence of the economy's recovery in the story of our own city."

Rhetorical questions often are used as sentence transitions because the question format invites audience members to consider possible answers, which are the subject of the next section. Bill Gates frequently uses rhetorical questions to move from one idea to another. In his presentation at a Consumer Electronics Show, he asked, "So what's driving the opportunity?" His next sentence provided the answer to the question and also served as a preview of where he was headed next: "The smart devices where the hardware costs are coming down and the intelligence is going up."[4]

Your commitment statement also can serve as a transition sentence because it fulfills the summarizing and previewing functions of a transition. The commitment statement often is placed at the end of the introduction of a presentation, where it leads from the preliminary material to the body of the presentation. For a presentation on the need to reevaluate the importance parents place on athletics in elementary school, you might begin with the story of the father who was beaten to death at his son's hockey game.[5] Your commitment statement would move your audience from that story into the body of your presentation: "Although most parents do not come to blows at their children's sporting events, I believe parents are placing too much emphasis on competitive sports at the elementary school level."

Phrases or Single Words

Phrases or single words also can function as transitions. Because these are brief, they most often are used to move between forms of elaboration that develop a main idea to suggest relationships among them. Transitions that make comparisons include words such as *similarly*, *likewise*, and *in comparison*. To move between two examples of overspending in a company, you might say, "Similarly, we can see another instance of overspending in the parts department."

Some transitions indicate a causal relationship between forms of elaboration, indicated by phrases such as *therefore*, *as a result*, and *consequently*. With the topic of overspending, you might move from making a point about bad accounting practices—an explanation—to a metaphor by means of a transition that stresses a causal connection: "As a result of bad accounting practices, we now find ourselves in hot water."

Other transition words or phrases focus on summary. Words such as *finally*, *in summary*, and *as we have seen* are examples of transitions of this type. For a presentation in which you have offered a problem-solution approach, for example, you might begin your conclusion by saying, "As we have seen, the problem of overcrowding in schools will not be fixed overnight."

As a speaker, you might be tempted to overuse certain transitions because they are familiar. Consequently, they have lost much of their impact. Many speakers use *next*, *furthermore*, or numbers (*first*, *second*, *third*) as transitions. They also use *in conclusion*, *I would like to say* as a way to move into their conclusions. Rather than serving as effective transitions, these do little more than tell your audience that you didn't take the time to think of a transition that effectively allows you to move from one idea to another. Saying *I see that my time is up* is equally unimpressive. Rather than assisting your audience in moving between segments of your presentation, you let time—or, more precisely, the lack of it—provide your transition. Transitions should be designed carefully to assist your audience in moving with you between the segments, main ideas, and forms of elaboration of your presentation. They should not be fillers you insert because you did not take the time to do the kind of planning your audience deserves.

Transitions provide your audience with crucial cues about the world you are creating with your presentation. As you incorporate explicit cues about the frame or structure into your presentation, you encourage your listeners to understand your perspective fully. In finalizing your transitions, the process of developing your presentation is complete, and you are ready to work on the most effective way to deliver it.

9

DELIVERING

Delivering your presentation is the final step in the process of preparing a presentation. Delivery means using your body and other presentational aids to help express the ideas that comprise the content of your presentation. The various components of delivery—mode of presentation, use of notes, practice, voice, bodily movement, personal appearance and dress, and presentational aids—can be thought of as tools to facilitate the full presentation of your perspective and to provide opportunities for transformation to your audience.

Functions of Delivery

The elements of delivery perform two primary functions for your presentation. Delivery assists you in the creation of an environment of freedom, safety, value, and openness. When your posture, gestures, and facial expressions communicate warmth and a genuine interest in audience members rather than combativeness, aloofness, or superiority, you are more likely to create an environment in which transformation is possible. When you use projection aids thoughtfully and carefully, you communicate that you value audience members and their capacity for understanding.

A second function of delivery is that it offers an additional means for you to give full expression to your perspective. The more attractive and appealing your perspective is because of how it is delivered, the more likely it will be accorded full consideration by others. Many elements of delivery communicate your message to your audience visually and thus reinforce what you are saying verbally. Audience members are able to remember your perspective more easily because they have been able to process it using more than one sensory channel.

Components of Delivery

Factors to consider in delivering your ideas include mode of presentation, use of notes, voice, practice, bodily movement, personal appearance and dress, and presentational aids.

Mode of Presentation

One of the first choices you make when considering how best to use the delivery options available to you is mode of presentation. The mode of presentation you are likely to use for most formal speaking situations is the **extemporaneous** mode. In this mode, you speak from notes of some kind, and not everything you plan to say is written out in those notes. Each time you give the presentation, it will be different as you spontaneously create the presentation from your notes. This mode of presentation allows you to present your ideas in a careful and thoughtful way but also to be conversational in tone and to adapt readily to the verbal and nonverbal responses of the audience.

Sometimes, you will choose to write your presentation out completely and to read from a text. The **manuscript** mode is used if there are strict time limits within which you must speak or when the wording of the ideas in your presentation is critical. This mode has the advantage of allowing you to present your ideas exactly as you have planned, using the precise language you intended. Generally, however, the disadvantages of this mode outweigh its advantages. Because your entire presentation is written out in advance, your ideas are more likely to be phrased in a written style, which is more formal and less conversational than your natural oral style. You also cannot adapt to your audience as easily during the presentation. Whatever happens in the course of the interaction, your inclination is to continue reading your manuscript no matter how the audience is responding.

If you choose to use a manuscript, begin by converting the written style into a conversational one so you can deliver your presentation as though you are speaking and not reading. Read the manuscript out loud and change formal language such as *do not* to more conversational constructions such as *don't*. Change passive voice to active voice—*I researched this topic extensively* rather than *research has shown*. Make your presentation, in other words, sound like you talk. As you practice speaking from the manuscript, think about your ideas as you say them and remind yourself of the feelings and emotions that led you to express ideas in particular ways. Don't be afraid to deviate from the manuscript if something occurs to you during the presentation.

A third presentational mode available to you is **impromptu** speaking. In this mode, you speak with little or no planning or preparation, forming your presentation at the time that you speak. This is the mode of presentation you use most often. When you speak in class; offer your ideas at a staff meeting; or explain, in response to a question from your supervisor, how your current project is progressing, you are engaged in impromptu speaking. There will be times, however, when you are asked to speak impromptu in more formal situations—to give a toast at a wedding, to say a few words at a memorial service, to accept an award, or to introduce someone, for example. Remember that you have been asked to speak because of your expertise or special connection to the occasion, so responding appropriately probably will not be too difficult in these situations. If you have time, find a quiet place to think for a few minutes and jot down a few main points that can serve as the basic structure for your presentation. You then can elaborate on each of those points as you speak, using a story, fact, example, or other form of elaboration.

Choice of Notes

Your choice of notes is an important element in creating a comfortable speaking situation for you. Although you may have been told at some time to use note cards, they often are not practical for an extensive presentation where you need to present a great deal of information. You may find that you prefer to use one or two sheets of paper rather than note cards so you aren't creating a distraction for your audience by shuffling many cards. Another advantage of larger sheets of paper over note cards is that if you are using a lectern, an 8½" x 11" sheet of paper will sit higher on the stand than will a note card, which means it is easier for you to read.

You also will find that certain approaches to your notes work better for you than others. Your notes may include key ideas, major points of elaboration, and transitions in a list; you may prefer a formal outline; or you may want to use a visual diagram. Whatever format you choose, your notes should be easy for you to read. Typing up your notes rather than handwriting them, double or triple spacing them, and using a bold font can make them easy to see as you glance down and then back to your audience. You also might find that writing notes to yourself about aspects of delivery you want to be sure to remember is helpful. If you tend to talk fast during presentations, for example, you might want to write *SLOW DOWN* in bold, colorful letters at the top of each page of notes. Writing *MOVE* on your notes to encourage you to move out from behind the lectern or *HAIR* if you have a tendency to play with your hair can help you manage elements of delivery that may be problematic for you.

Time Limits

When you are asked to speak, you most likely will be given a length of time for your presentation. Perhaps you are speaking at a luncheon meeting and are scheduled to talk for 20 minutes, or perhaps you are lecturing to a class that meets for 50 minutes. Staying within the time frame given you is critical because time limits create expectations on the part of the audience, and audience members can become irritated and restless if you violate time limits. Acceptance speeches at the Academy Awards ceremony are examples of a presentational situation in which maintaining strict time limits is important if the ceremony is to end at a reasonable hour. By staying within the time limits you are given, you will be communicating that you are considerate of your audience members' needs and interests.

Paying close attention to time constraints also means you must be able to fit your perspective on your subject into whatever time is available for your presentation. You need to consider carefully what to leave in and what to take out. When you refuse to omit aspects of your perspective, you are forced to talk very fast or go overtime to get all of your ideas into your presentation. This approach works against rather than accomplishes your goal of giving full expression to your perspective. Attending to time limits, then, not only communicates to your audience members that you are respectful of their time, but it also helps you hone your perspective so that you can offer it as fully as possible in the time that you have.

Practice

For presentations other than impromptu, practice facilitates the creation of an environment of freedom, safety, value, and openness and the full articulation of your perspective. Practice under the most realistic conditions possible. You may find that practicing in front of real people—someone such as your roommate or partner—is helpful. The feedback of a live audience better approximates what you will experience in front of your audience during the actual presentation. If you will be standing to give your presentation, stand up to practice it. Each time you practice, deliver your presentation all the way through without stopping. If you stumble over a word or idea, don't start the presentation over. Instead, think about what you would do if that happened in front of your actual audience, and go on from there. We suggest practicing in front of a mirror a time or two and, if possible, videotaping a practice session. Both of these types of practice will show you if you have gestures or mannerisms that distract from the presentation of your ideas.

Practice, then, is a major factor in your ability to create a potentially transformative environment and to ensure that your perspective is presented fully. For a major presentation, practice your talk at least once and even twice a day for the week or so before the presentation. Even short presentations of four-to-six minutes in length deserve at least five or six practice sessions. The more times you give your presentation, the more familiar and comfortable you are with it, and the more confident you can be that your delivery will enhance rather than detract from the full articulation of your perspective.

Bodily Elements

Elements of your body that contribute to or detract from the delivery of your presentation include voice, movement, and personal appearance and dress. **Voice** includes the factors of volume, rate, pitch, and pausing. Volume is the degree of loudness or intensity of sound, and rate is the speed at which you speak. Pitch is the tone or register of vocal vibration, and pausing is the length of time between words or sentences.

Movement involves posture, gestures, facial expressions, and general body movement. Posture is how you carry your body, and gestures are movements of the hands, arms, body, and head. Facial expressions are the use of the face and eyes to communicate, and movement includes the general actions of your body, such as when you walk, stand, or sit.

Personal appearance and dress is another way in which your message is delivered. Personal hygiene, hairstyle, clothing, jewelry, and accessories are elements of personal appearance and dress. Personal hygiene concerns issues of health, cleanliness, and neatness. For many audiences, body odor, dirty or unkempt hair, scruffy beards, and wrinkled clothing detract from delivery. Hairstyle, clothing, jewelry, and accessories are the ways in which you decorate your body, including what you wear and the other decorative items you select as adornment—earrings, rings, bracelets, necklaces, pins, cuff links, hats, scarves, and ties, for example.

Offering specific guidelines for every bodily element of delivery is not possible because what is appropriate in one situation is inappropriate in another. For example, many audiences in the United States expect eye contact. It is a primary way to communicate that you sincerely want your audience members to understand your ideas and that you are interested in their responses to your perspective. If your audience members are from cultures in which direct eye contact is regarded as insulting or disrespectful, however, efforts to create an environment in which they feel safe and valued would need to assume a different form. In that case, you might choose to sit in a circle with audience members, where you can look down easily and naturally while others are talking.

Although there are no rules of delivery that apply to every situation, there are two general guidelines that can assist you as you think about your body as an aspect of delivery. No element should be: (1) sustained; or (2) distracting. If any aspect of your delivery is repeated over and over again, it is sustained and, in all likelihood, will dominate audience members' attention and make fulfilling the functions of your presentation difficult. If you use one gesture repeatedly or pace back and forth in the front of the room, for example, those sustained elements distract the audience from the goals you have for your presentation. Running back and forth between the slide projector, the lights, and the lectern is another instance of a sustained activity that is detrimental to the presentation of your message. Any element that is repeated to this degree calls attention to itself rather than to your perspective and thus is a distraction.

Some elements of delivery do not need to be repeated to be distracting. Showing a poster that is too small to be seen, playing with your hair, wearing a noisy bracelet, or using obnoxious sound effects in a computer-projection presentation increase the chances that your audience will pay attention to the distraction rather than to the content of your presentation.

Presentational Aids

Presentational aids are any audiovisual aids you use to supplement the content of your presentation. They include objects, models, diagrams, graphs and charts, maps, pictures, and audio and video clips. **Objects** are items that illustrate some feature of your speech. Showing a fossil to explain plant life in an earlier geologic period or a quilt made by your grandmother in a presentation on sewing as a form of communication are examples of using objects as presentational aids. A three-dimensional representation of something such as a building is making use of a **model** and might be used in a presentation about architecture or the revitalization of a downtown neighborhood. **Diagrams** show how something works; you might use diagrams in a presentation about how information travels in an organization or how the computers in your office could be networked.

Graphs and charts show information in numerical form. **Graphs** often are used to show relationships among components. For a speech on water conservation, you might use a graph that shows how conservation has reduced water use over the past five years. **Charts** also organize information in a visual format; a company's organizational chart is an example of this kind of aid that could be used in a presentation about where layoffs will occur. **Maps** display geographical areas. You could use a map of the United States in a speech about college recruitment to show how your university draws students from all 50 states. **Pictures,** which include paintings and photographs, are two-dimensional representations of people, places, and things. A photograph of a street scene in Beijing could be used to illustrate the increase of auto traffic in China, or painted self-portraits by several renowned artists could serve as aids in a presentation about the artistic genre of self-portraits. **Audio and visual clips** are short recordings of music, sounds, speech, or excerpts from movies, television, and radio. Playing a segment from the movie *Iris* to demonstrate the impact of Alzheimer's disease on family members is an example of the use of an audiovisual clip as a presentational aid.

Presentational aids can be displayed in various ways for your audience. Overhead transparencies, slides, flip charts, chalkboards, posters, handouts, and computer-generated graphics are some of the most common display media. A picture, map, chart, or graph, for instance, can be presented via slides, computer-projection software, overhead transparencies, a handout, or a poster.

Regardless of the type and medium for presentation of your aids, they should be supplemental. They should elaborate on ideas in the presentation but should not constitute the presentation itself. If you discover that your video clip consumes over half of your presentation, you need to cut it down so that it becomes a form of elaboration and not the speech itself. Likewise, a presentation that consists solely of showing slides and explaining each one is a presentation in which the aids have become the presentation. You also need to be prepared in case your presentational aids fail or are not available. Perhaps the computer does not work, your portfolio of charts was ruined in a rainstorm, or you left your slides at home. If you can give the presentation without any aids at all and it still makes sense, you will be prepared for any contingency and will be confident that your presentation is more than just a visual display.

The components of delivery are ways to assist in the full presentation of your perspective and in the audience's retention of your message. Whether these concern your use of notes, bodily elements, or presentational aids, components of delivery assist you in creating a potentially transformative environment for both you and your audience.

Twirks

Although there are no absolute rules for the use of elements of delivery, there is a category of elements or conditions called *twirks* that can interfere with delivery. *Twirk* is an arcane word that linguist Suzette Haden Elgin discovered and uses to refer to *"a feature of language behavior which attracts so much attention to itself that it outweighs both the content and the form of the speech."*[1] According to Elgin, twirks are anything that provokes a reaction not based on the content of your presentation. Twirks, in other words, are elements of delivery that are sustained or distracting. Elgin offers the following example of a twirk:

> Suppose you make an interesting, rational, and compelling speech, and you do that while wearing a purple velvet floppy hat with rabbit ears and scarlet satin roses. Then that hat is a *twirk*—and it will seriously interfere with the manner in which your speech is heard and understood by your audience. You could be the greatest orator since Demosthenes, and that hat would still undercut you and cancel out the power of your words and all the nonverbal communication that went with them.[2]

The purple hat—or whatever the object or condition that constitutes a twirk—is not in itself good or bad, positive or negative. But certain elements associated with delivery have the potential to interfere with the full presentation and reception of your perspective. Analyze all aspects of your planned delivery to recognize and eliminate the twirks that could hinder the transformative possibilities of your presentation.

Twirks assume a variety of forms. Some that are most likely to affect a speaking presentation involve: (1) communication anxiety; (2) language; (3) clothing and adornment; (4) permanent physical conditions; and (5) presentational aids.

Communication Anxiety

When you become so nervous that it interferes with your ability to present your perspective effectively, you are experiencing communication anxiety or stage fright. When you perceive that you are in a challenging, frightening, or new situation, one way your body responds is by producing adrenaline. Adrenaline sets you up to respond by "fight or flight," but in a communication situation, of course, you can do neither, so the adrenaline in your body seeks some kind of release. Manifestations of adrenaline take the form of the symptoms we associate with communication anxiety, such as shaking hands and knees, a dry mouth, butterflies in the stomach, an accelerated heartbeat, or blushing. If these symptoms are obvious to an audience as you are speaking, they may function as twirks.

Some degree of anxiety about communicating is normal; in fact, there are many legitimate reasons why you might feel anxious. One reason is that there is the expectation, when you are asked or choose to speak, that you will have given some thought to what you want to say and that it will offer a perspective or viewpoint that, if not novel, is at least interesting and of value to the audience. You may not be entirely confident that your perspective will be accepted and appreciated by your audience.

A lack of preparation also may trigger feelings of anxiety. If you are not as ready as you would like to be for a speaking situation—you have not had adequate preparation time, did not know you would be asked to speak, procrastinated in preparing your presentation, or did not practice your presentation very much—you probably will find yourself experiencing some anxiety. Even when you are well prepared, you still may experience anxiety because of uncertainties related to your presentation. Perhaps you are planning a presentation with an interactional goal of discovering knowledge and belief. You have prepared fully for the discussion, but it is a mode you do not use very often, and thus it generates anxiety for you. Perhaps your perspective itself is undergoing major shifts, and you feel a natural anxiety about articulating it in its changing form to an audience.

Perhaps you are experiencing anxiety because you feel you have nothing to contribute to the interaction. This feeling may be the result of having been silenced in the past, of feeling devalued in a group, or of not having the communication tools to express your perspective adequately. You also may believe that others will articulate the perspective you would offer and see no particular reason to speak up yourself. All of these feelings are legitimate and may provoke feelings of anxiety before and during your presentation.

There are other sources of anxiety, however, that basically are irrational. Fearing being in a car accident on a very foggy night or fearing for your life on a battlefield are legitimate sources of anxiety. Anxiety of an irrational sort consists of exaggerated or needless fear. Most irrational concerns arise not because of fear of possible physical harm or injury but because of an *"overconcern for what someone thinks about you."*[3] This kind of anxiety is self-defeating because the worry and fretting themselves are usually far worse than the actual event. If you experience anxiety of this sort, you are likely to exaggerate the possible outcomes of a speaking situation, and the worry itself increases the likelihood of something unexpected occurring.[4] You may worry, for example, about tripping on the way to the lectern and falling flat on your face. That this will occur is extremely unlikely, but stewing about it—focusing on it—will not keep it from happening.

Whether your anxiety has a legitimate basis or is largely irrational, it can be managed. You may have been given all sorts of advice for dealing with communication anxiety. Not all of it, however, helps create an environment of freedom, safety, value, and openness. You may have been told, or example, to look over the heads of your audience members; to imagine them sitting before you in their underwear; or to say over and over to yourself before you speak, "I'm a better person than they are." All of these techniques create just the opposite conditions from the ones you are attempting to foster. They require you to see yourself as superior to your audience rather than as a participant in an interaction in which everyone's perspective is welcomed and valued. They also assume a generally hostile and inhospitable environment. Such an environment is not likely to exist, but if it does, your presentation can help to change that situation.

Some ways of managing communication anxiety do allow you to contribute to the creation of the conditions of freedom, safety, value, and openness. One way is simply to deal with the symptoms you tend to experience so that your discomfort with or embarrassment about them does not interfere with your efforts to communicate. If your mouth tends to be dry when you speak, bring water with you to sip throughout your presentation. If your neck turns red when you speak, wear a turtleneck or a scarf that covers it. If shakiness is your body's preferred symptom of speech anxiety, try to engage in some physical activity before your presentation to rid your body of excess energy—take a walk, breathe deeply, or move your head and arms. Once you know that you have addressed your body's symptoms of communication anxiety, you will feel more comfortable and can concentrate on creating the kind of environment you desire.

Practicing your presentations also can lessen your communication anxiety. As you listen to yourself speak, your perspective will become increasingly clear, and you will become more confident about expressing it. Voicing your perspective whenever you get the opportunity is another way to decrease communication anxiety. Whenever you are given the chance to present your ideas, take it. The first several or perhaps the first hundred times you accept the opportunity to share your perspective, you might be uncomfortable and might experience the symptoms of anxiety that are familiar to you. Gradually, however, they will begin to disappear. You will feel more comfortable with the process of presenting ideas orally, will discover that you have good ideas to contribute, and will find that others appreciate your input into various interactions. We hope you will reach a point where you enjoy the experience of presenting ideas orally because of the insights you gain from the exchange of ideas and the possibilities for transformation that result.

If your stage fright is irrational because it assumes the form of exaggerated and needless worry, rational self-talk may be your best response. Recognizing the degree to which you can control how you interpret a situation may be the first step toward reducing irrational anxiety. Rather than reinforcing anxiety by dwelling on and worrying about the things that might go wrong in a presentation, you can minimize or even dispel it by focusing your attention elsewhere. One of the ways to do this is to put the presentation in perspective. It is only a presentation, and if it does not go perfectly, it is not the end of the world. That perfection is not the goal of the presentation might be another statement that is part of your positive self-talk. You also might turn your attention to the presentation itself and construct messages to yourself that reinforce the positive features of the presentation—how much you enjoy the opportunity to discuss the subject, how exciting it will be to hear others' perspectives on the same issue, or how delighted you are to have the opportunity to talk to a particular audience. Spending your time preparing for your presentation rather than worrying about it will focus your attention where it will do some good.

Just because you have addressed your speech anxiety, however, does not mean you can eradicate it entirely or forever. Even the most experienced speakers can experience some symptoms of anxiety in particularly difficult or challenging speaking situations. By understanding why the anxiety is surfacing and reminding yourself of what you have going for you in your presentation, how much you have practiced, and how much you want to give expression to your perspective, those anxieties will dissipate and probably disappear.

Language

Twirks of language relate to how something is said and include pronunciation, grammar and usage, jargon, obscenities, and fillers. **Pronun-**

ciation associated with a particular dialect often functions as a twirk. The way of pronouncing a certain vowel can be a twirk if the pronunciation is different from that of the dialect of your audience members. Dropping the endings of words or eliding words—*gonna* instead of *going to*—can be twirks for some audiences.

Grammar and usage also function as potential twirks, usually when violations of standard grammar and usage occur. Saying *ain't* instead of *isn't* or using the double negative—*I don't have no money*—are examples of such violations. For some cultural groups, grammatical errors interfere with the creation of an environment of freedom, safety, value, and openness.

Jargon might be seen as the opposite of poor grammar in the sense that it involves language that exceeds conversational standards and norms. Jargon is the use of a highly technical vocabulary characteristic of one field of activity. Virtually every discipline and field has its jargon, but use of that vocabulary with an audience not familiar with that field is a twirk. In a presentation about the military to a non-military audience, discussing *Batts, gunnery sergeants, master petty chief officers,* and *midshipmen* without defining terms, for example, constitutes jargon.

Obscenities also function as twirks for many audiences, although other audiences are accustomed to hearing such language. Obscenities are utterances that are offensive and violate a culture's norms for polite or appropriate speech. If you are not sure how an audience will respond to an obscenity, err on the side of caution and don't use it. For many audiences, obscenities are major detractors from the content of the presentation and affect audience members' attitudes toward you as a speaker. When an audience dismisses you because of your use of obscenities, your perspective is not given a full hearing, and your audience does not feel safe and valued.

Fillers are words that are inserted between phrases or sentences to avoid silence. Some common fillers are *you know, uh, um,* and *like.* Because these are natural elements in informal conversation, they are not twirks for most audiences unless they appear so frequently that they become distracting. When this occurs, audience members may start waiting for the next filler to occur instead of listening to the content of the speech itself. One of Karen's students had a professor who said *actually* a lot. One day, the student wrote down each instance of *actually* the professor said and became so focused on this task that he did not hear when the professor called on him. The professor walked over to his desk, asked what he was doing, and discovered the long list. Until this moment, the professor had no idea that he overused *actually,* and he made a concerted effort after that to excise it from his vocabulary.

Linguistic twirks are among the most manageable because, with awareness, you can make changes in your language so that particular aspects of your speech do not become twirks. You can practice your presentation, for example, so that many of your fillers disappear and, with vigilance, can catch and change grammatical errors. Taping your presentation or asking for feedback from those who hear you practice also can help you become aware of twirks. Language is the vehicle through which your presentation is offered. If you can prevent your language from producing twirks for your audience, your perspective will have a better chance of being heard.

Clothing and Adornment

Your clothing and other forms of adornment can become twirks if they are unacceptable, unusual, or inappropriate for your audience. Clothing becomes a twirk when it is outside the clothing norms of a particular group. Speaking in a short-sleeved shirt and khakis when everyone else is wearing a suit is a twirk, just as is presenting in a suit when everyone else is in shorts and T-shirts. There is a norm that, for a formal presentation, a speaker should be dressed at or slightly above the dress level of the audience, and major discrepancies in clothing between you and your audience tend to make you and your audience uncomfortable.

Personal hygiene can become an issue, too, if your deodorant has failed you, you have not had a chance to bathe or wash your hair before your presentation, or you spilled spaghetti sauce on your tie or dress at the luncheon right before you have to speak.

Bodily adornments in the form of tattoos and body piercings are twirks for some audiences. The tattoo on your hand—no matter what the image—may keep some employers from taking you seriously at a job interview no matter how well you present your ideas. Any tattoo that cannot be covered is a potential twirk, as is an eyebrow ring, tongue stud, nose ring, or pierced lip. Even earrings on men are considered inappropriate by some audiences and would function as twirks in those settings.

At times, hair style or hair color can function as a twirk. Hair that is dyed an unusual color—pink, purple, or green—is a twirk if it is all the audience members can see and think about during your presentation. For other audiences, an unusual hairstyle or dated style—a beehive, for example—might keep an audience from focusing on what you are presenting. In the movie *There's Something About Mary*, the main character arrives for a date not knowing he has semen in his hair, a definite twirk in that situation. Long strands of hair combed over a man's bald spot can be a twirk because they cause audience members to spend their time wondering why he thinks the few strands of hair are hiding anything.

Twirks relating to clothing and adornment also can include temporary conditions that affect appearance such as spinach between or lipstick on the teeth, a loose hem, a tie that has inadvertently flipped over, a collar that is up instead of down, or an unzipped zipper. If, as a speaker, you become aware of these, they can be fixed with relative ease and are not likely to remain twirks for very long.

Conditions related to clothing and appearance that can become twirks usually can be managed with some forethought. Talking with whomever asked you to speak so that you can gauge the kind of dress appropriate for the occasion can be helpful. If your analysis of the speaking situation tells you that adornments such as earrings, piercings, and tattoos will constitute twirks for your audience, remove or cover them for your presentation, if possible. Checking yourself in a mirror immediately before a presentation to make sure there are no temporary problems is also a good idea.

Permanent Physical Conditions

There are also twirks that are permanent features, and these can function as distractions for the audience when you get up to speak. Physical conditions of various kinds fall under this category and range from disfigurements such as having no arms, being in a wheelchair, or having a birthmark on your face to physical limitations such as being hard of hearing, deaf, blind, or cerebral palsied. The weight of a speaker who is obese or severely anorexic also can be a twirk for some audiences if it distracts from the content of the presentation. Speaking in a strong foreign accent also can be seen as a kind of permanent condition that can function as a twirk. Although accents can be changed, to eliminate an accent entirely is difficult for an adult.[5] If an audience cannot understand you and focuses on that difficulty, your accent has become a twirk.

The best way to manage permanent physical twirks is directly. You may want to explain to the audience near the beginning of your presentation, for example: "I have cerebral palsy" (or "I am a stutterer" or "I don't hear well"). You then can let your audience know how to handle the situation: "Because this may interfere with our communication, please feel free to ask me to repeat or explain whenever necessary. I won't be offended, and I appreciate your patience."[6] By dealing with the twirk directly, you reduce the discomfort of your audience, make the condition something that can be addressed directly, and, as the interaction proceeds, encourage audience members to think less and less about it. Instead of spending their time wondering whether to ask if you need help with your wheelchair or whether they can ask you to repeat something they missed because of your accent, you have made the condition something that can be talked about. Audience members then can turn their attention to the presentation itself rather than worrying that something they do or say will offend you or make you uncomfortable.

Your sex—whether you are male or female—constitutes another potential permanent twirk because the expectations for speaking differ for the sexes. Although gendered associations with sex vary greatly across cultures and time periods, biological sex can be a twirk in some situations. Just over 100 years ago, women were not even allowed to speak in public.

Not only was speaking considered unladylike for a woman, but it generally was considered a physical impossibility. Women were seen as not having the stamina or temperament to manage a public speaking role.[7]

Although women now speak in every kind of context, there are some audiences who might begrudge a woman a position of power or influence or who might perceive the same statement from a man and a woman in different ways. A man who reveals emotion might be seen as sensitive; a woman who does so might be viewed as hysterical or as governed by her emotions. A man who is assertive might be seen as commanding, while a woman who is assertive might be viewed as domineering. Whether you are a woman or a man, then, may function as a twirk for certain audiences, especially if you are speaking on subjects that have not been typical for members of your sex or if you are violating gender norms in some way. If you are a woman, dressing in ways that conform to feminine expectations may temper an audience's perception of inappropriateness if your topic is especially unusual for a woman to be discussing. Consciously choosing to dress so that you can't be categorized also may allow your audience to be more open to a variety of perspectives.

Another permanent condition that can become a twirk is an extraordinary appearance—the opposite of the physical impairments and conditions that engender uncomfortable responses in many audiences. Being spectacularly beautiful, being endowed with magnificent green eyes, or having an unusually resonant voice can be so distracting that audience members don't hear what you're saying. Although these kinds of conditions may not seem as if they could be twirks, they may function as twirks if these characteristics are so striking that they are distracting for audiences.

If you do have a feature that is especially striking, you may make a deliberate decision not to call attention to it and perhaps even to minimize it. If you have an especially good figure, you might decide not to wear a fitted suit but instead select a long dress and jacket that is attractive but that does not reveal the figure. Karen once worked with a teaching assistant who had this difficulty. She was particularly attractive and highlighted her figure by wearing extremely short mini-skirts, fitted tops, and sleeveless blouses. She then wondered why her students did not take her seriously. Again, you can make choices that almost assure that such features do or do not become twirks for a given audience.

Presentational Aids

Sometimes, twirks result from the misuse of an aspect of delivery that typically is of use or value in a presentation. This is the case with presentational aids. Presentational aids can become twirks under three conditions: (1) when aids are of poor quality; (2) when aids are overused; and (3) when aids take too much attention away from you as the speaker.

If, because of poor quality, an aid does not fulfill its function—to *aid* in the understanding of the content of the presentation—it becomes a twirk. The chart that is too small to be seen, the overhead transparency that is blurry, or the presentational equipment that blocks audience members' view of the speaker are some situations in which presentational aids function as twirks. Rather than assisting in the full articulation of your perspective, these aids are likely to irritate your audience and decrease their attention to the perspective you are offering.

The overuse or excessive use of presentational aids also constitutes a twirk. When an excerpt from a movie consumes the time allotted for your entire presentation, your audiovisual aid is functioning as a twirk. Similarly, when you give audience members handouts that duplicate the screens of your PowerPoint presentation, you are overusing aids, and they lose their impact. Even using PowerPoint because "everyone else does" may be too much of a good thing because computer-generated presentations have become largely homogeneous in terms of format. Audiences are given the same graphics, the same layout, the same color schemes, and even the same outlining formats over and over by different speakers, creating a limited number of ways of viewing the world. As a result, the presentational software not only loses its effectiveness but becomes a twirk.

Any time you take attention away from you as the speaker, you are creating yet another potential twirk because the whole range of elements of delivery no longer is available to you. Turning off the lights in the room for presentational software, overhead transparencies, slides, or video clips limits the variety of ways in which you can express your perspective. Without access to the full range of delivery components, audience members more easily can begin thinking about things other than your presentation, their energy level often drops, and they may fall asleep. The use of a deaf or foreign-language interpreter can become a twirk because the attention is on the interpreter and not on you as a speaker. Again, in such a situation, audience members miss the personal resources related to the body that you have developed to aid in the presentation of your perspective.

You can keep presentational aids from becoming twirks by keeping their use to a minimum and remembering that the content of your perspective is what is most important. Use a few distinctive slides, photographs, or images that truly reinforce a point, and do not simply read exactly what is on your chart or overhead to your audience. Your presentation should be more than what is shown on the screen or the chart. Talk to your listeners, allowing the outline or points on your screen to reinforce and restate what you are saying. Turn off the equipment and turn on the lights whenever possible during the presentation to allow all of your personal resources to come back into play in the speaking situation. Limiting your use of presentational aids allows them to function as intended—to enhance understanding.

The delivery of your presentation is more than the means by which your ideas are expressed. It is an additional resource available to you for creating an environment of freedom, safety, value, and openness and for enhancing the articulation of your perspective. Attention to the various components of delivery and how they can become twirks creates a presentation that helps your audience members both understand and remember your presentation.

10

ASSESSING CHOICES

You now have made decisions about all aspects of your presentation in terms of focus, frame, forms of elaboration, transitions, and delivery. Your final task, before the actual delivery of your presentation, is to write your speaking plan. The speaking plan is an assessment tool you can use to evaluate the decisions you have made about your presentation. It summarizes what you plan to do in your presentation. As a representation of your understanding of your presentation, the speaking plan encourages you to think carefully about all of the components of your presentation. One way to think about this plan is as a path through your understanding of your ideas. Obviously, there are many presentations you give when you do not have the opportunity to write a speaking plan. If you are able to complete this step, it will tell you if what you have planned for your presentation will accomplish your interactional goal and create the environment of freedom, safety, value, and openness required for transformation.

Creating the Speaking Plan

Your speaking plan should include the 11 basic components of the process of creating a presentation:

1. **Audience**. Identify your audience.
2. **Setting**. Identify the setting for your presentation.
3. **Interactional goal**. State your interactional goal for the presentation. (Review pages 23–33.)

119

4. **Commitment statement**. Write a commitment statement that captures the perspective on your subject that you plan to develop in the presentation. (Review pages 50–53.)

5. **Organizational pattern**. State the organizational pattern you are using to organize your major ideas. (Review pages 60–72.)

6. **Major ideas**. State the major ideas you will develop in the presentation. This section is the most extensive part of your speaking plan because it includes the major ideas and primary elaborating ideas of your presentation. Many different formats exist for depicting the major ideas and the relationships among them. One way is to outline them. Translate your major and minor ideas into key words or phrases and arrange them hierarchically in groups of points and subpoints. Your major ideas are major headings, and the elaborations of them—the minor ideas—are subpoints under them in the outline.

Sometimes, you will find that an outline form cannot capture the vision you have for your presentation because an outline requires that your ideas be structured in a linear, hierarchical way. In such a case, a visual diagram will serve you better than an outline to present the major ideas, their elaborations, and the relationships among them. A visual diagram involves summarizing your major ideas with key words and phrases and laying them out in the structure in which you see them related. Lines and arrows indicate the relationships among the ideas. Both forms of presenting major ideas are illustrated in the sample speaking plans that follow.

7. **Major forms of elaboration**. List the names of the forms of elaboration you use to develop your major ideas. (Review pages 74–86.)

8. **Introduction**. Indicate the type of introduction you are planning to use. (Review pages 88–91.)

9. **Conclusion**. Indicate the type of conclusion you are planning to use. (Review pages 92–96.)

10. **Transitions**. Write out the paragraph, sentence(s), or words you will use to move from the introduction to the body and from the body to the conclusion of your presentation. You will want to plan other transitions for moving between the main ideas and the forms of elaboration in the body of your presentation, but these do not need to be included in the speaking plan.

11. **Delivery**. List major strengths and weaknesses you bring to the delivery of your presentation. Strengths are aspects of your delivery that you believe will facilitate the accomplishment of your goals for the presentation and the creation of the conditions of freedom, safety, value, and openness. For example, you may see

as strengths the audiovisual aid you have prepared, the amount of time you practice your presentations, and your ability to think on your feet to adapt to what is happening in the audience. Weaknesses are aspects of your delivery you want to eliminate or neutralize in your presentation because they make achieving your goals for your presentation more difficult. For example, you may see as weaknesses your tendency to speak too softly, your speech anxiety, and the twirk of using *um* frequently.

Sample Speaking Plans

Below are seven sample speaking plans. They show different interactional goals, different styles of presenting major ideas, and a variety of organizational patterns and forms of elaboration.

Speaking Plan for "Who Is a True Friend?"

1. **Audience**. Junior-high-school students
2. **Setting**. Sunday school class
3. **Interactional goals**. To discover knowledge and belief, to articulate a perspective
4. **Commitment statement**. Let's develop a definition of friendship and see in what ways God can be a friend.
5. **Organizational pattern**. Multiple perspectives (non-oppositional perspectives)
6. **Major ideas**.
   - I.   Audience's perspectives on friendship
   - II. My definition of friendship
     - A.   Someone who will respect what I say
     - B.   Someone who is there for me
   - III. What the Bible says about friends
     - A.   Proverbs 18:24
     - B.   Proverbs 27:10
   - IV. How we can be true friends
     - A.   Keep secrets
     - B.   Be trustworthy
   - V.   God is a trustworthy friend
7. **Major forms of elaboration**. Participation (discussion), comparison and contrast, definition, exaggeration, examples, questions (substantive)

8. **Introduction**. Reference to speaking situation (audience), questions (substantive)

9. **Conclusion**. Summary of basic theme

10. **Transitions**.

    I. **Transition from introduction to body**. These are all excellent ideas about friendship. I hold a similar perspective to yours on friendship.

    II. **Transition from body to conclusion**. At the beginning of my presentation, you shared with me your perspectives on friendship. I hope you can see how God can be a friend in much the same way to you.

11. **Delivery**.

    I. **Strengths**. I know the people in the audience well, so I'll feel comfortable asking them questions and presenting my perspective.

    II. **Weaknesses**. I tend to experience speech anxiety; frequent use of *um* is a twirk for me.

This speaking plan was adapted from one developed by Christa C. Porter at Ohio State University. The speech for which this speaking plan was developed is included in the speeches at the end of the book.

Speaking Plan for "The Pre-Season Speech"

1. **Audience**. Thirty soccer players, ranging in age from 16 to 18 years old

2. **Setting**. First day of school, August 20

3. **Interactional goal**. To build community

4. **Commitment statement**. If we work together, we can build an excellent team this year.

5. **Organizational pattern**. Category

6. **Major ideas**.

    I. We are getting better in all aspects of the game

        A. Practiced hard all summer

        B. Several experienced players

        C. Cohesive team

    II. My expectations for the team

        A. Play with a sense of urgency

            1. Anticipate and play with intensity

            2. Make each other better players

   B. Communicate on the field
       1. Let each other know where you are
       2. Move without the ball
   C. Special responsibilities for the seniors
       1. Step up and take responsibility
       2. Set an example
III. Team goals for the season
   A. Improve individual scoring
   B. Place in regional tournament
   C. Have fun

7. **Major forms of elaboration**. Explanation, repetition and restatement

8. **Introduction**. Reference to speaking situation (occasion)

9. **Conclusion**. Summary of main ideas

10. **Transitions**.

   I. **Transition from introduction to body**. We can have a winning season this year if we are willing to develop as a team in three areas: Play with a sense of urgency, communicate on the field, and expect our seniors to do a bit extra.

   II. **Transition from body to conclusion**. I have outlined some ambitious goals for the season, but I am confident that we can accomplish them.

11. **Delivery**.

   I. **Strengths**. Feel comfortable giving presentations; use lively bodily movement and gestures naturally

   II. **Weaknesses**. Have a tendency to go over my time limit; get so excited about my ideas that I sometimes forget to pay attention to my audience members and their perspectives

This speaking plan was adapted from one developed by Wes Zunker at the University of New Mexico.

Speaking Plan for "Violations of the Covenants"

1. **Audience**. Homeowners and representatives from Grubb and Ellis (Grubb and Ellis regulates the homeowner association for my subdivision)

2. **Setting**. A meeting for concerned homeowners to voice concerns to Grubb and Ellis

3. **Interactional goals**. Articulate a perspective, seek adherence, build community

4. **Commitment statement**. In my opinion, unintended and uncorrected violations of the covenants allow for the deterioration of the subdivision, and we should all work to see that these violations are corrected.

5. **Organizational pattern**. Metaphor

6. **Major ideas**.

I. Broken windows as metaphor for decline in neighborhood

II. Explanation of broken-windows theory

III. Examples of broken-windows theory

IV. Violations of covenants in neighborhood as "broken windows"

7. **Major forms of elaboration**. Figure of speech (metaphor), sensory images, explanation, participation (discussion)

8. **Introduction**. Reference to speaking situation (audience)

9. **Conclusion**. Call to action

10. **Transitions**.

I. **Transition from introduction to body**. Unintended and uncorrected violations of the covenants allow for the deterioration of the subdivision, as the broken-window theory of community development suggests.

II. **Transition from body to conclusion**. The broken-window theory suggests that broken windows are a metaphor for the decline of neighborhoods. So, too, the violations of the covenants of our community, if left unchecked, can lead to the decline of our community.

11. **Delivery**.

I. **Strengths**. I have a style of delivery that many people see as warm and friendly

II. **Weaknesses**. My hair color may distract the audience; I tend to talk too fast

This speaking plan was adapted from one developed by Joanne Villa at the University of New Mexico.

Speaking Plans for "First Day of Class"

1. **Audience**. College students in an Anthropology 101 class

2. **Setting**. The first day of the semester

3. **Interactional goal**. Assert individuality, seek adherence

4. **Commitment statement**. I want to communicate my goals, assignments, and policies for Anthropology 101.

5. **Organizational pattern**. Web

6. **Major ideas**.

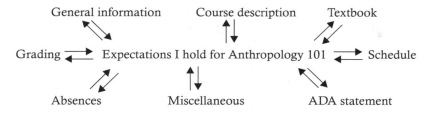

7. **Major forms of elaboration**. Definition, example, explanation, humor, audiovisual aids, credentials

8. **Introduction**. Questions (substantive), reference to speaking situation (audience, occasion)

9. **Conclusion**. Summary of main ideas

10. **Transitions**.

    I. **Transition from introduction to body**. I'd like to go over the syllabus now to see if you have any questions about the course and my expectations for you in this course.

    II. **Transition from body to conclusion**. These are my plans and expectations for the course.

11. **Delivery**.

    I. **Strengths**. I am able to speak conversationally while giving presentations; I move around the room to make my presentation lively

    II. **Weaknesses**. The fact that I'll be going over a syllabus may keep me too tied to this handout, diminishing my movement and eye contact

This speaking plan was adapted from one developed by Madalena Salazar at the University of New Mexico.

Speaking Plan for "Creating an Educational Foundation"

1. **Audience**. Crownpoint High School students

2. **Setting**. Student assembly

3. **Interactional goal**. To articulate a perspective

4. **Commitment statement**. It is important to create a firm educational foundation in preparation for college.

5. **Organizational pattern**. Problem-solution

6. **Major ideas**.

    I. Problem: Native Americans sometimes have difficulty in college

       A. Different values

    B. Lack of adequate preparation

    C. Lack of role models for success in college

 II. My perspective on education

    A. Education has always been important to me

        1. To set a good example for my younger sister and older brother

        2. To prove to my parents that I could do it

        3. To get a good job

 III. Solution: It's important to get a good education

    A. Take pride in who you are

    B. Don't let school get in the way of your education

    C. Approach each situation with a positive mind

    D. Do more than you are expected to do with any assignment you are given or any task you face

7. **Major forms of elaboration**. Examples, explanation, narratives

8. **Introduction**. Reference to speaking situation (self)

9. **Conclusion**. Call to action

10. **Transitions**.

    I. **Transition from introduction to body**. I once held the same view of education that most of you do. I've since developed a new perspective and would like to suggest that it's important to create a firm educational foundation in preparation for college.

    II. **Transition from body to conclusion**. I did the best I could when I was in high school to make good use of what my teachers had to offer, but I know now there were many other things I could have done. Taking pride in who you are, refusing to let school get in the way of your education, approaching each situation with a positive mind, and doing more than expected at any task are ways that anyone can create a firm educational foundation for college.

11. **Delivery**.

    I. **Strengths**. I'm enthusiastic about my subject, which should come out in my gestures and voice; I practice my presentations a lot so they flow easily

    II. **Weaknesses**. I don't have much vocal variation.

This speaking plan was adapted from one developed by Tracy J. Tsosie at the University of New Mexico.

Speaking Plan for "Medical School Interview"

1. **Audience**. Interviewers at medical school asking the question, "What influenced you to want to become a doctor?"

2. **Setting**. Office/small meeting room at medical school

3. **Interactional goal**. Assert individuality, seek adherence

4. **Commitment statement**. I want to share how my life experiences have led me to want to become a pediatrician.

5. **Organizational pattern**. Narrative progression

6. **Major ideas**.

   I.   Babysitting

      A.   Story about babysitting sick nephew

   II.   Past volunteer work

      A.   Story about work at Camp Fire day camp

      B.   Story about volunteering at hospital

   III.   Summer job

      A.   Story about life guarding at swimming pool

   IV.   Religious experience

      A.   Story about experience at hospital chapel

   V.   Education

      A.   Story about fifth-grade science project

      B.   Story about internship in college

   VI.   Current volunteer work

      A.   Story about work with Doctors Without Borders

7. **Major forms of elaboration**. Stories, questions (substantive)

8. **Introduction**. Reference to speaking situation (occasion)

9. **Conclusion**. Summary of main ideas

10. **Transitions**.

    I.   **Transition from introduction to body**. What I hope to convey to you in the short time I have here is how my life experiences have led me to want to become a pediatrician.

    II.   **Transition from body to conclusion**. I've told you a number of stories of various experiences I've had that show how my interest in becoming a pediatrician developed.

11. **Delivery**.

    I.   **Strengths**. I know my stories well and have told them many times, so I should be able to tell them in a way that suggests my passion and excitement for my topic.

II. **Weaknesses**. I have a tendency to keep going once I start, so I need to watch the time and pay attention to the response I'm getting from the interviewer as I tell the stories.

This speaking plan was adapted from one developed by Cuoghi Edens at the University of New Mexico.

Speaking Plan for "Increased Funding for the Colorado Council on the Arts"

1. **Audience**. Representatives in the Colorado legislature
2. **Setting**. Hearing room in state capital
3. **Interactional goal**. To articulate a perspective, to seek adherence
4. **Commitment statement**. There should be an increase in the legislature's appropriation to the Colorado Council on the Arts.
5. **Organizational pattern**. Circle
6. **Major ideas**.

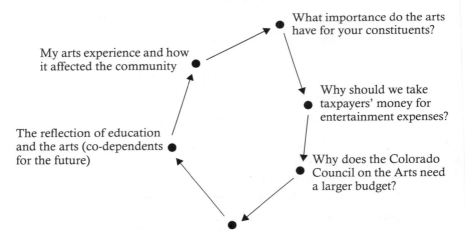

What importance do the arts have for your constituents?

My arts experience and how it affected the community

Why should we take taxpayers' money for entertainment expenses?

The reflection of education and the arts (co-dependents for the future)

Why does the Colorado Council on the Arts need a larger budget?

The future of the arts in Colorado

7. **Major forms of elaboration**. Explanation, examples, stories, audiovisual aids
8. **Introduction**. Narrative
9. **Conclusion**. Call to action.
10. **Transitions**.
    I. **Transition from introduction to body**. Why am I suggesting that the budget of the Colorado Council on the Arts be increased? Because of the importance of the arts for your constituencies.

   II. **Transition from body to conclusion**. I've suggested many reasons why the arts are important in our communities. That's why I'm asking for your support for an increase in the legislative appropriation to the Colorado Council on the Arts.

11. **Delivery**.

   I. **Strengths**. Visual aid provides a clear summary of the budget, so the audience will be able to understand my perspective easily; I practice my presentations a lot

   II. **Weaknesses**. I will experience speech anxiety because this is a very important presentation, and I've never testified before the legislature before. My hands tend to shake and my face turns red when I experience stage fright.

This speaking plan was adapted from one developed by Jason Renak at the University of Colorado at Denver.

Assessing Your Speaking Plan

Your speaking plan allows you to assess the results of your process of developing a presentation and to discover whether how you have planned the presentation matches up with the mental vision you have for it. It also allows you to do a final check of whether the options you have selected facilitate or impede the creation of an environment in which transformation may occur—whether they contribute to the creation of freedom, safety, value, and openness in the interaction. The following questions will help you determine if the various decisions you have made about your presentation create or inhibit possibilities for transformation. If a check of your speaking plan reveals any problems, this is the time to revise it. Do not be afraid to change or abandon parts of the plan and thus your speech if you discover that some of the decisions you have made about your presentation do not contribute to the accomplishment of your goals for the interaction.

Audience. How carefully have you considered the characteristics of your audience members, their interest in this interaction, and their willingness to be changed as a result of it?

Setting. What have you done to minimize distracting environmental factors that might inhibit or negate your efforts at establishing the conditions of freedom, safety, value, and openness?

Interactional goal. Does your interactional goal promote the creation of conditions that maximize possibilities for transformation? If your audience members' interactional goals are at odds with creating a transformative environment, do you attempt to re-shape their expectations, encouraging them to join you in working to create such an environment?

Commitment statement. Do you convey to audience members your willingness to yield your tentative commitments as a result of your interaction with them? Do you suggest that you are willing to follow the inter-action wherever it goes and to be transformed in the process? In commu-nicating your commitment statement, do you suggest that you value the commitments of audience members if they are different from yours?

Organizational pattern. Does your organizational pattern open or restrict the terms of the interaction? Does it enable audience members to participate, if they wish, in the interaction? Do you provide sufficient unity and coherence in your presentation so your audience members can follow you without difficulty and understand your perspective easily?

Major ideas. Do your major ideas communicate the essence of your perspective so that your audience members can understand it?

Forms of elaboration. Do your forms of elaboration provide suffi-cient development of your ideas so your audience members are able to understand your perspective? Are your forms of elaboration relevant to the ideas they develop so that the audience can understand those ideas? Are the feelings you evoke through your choice of forms of elaboration ones that facilitate or impede the possibility of transformation? Do your forms of elaboration silence other participants because they are pre-sented, for example, in technical jargon? Do the forms of elaboration you have chosen encompass sufficient variety so that they maintain audience members' interest in hearing about your perspective?

Introduction. Does your introduction function to orient your audi-ence to your topic and begin to establish the conditions of freedom, safety, value, and openness?

Conclusion. Does your conclusion function to reemphasize your main idea and convey what you would like to have happen next in the interaction?

Transitions. Do the transitions you are planning for your presenta-tion move you from the introduction to the body and from the body to the conclusion so that audience members can follow your ideas and thus understand your perspective easily?

Delivery. How do you plan to use the strengths you've identified con-cerning your delivery to facilitate your goals for your presentation? How are the weaknesses you've identified likely to have negative impacts on your presentation? What can you do to ensure that you minimize them as much as possible?

You now have the basic information you need to create and deliver a presentation that invites your audience members to consider your per-spective and that facilitates your understanding of their perspectives. You know the characteristics of the invitational mode of rhetoric in which to frame your presentation, the options you have for interactional goals in presentations, and how to create a speaking environment of freedom, safety, value, and openness. You know how to develop your commitment statement, how to form your ideas into an organizational frame, and how to elaborate those ideas in various ways. You have completed the frame of your presentation with an introduction and a conclusion and know the importance of transitions to disclose the frame of your presentation to your audience. If your choices in these areas contribute to the creation of freedom, safety, value, and openness, the interaction that results as your audience members respond to your invitation will enable everyone involved to understand one another better and to consider choosing to change. The result will be further conversations that produce greater understanding, more creative solutions to problems, and ever more opportunities for transformation.

SAMPLE
PRESENTATIONS

Asserting Individuality

Retailing Clothing and Cosmetics:
Response to an Interview Question

Liz Stroben
Student, Ohio State University

In this presentation, Liz Stroben is responding to a question as part of an interview for a position with a retail firm that sells clothing and cosmetics. The question is: "What inspired you or led you to pursue a career in women's fashion and cosmetics?"

When I think back over my life and my experience, three specific times in my life come to mind that have emphasized my interest in a career in retail. First, when I was about five years old, my mom took me to an antique shop owned by a friend of hers. As you know, antique stores are often small and have lots of objects in them—lots of glass, lots of plates, lots of things that are breakable. As you can imagine, my mom was watch-

This presentation was given at Ohio State University, Columbus, Ohio, spring, 1993. Used by permission of Liz Stroben.

ing me closely so I didn't run around too much. But I was mesmerized by one table, and as my mom and her friend were talking, they realized that I had started to arrange the different items on the table. They didn't say anything to me because I was being very careful in moving the things around and doing so very slowly. When I was done, they asked me, "Liz, why did you rearrange that table?" And I said, "Well, I like it this way." My mom's friend looked at it and said, "I like it, too—but I can't believe a five-year-old is merchandising my antique store." She led me around that day to different tables, and I got to arrange them as well. From the age of five through high school, then, I went twice a month to her store and did all of her displays as well as some designs for her customers who wanted ideas for how to arrange their furniture and antiques. This experience really helped me later on as I moved into my official retailing career, where I did floor plans and rearranged stores to help customers find things more easily and to help sales. That was my start in the retailing business.

Around the age of 12 or 13—the age when a lot of young women get into clothing and make-up—my friends and I were no different. Every Friday, we'd go to a different person's house, and we'd do what we called *fashion show.* We'd all bring our suitcases with a bunch of clothes, and we'd mix and match them and play fashion show. I was the person who would create the different outfits for everybody. So, again, I learned how to put things together—colors and textures—and I also learned something that really helped me later. I learned that I really like working with people, and I like helping clients choose things for themselves. That's what helped me later on when I worked in various stores. I really enjoy customer contact and the positive feedback from the people I've helped. This experience, then, pretty much solidified the fact that I was going to stay in retailing.

The most recent experience—and probably the most important experience that confirmed my interest in fashion retailing—was my work with Calvin Klein. This was an official working position. It wasn't playtime or me at the age of five. And what I learned in this position was that you really can combine clothing and cosmetics in a single business because, as you know, they have a couture line, a sportswear line, and a cosmetics and fragrance line. At Calvin Klein, I also learned that clothing is not just an outer shell. When you see someone, you think, "Oh, they have a sweater on," or "Oh, they have a T-shirt on." But clothing and cosmetics are not just a superficial way of expressing your personality. They are really an expression of you; they are not just something superficial. Most women and most men don't do clothing for someone else—they do it for themselves—as a way to express their personalities.

Obviously, my most recent experience has been with you as a summer intern, and this work has had the most impact on my career thus far. It has been an incredible learning experience because it has been my first time working in a corporate setting instead of in the store setting with clients. The personnel have been incredible; they are really, really support-ive; they've helped me any time I've asked; and they answered any questions I had, no matter how trivial; and they made me feel important. Your company image is very much in keeping with the image that I have for the kind of place in which I'd like to work. Not only do you have a clothing line, but you have also added a new division—a cosmetics and body-care line.

One of the questions you asked me earlier and that I'd like to incorpo-rate into this answer as well is, "Would I be the right person for this job?" I believe that I've explained how, from a very early age, I've had the incli-nation and the desire to design, to arrange things, and to sell things. These have been very important to me, and I'd like to keep doing them as part of your company.

Exhibiting With Pride

Janet K. Hughes
Artist

This presentation was given as part of a panel discussion of artists whose work had been selected for inclusion in the Missouri Visual Artists' Biennial. The artists were asked to discuss their work prior to the opening of the exhibition.

She's an exhibitionist
She exhibits with pride
She exhibits her work in the Missouri Visual Artists' Biennial.

She collected her thoughts
>   dust
>   and her award.

She means what she says
She means well
She now has the means to continue and expand her work.

For her it was a time of renewal
She renewed her spirit
>   an old acquaintance
>   and her contract at Indiana State University.

She moved from private to public
and enjoyed the exposure.
The exposure was wide.
She exposed herself.
She was well read.

She became widely read.
She painted the town
>   the picture
>   and her lips.
Her lips were read.
Her lips were red.

She moved from the margin
Into the center
And preferred the view.

This presentation was given at the University of Missouri, Columbia, Missouri, March 5, 1993. Used by permission of Janet K. Hughes.

I am a Man, a Black Man, an American

Clarence Thomas
Justice, U.S. Supreme Court

Thirty years ago, we all focused intently on this city as the trauma of Dr. King's death first exploded, then sank into our lives. For so many of us who were trying hard to do what we thought was required of us in the process of integrating this society, the rush of hopelessness and isolation was immediate and overwhelming. It seemed that the whole world had gone mad.

I am certain that each of us has his or her memories of that terrible day in 1968. For me it was the final straw in the struggle to retain my vocation to become a Catholic priest. Suddenly, this cataclysmic event ripped me from the moorings of my grandparents, my youth and my faith and catapulted me headlong into the abyss that Richard Wright seemed to describe years earlier.

It was this event that shattered my faith in my religion and my country. I had spent the mid-'60s as a successful student in a virtually white environment. I had learned Latin, physics and chemistry. I had accepted the loneliness that came with being "the integrator," the first and the only. But this event, this trauma I could not take, especially when one of my fellow seminarians, not knowing that I was standing behind him, declared that he hoped the SOB died. This was a man of God, mortally stricken by an assassin's bullet, and one preparing for the priesthood had wished evil upon him.

The life I had dreamed of so often during those hot summers on the farm in Georgia or during what seemed like endless hours on the oil truck with my grandfather expired as Dr. King expired. As so many of you do, I still know exactly where I was when I heard the news. It was a low moment in our nation's history and a demarcation between hope and hopelessness for many of us.

But three decades have evaporated in our lives, too quickly and without sufficient residual evidence of their importance. But much has changed since then. The hope that there would be expeditious resolutions to our myriad problems has long since evaporated with those years. Many who debated and hoped then now do neither. There now seems to be a broad acceptance of the racial divide as a permanent state. While we once celebrated those things that we had in common with our fellow citizens who did not share our race, so many now are triumphal about our differences, finding little, if anything, in common. Indeed, some go so far as to all but define each of us by our race and establish the range of our thinking and our opinions, if not our deeds by our color.

This presentation was given to the National Bar Association, Memphis, Tennessee, July 29, 1998. Available at http://douglass.speech.nwu.edu/thom_b30.htm

I, for one, see this in much the same way I saw our denial of rights—as nothing short of a denial of our humanity. Not one of us has the gospel. Nor are our opinions based upon some revealed precepts to be taken as faith. As thinking, rational individuals, not one of us can claim infallibility, even from the overwhelming advantage of hindsight and Monday morning quarterbacking.

This makes it all the more important that our fallible ideas be examined as all ideas are in the realm of reason, not as some doctrinal or racial heresy. None of us—none of us have been appointed by God or appointed God. And if any of us has, then my question is why hasn't he or she solved all these problems.

I make no apologies for this view now, nor do I intend to do so in the future. I have now been on the court for seven terms. For the most part, it has been much like other endeavors in life. It has its challenges and requires much of the individual to master the workings of the institution. We all know that. It is, I must say, quite different from what I might have anticipated if I had the opportunity to do so. Unlike the unfortunate practice or custom in Washington and in much of the country, the court is a model of civility. It's a wonderful place. Though there have been many contentious issues to come before the court during these initial years of my tenure, I have yet to hear the first unkind words exchanged among my colleagues. And quite frankly, I think that such civility is the sine qua non of conducting the affairs of the court and the business of the country.

As such, I think that it would be in derogation of our respective oaths and our institutional obligations to our country to engage in uncivil behavior. It would also be demeaning to any of us who engaged in such conduct. Having worn the robe, we have a lifetime obligation to conduct ourselves as having deserved to wear the robe in the first instance.

One of the interesting surprises is the virtual isolation, even within the court. It is quite rare that the members of the court see each other during those periods when we're not sitting or when we're not in conference. And the most regular contact beyond those two formal events are the lunches we have on conference and court days. Also, it is extraordinarily rare to have any discussions with the other members of the court before voting on petitions for certiorari or on the merits of the cases. And there is rarely extended debate during our conferences. For the most part, any debate about the cases is done in writing. It has struck me as odd that some think that there are cliques and cabals at the court. No such arrangements exist. Nor, contrary to suggestions otherwise, is there any intellectual or ideological pied piper on the court.

With respect to my following, or, more accurately, being led by other members of the Court, that is silly, but expected since I couldn't possibly think for myself. And what else could possibly be the explanation when I fail to follow the jurisprudential, ideological and intellectual, if not anti-intellectual, prescription assigned to blacks. Since thinking beyond this prescription is presumptively beyond my abilities, obviously someone must be putting these strange ideas into my mind and my opinions.

Though being underestimated has its advantages, the stench of racial inferiority still confounds my olfactory nerves.

As Ralph Ellison wrote more than 35 years ago, "Why is it so often true that when critics confront the American as Negro, they suddenly drop their advance critical armament and revert with an air of confident superiority to quite primitive modes of analysis?" Those matters accomplished by whites are routinely subjected to sophisticated modes of analysis. But when the selfsame matters are accomplished by blacks, the opaque racial prism of analysis precludes such sophistication and all is seen in black and white. And some who would not venture onto the more sophisticated analytical turf are quite content to play in the minor leagues of primitive harping. The more things change, the more they remain the same.

Of course there is much criticism of the court by this group or that, depending on the court's decisions in various highly publicized cases. Some of the criticism is profoundly uninformed and unhelpful. And all too often, uncivil second-guessing is not encumbered by the constraints of facts, logic or reasoned analysis. On the other hand, the constructive and often scholarly criticism is almost always helpful in thinking about or rethinking decisions. It is my view that constructive criticism goes with the turf, especially when the stakes are so high and the cases arouse passions and emotions, and, in a free society, the precious freedom of speech and the strength of ideas. We at the court could not possibly claim exemption from such criticism. Moreover, we are not infallible, just final.

As I have noted, I find a thoughtful, analytical criticism most helpful. I do not think any judge can address a vast array of cases and issues without testing and re-testing his or her reasoning and opinions in the crucible of debate. However, since we are quite limited in public debate about matters that may come before the court, such debate must, for the most part, occur intramurally, thus placing a premium on outside scholarship. Unfortunately, from time to time, the criticism of the court goes beyond the bounds of civil debate and discourse. Today it seems quite acceptable to attack the court and other institutions when one disagrees with an opinion or policy. I can still remember traveling along Highway 17 in south Georgia, the Coastal Highway, during the '50s and '60s and seeing the "Impeach Earl Warren" signs.

Clearly, heated reactions to the court or to its members are not unusual. Certainly, Justice Blackmun was attacked repeatedly because many disagreed, as I have, with the opinion he offered on behalf of the Court in Roe vs. Wade. Though I have joined opinions disagreeing with Justice Blackmun, I could not imagine ever being discourteous to him merely because we disagreed.

I have found during my almost 20 years in Washington that the tendency to personalize differences has grown to be an accepted way of doing business. One need not do the hard work of dissecting an argument. One need only attack and thus discredit the person making the argument. Though the matter being debated is not effectively resolved, the debate is reduced to unilateral pronouncements and glib but quotable clichés. I, for one, have been singled out for particularly bilious and venomous assaults. These criticisms, as near as I can tell, and I admit that it is rare that I take notice of this calumny, have little to do with any particular opinion, though each opinion does provide one more occasion to criticize. Rather, the principal problem seems to be a deeper antecedent offense.

I have no right to think the way I do because I'm black. Though the ideas and opinions themselves are not necessarily illegitimate if held by non-black individuals, they, and the person enunciating them, are illegitimate if that person happens to be black. Thus, there's a subset of criticism that must of necessity be reserved for me, even if every non-black member of the court agrees with the idea or the opinion. You see, they are exempt from this kind of criticism, precisely because they are not black. As noted earlier, they are more often than not subjected to the whites-only sophisticated analysis.

I will not catalogue my opinions to which there have been objections since they are a matter of public record. But I must note in passing that I can't help but wonder if some of my critics can read. One opinion that is trotted out for propaganda, for the propaganda parade, is my dissent in Hudson vs. McMillian. The conclusion reached by the long arms of the critics is that I supported the beating of prisoners in that case. Well, one must either be illiterate or fraught with malice to reach that conclusion. Though one can disagree with my dissent, and certainly the majority of the court disagreed, no honest reading can reach such a conclusion. Indeed, we took the case to decide the quite narrow issue whether a prisoner's rights were violated under the "cruel and unusual punishment" clause of the Eighth Amendment as a result of a single incident of force by the prison guards which did not cause a significant injury. In the first section of my dissent, I stated the following. "In my view, a use of force that causes only insignificant harm to a prisoner may be immoral; it may be tortuous; it may be criminal, and it may even be remediable under other provisions of the Federal Constitution. But it is not cruel and unusual punishment."

Obviously, beating prisoners is bad. But we did not take the case to answer this larger moral question or a larger legal question of remedies under other statutes or provisions of the Constitution. How one can extrapolate these larger conclusions from the narrow question before the court is beyond me, unless, of course, there's a special segregated mode of analysis.

It should be obvious that the criticism of this opinion serves not to present counter-arguments, but to discredit and attack me because I've deviated from the prescribed path. In his intriguing and thoughtful essay on "My Race Problem and Ours," Harvard law professor Randall

Kennedy, a self-described Social Democrat, correctly observes that "If racial loyalty is deemed essentially and morally virtuous, then a black person's adoption of positions that are deemed racially disloyal will be seen by racial loyalists as a supremely threatening sin, one warranting the harsh punishments that have historically been visited upon alleged traitors." Perhaps this is the defensive solidarity to which Richard Wright refers. If so, it is a reaction I understand, but resolutely decline to follow.

In the final weeks of my seminary days, shortly after Dr. King's death, I found myself becoming consumed by feelings of animosity and anger. I was disenchanted with my church and my country. I was tired of being in the minority, and I was tired of turning the other cheek. I, along with many blacks, found ways to protest and try to change the treatment we received in this country. Perhaps my passion for Richard Wright novels was affecting me. Perhaps it was listening too intently to Nina Simone. Perhaps, like Bigger Thomas, I was being consumed by the circumstances in which I found myself, circumstances that I saw as responding only to race.

My feelings were reaffirmed during the summer of 1968 as a result of the lingering stench of racism in Savannah and the assassination of Bobby Kennedy. No matter what the reasons were, I closed out the '60s as one angry young man waiting on the revolution that I was certain would soon come. I saw no way out. I, like many others, felt the deep chronic agony of anomie and alienation. All seemed to be defined by race. We became a reaction to the "man," his ominous reflection.

The intensity of my feelings was reinforced by other events of the late '60s, the riots, the marches, the sense that something had to be done, done quickly to resolve the issue of race. In college there was an air of excitement, apprehension and anger. We started the Black Students Union. We protested. We worked in the Free Breakfast Program. We would walk out of school in the winter of 1969 in protest.

But the questioning for me started in the spring of 1970 after an unauthorized demonstration in Cambridge, Mass., to "free the political prisoners." Why was I doing this rather than using my intellect? Perhaps I was empowered by the anger and relieved that I could now strike back at the faceless oppressor. But why was I conceding my intellect and rather fighting much like a brute? This I could not answer, except to say that I was tired of being restrained. Somehow I knew that unless I contained the anger within me I would suffer the fates of Bigger Thomas and Damon Cross. It was intoxicating to act upon one's rage, to wear it on one's shoulder, to be defined by it. Yet, ultimately, it was destructive, and I knew it.

So in the spring of 1970 in a nihilistic fog, I prayed that I'd be relieved of the anger and the animosity that ate at my soul. I did not want to hate any more, and I had to stop before it totally consumed me. I had to make a fundamental choice. Do I believe in the principles of this country or not? After such angst, I concluded that I did. But the battle between passion and reason would continue, although abated, still intense.

Ironically, many of the people who are critics today were among those we called half-steppers, who had co-opted by "the man" because they were part of the system that oppressed us. When the revolution came, all of the so-called Negroes needed to be dealt with. It is interesting to remember that someone gave me a copy of Prof. Thomas Sowell's book, "Education, Myths and Tragedies," in which he predicted much of what has happened to blacks and education. I threw it in the trash, unread, declaring that he was not a black man since no black could take the positions that he had taken, whatever they were, since I had only heard his views were not those of a black man.

I was also upset to hear of a black conservative in Virginia named Jay Parker. How could a black man call himself a conservative? In a twist of fate, they both are dear friends today, and the youthful wrath I visited upon them is now being visited upon me, though without the youth. What goes around does indeed come around.

The summer of 1971 was perhaps one of the most difficult of my life. It was clear to me that the road to destruction was paved with anger, resentment and rage. But where were we to go? I would often spend hours in our small efficiency apartment in New Haven pondering this question and listening to Marvin Gaye's then new album, "What's Going On?" To say the least, it was a depressing summer.

What were we to do? What's going on?

As I think back on those years, I find it interesting that many people seemed to have trouble with their identities as black men. Having had to accept my blackness in the cauldron of ridicule from some of my black schoolmates under segregation, then immediately thereafter remain secure in that identity during my years at an all-white seminary, I had few racial identity problems. I knew who I was and needed no gimmicks to affirm my identity. Nor, might I add, do I need anyone telling me who I am today. This is especially true of the psycho-silliness about forgetting my roots or self-hatred. If anything, this shows that some people have too much time on their hands.

There's a rush today to prescribe who is black, to prescribe what our differences are or to ignore what our differences are. Of course, those of us who came from the rural South were different from the blacks who came from the large northern cities, such as Philadelphia and New York. We were all black. But that similarity did not mask the richness of our differences. Indeed, one of the advantages of growing up in a black neighborhood was that we were richly blessed with the ability to see the individuality of each black person with all its fullness and complexity. We saw those differences at school, at home, at church, and definitely at the barbershop on Saturday morning.

Intraracially, we consistently recognized our differences. It is quite counter-factual to suggest that such differences have not existed throughout our history. Indeed, when I was on the other side of the ideological divide, arguing strenuously with my grandfather that the revolution was imminent and that we all had to stick together as black people, he was quick to remind me that he had lived much longer than I had and during far more difficult times, and that, in any case, it took all kinds to make a world.

I agree with Ralph Ellison when he asked, perhaps rhetorically, why is it that so many of those who would tell us the meaning of "Negro," of Negro life, never bothered to learn how varied it really is. That is particularly true of many whites who have elevated condescension to an art form by advancing a monolithic view of blacks in much the same way that the mythic, disgusting image of the lazy, dumb black was advanced by open, rather than disguised, bigots. Today, of course, it is customary to collapse, if not overwrite, our individual characteristics into new, but now acceptable stereotypes. It no longer matters when one is from urban New York City or rural Georgia. It doesn't matter whether we came from a highly educated family or a barely literate one. It does not matter if you are a Roman Catholic or a Southern Baptist. All of these differences are canceled by race, and a revised set of acceptable stereotypes has been put in place.

Long gone is the time when we opposed the notion that we all looked alike and talked alike. Somehow we have come to exalt the new black stereotype above all and to demand conformity to that norm. It is this notion that our race defines us that Ralph Ellison so eloquently rebuts in his essay, "The World and the Jug." He sees the lives of black people as more than a burden, but also a discipline, just as any human life which has endured so long is a discipline, teaching its own insights into the human condition, its own strategies of survival. There's a fullness and even a richness here. And here despite the realities of politics, perhaps, but nevertheless here and real because it is human life.

Despite some of the nonsense that has been said about me by those who should know better, and so much nonsense, or some of which subtracts from the sum total of human knowledge, despite this all, I am a man, a black man, an American. And my history is not unlike that of many blacks from the deep South. And in many ways it is not that much different from that of many other Americans. It goes without saying that I understand the comforts and security of racial solidarity, defensive or otherwise. Only those who have not been set upon by hatred and repelled by rejection fail to understand its attraction. As I have suggested, I have been there.

The inverse relationship between the bold promises and the effectiveness of the proposed solutions, the frustrations with the so-called system, the subtle and not-so-subtle bigotry and animus towards members of my race made radicals and nationalists of many of us. Yes, I understand the reasons why this is attractive. But it is precisely this in its historic form, not its present-day diluted form, that I have rejected. My question was whether as an individual I truly believed that I was the equal of individuals who were white. This I had answered with a resounding "yes" in 1964 during my sophomore year in the seminary. And that answer continues to be yes. Accordingly, my words and my deeds are consistent with this answer.

Any effort, policy or program that has as a prerequisite the acceptance of the notion that blacks are inferior is a non-starter with me. I do not believe that kneeling is a position of strength. Nor do I believe that begging is an effective tactic. I am confident that the individual approach, not the group approach, is the better, more acceptable, more supportable and less dangerous one. This approach is also consistent with the underlying principles of this country and the guarantees of freedom through government by consent. I, like Frederick Douglass, believe that whites and blacks can live together and be blended into a common nationality.

Do I believe that my views or opinions are perfect or infallible? No, I do not. But in admitting that I have no claim to perfection or infallibility, I am also asserting that competing or differing views similarly have no such claim. And they should not be accorded a status of infallibility or any status that suggests otherwise.

With differing, but equally fallible views, I think it is best that they be aired and sorted out in an environment of civility, consistent with the institutions in which we are involved. In this case, the judicial system.

It pains me deeply, or more deeply than any of you can imagine to be perceived by so many members of my race as doing them harm. All the sacrifice, all the long hours of preparation were to help, not to hurt. But what hurts more, much more is the amount of time and attention spent on manufactured controversies and media sideshows when so many problems cry out for constructive attention.

I have come here today not in anger or to anger, though my mere presence has been sufficient, obviously, to anger some. Nor have I come to defend my views, but rather to assert my right to think for myself, to refuse to have my ideas assigned to me as though I was an intellectual slave because I'm black. I come to state that I'm a man, free to think for myself and do as I please.

I've come to assert that I am a judge and I will not be consigned the unquestioned opinions of others. But even more than that, I have come to say that isn't it time to move on? Isn't it time to realize that being angry with me solves no problems? Isn't it time to acknowledge that the problem of race has defied simple solutions and that not one of us, not a single one of us can lay claim to the solution? Isn't it time that we respect ourselves and each other as we have demanded respect from others? Isn't it time to ignore those whose sole occupation is sowing seeds of discord and animus? That is self-hatred.

Isn't it time to continue diligently to search for lasting solutions?

I believe that the time has come today. God bless each of you, and may God keep you.

City Planning as a Career

Andrea Armstrong
Student, Ohio State University

In this presentation, Andrea Armstrong assumed the role of a city planner, speaking to first-grade students on career day.

Hi, I'm Ms. Armstrong, and I'm a city planner for the city of Columbus. I'd like to ask you a couple questions. Do any of you have a favorite city?
Student: Columbus.
Columbus? Anybody else?
Student: Chicago.
Chicago? Yes?
Student: Las Vegas.
What do you all like about Columbus, since that's where we're living right now?
Student: The zoo.
Student: I like the playgrounds.
The playgrounds? Anything else?
Student: It doesn't take long to get anywhere.
Student: The fair.
The fair—the state fair. You like going to the fair? I like going to the fair, too. OK, those are some of the things you like about Columbus, but a long time ago, cities weren't such nice places to be. There were a lot of factories, there was a lot of smoke, cities were crowded, and there weren't very many parks. Kids actually used to have to play in cemeteries because there weren't parks in their neighborhoods to play in—that was the only green space they could find. That was before planning. What planners try to do is to make places nicer for people. They make cities places where people want to live and want to be.

Planners try to make cities better in a lot of different ways. For instance, they try to decide where schools should be. They try to make sure that there are enough parks and playgrounds in neighborhoods for families and friends to play in. They have to make sure there are police and fire services for everyone in the city. They need to make sure that there are enough water lines and sewer lines. They have to make sure that buildings are built correctly.

This presentation was given at Ohio State University, Columbus, Ohio, spring, 1993. Used by permission of Andrea Armstrong.

City planners have to know a lot about a lot of things. They have to know about law because they have to know laws that affect where and how things can be built. City planners also have to be good public speakers because they have to explain ideas and plans to people. They need to be architects and engineers—they need to know how things are built and how they can be built. They need to be computer users; they use computers to figure things out. They need to be demographers—they need to know how to use numbers and statistics and to figure out how many people are in cities.

City planners also need to be mapmakers. I've brought along a few of the maps I use at work every day. These are the kinds of maps that planners use and make. The first map is an annexation map. Annexation is how a city grows—how it gets more land. The purple area in this map shows Columbus in 1900; that's all the bigger Columbus was in 1900. If any of you have a grandmother who is 93 years old, that's how big Columbus was when she was born. Today, Columbus is as big as all the areas that are colored on this map. Planners need to know this, and they need to be able to provide services in all these areas. They need to make sure that there are police, fire, water, and roads and everything for all this area.

Your school is in this area, near the river. City planners need to know where the flood plain is for the river. We have something called 100- and 500-year floods. That means that we have a 1-in-100 chance to get a flood or a 1-in-500 chance to get a flood, which means the river will go outside of its banks. We need to know this so we don't build in those flood plains—people lose their houses and belongings if they do. Ohio State University's campus is located right here. It is in part of the flood plain, so part of this land may flood. We need to know that ahead of time.

This map shows flight contours for the airport, which is west of town—Port Columbus Airport. Every line on here is how loud the noise is from the air traffic in the air. We need to know this because nobody wants to live within these noise contours because it's loud, it hurts our ears, it's not good for our health. We need to make sure we don't build in those areas—it's not good for us.

Finally, we need to know where fire stations are located in our city. We need to make sure that if your house catches on fire, there's a fire station nearby that will be able to put the fire out. All the red circles are Columbus fire stations.

There are planning issues going on now that you might have heard about in the news or from your parents. The Tuttle Crossing area is a planning issue in Columbus. This is a mall that's being developed on the north side of town. It involves city planners who are trying to do all the things necessary to make sure the mall is a nice place.

So, planners do a lot of different things in their jobs. They have to know a lot of different things. Planning is a good profession for people who are curious. So, if you're a curious person and like to do a lot of different things, planning might be a profession for you someday.

Whose Woods These Are

Sally Miller Gearhart
Professor Emeritus, San Francisco State University

*This presentation was a response to papers presented on the program,
"Narrative as Communication. "It was partly inspired by "It Was a
Dark and Stormy Night; or, Why Are We Huddling About the Camp-
fire?" by Ursula K. Le Guin.*

The big stand-off was about to be over. The showdown was here. The
heads of three world powers each held a thumb over a doomsday button.
They had tried everything. And everything hadn't worked. Now, no one
of them willing to give an inch, they prepared to send the planet into its
total annihilation. The only question was, which of them would have the
satisfaction of being the last to die.

Suddenly one of them, Thomas Ivanovitch Woo by name but Ivan for
short, remembered a promise that in a weak moment he had made to his
wife. "Wait a minute, fellows," he said. "Before we do this number we
might as well give the women a chance. We got nothing to lose." The others agreed.

So Ivan called his wife and asked her how to get in touch with this
Great Mother she was always talking about. His wife gave him three
instructions: "Hush. Go into the woods. And listen."

So Ivan hushed, went into the only forest left on the planet and stood
and listened. Pretty soon he sensed some sort of presence and he asked an
old, old question: "What must we do?"

The answer was prompt and fairly direct: "Disarm."

Since that was clear enough Ivan went back to his colleagues and told
them what the Great Mother had said. And they all disarmed their
nations, right down to the last bullet. Ivan went back to the woods and
asked the same question again. This time the answer was equally prompt:
"Decentralize."

And so the world decentralized its population, its business and government. Time and again Ivan went back to the woods and time and
again the Great Mother directed him in the re-making of the world. He
did not even argue with some things that seemed of a strictly personal
concern to her like the requirement that women be given all the say-so
about sex and reproduction, and the requirement that all future planning
hold the male population to twenty percent, or that the whole world
acknowledge the primacy of the female of the species and embrace the
values of nonviolence, nurturance, and cooperation.

This presentation was given at the Western Speech Communication Association Convention, Portland, Oregon, February 18, 1980. Used by permission of Sally Miller Gearhart.

"Yeah, yeah, yeah," said Ivan, pretty tired of it all by this time. Off he went and saw to it that all these things were accomplished.

One day when he came back to the Great Mother he was pretty smug. "Say, G.M.," he began. "It's really working. There's a pretty good world out there. Thanks a lot." And he started to go.

"Just a minute."

Ivan turned back.

"You haven't even started yet."

"Whaddya mean?"

"I've had to be pretty directive up to this point. But I won't do that much longer. It's time now for you to begin cleaning up your communication."

"My what?"

"Hush. Go deeper into the woods. Listen harder."

So Ivan went deeper into the woods and tried to listen harder. He sat for many days in the forest trying to listen. It was not at all easy. Finally a big oak tree said to him: "Hello." Ivan was so relieved that he sprang up and hugged the tree, an action pleasing to the tree since in all its experience the one thing that men do not do to trees is hug them, much less with tears running down their cheeks.

When he sat down again Ivan remembered that his mission was communication, so he tried to decide on his general purpose. Should he entertain, inform or persuade the tree? Since he had been in politics all his life he naturally decided on the persuasive mode. "Tree," he began, moving straight to his proposition, "you must help me and the rest of mankind with our communication problem. "

In response the tree cried out in pain and shrank away from him. Clearly he had done the wrong thing. "What is it, what is it? What did I do?"

"Too violent," wailed the tree. "You're trying to change me, and that hurts."

"By asking you to help me?".

"You didn't ask. You didn't even say you wanted or needed something. You told me what I must do."

"Oh," said Ivan. This was going to be difficult. He sat for a while and finally it dawned on him—if he simply opened up, said only what he wanted or needed, and was himself willing to change, then maybe he and the tree could change together. Ivan was ecstatic at this idea, and having been through EST training he was undaunted and eager to try again.

"Well, tree," he said. "I won't persuade. I'll inform you. I want to tell you something. About . . . about trees. Trees. Trees are a type of vegetation found. . . ."

Again the tree reacted, somewhat more mildly this time but enough to let him know that he was still behaving violently. "You're still trying to do something to me," said the tree. "You might just as well put a chain saw to my throat. Instead of trying to inform me you could. . . ."

"I could . . . ?" prompted Ivan.

The tree was silent.

"I could . . . ?"

"Do just what you're trying to do now?" suggested the tree.

Ivan exploded. "What I'm trying to do now? What I'm trying to do now is find out something." He stopped abruptly.

The tree seemed to smile.

And then Ivan was truly in despair. "What can I do," he said to himself. "What is there left? If I can't persuade but can only be open to change, if I can't instruct but must only discover, what can be the nature of my discourse with others?" Truly a puzzle.

He sat for many hours, thinking and listening, thinking to himself, listening to the trees, the grass, the small animals. Finally he said to the tree, "Tree, I've been sitting here for hours puzzling over this thing. First I tried reasoning it out but that didn't work. Then I tried getting in the mood of being all vulnerable and open, not trying to persuade you at all but being willing to change with you. But still nothing happened. Then I tried getting in the mood of just plain learning from you or with you but that didn't work either. Now here I sit, dog tired, and still not able to communicate with you without hurting you."

"Well, you just did it," said the tree.

"???????" said Ivan.

"You just told me a story. About what you've been going through in your head. It was in chronological order. That's the best beginning you've made."

"A story?" Then again Ivan was blessed with illumination. "Yeah! Yeah! You mean I entertained you! That's it! The only nonviolent way to communicate is to entertain! Telling stories—that's what the Toastmaster Club said all along!" He jumped up in exuberance and in sheer release of tension he began to do a buck-and-wing for the tree. "Let me entertain you," Ivan sang.

Again the tree shrank back as if offended.

Ivan stopped abruptly, mid-kick, his face a mask of astonishment. "I'm still trying to do something to you right?" he said to the tree. "*To you*, and not *for us*."

"Right."

Ivan collapsed again to his thinking/listening position. So even stories could hurt if they tried to change people or things. There must be a difference, he mused, between wanting things to change and wanting to change things. The moment he thought that, a good feeling washed over him. Then instead of entertaining the tree he could simply express himself. And then if the tree expressed itself. . . .

He tried it. "Tree, I want to tell a story." And he picked the first fairy tale that occurred to him, one that he barely remembered. But as he warmed to his task of the telling, he found that the words he was uttering themselves generated other words. Soon he began remembering easily and soon there were brand new images, new ideas and feelings that flew by so fast within him that he had trouble getting them out. He paid less and less attention to what he wanted the tree to think of him, even though he was of course still very much aware of the tree's presence, and more and more attention to the story he was telling. He began to enjoy the telling and when he had finished he was sure he heard sighs of appreciation and excitement.

To his amazement another tree in the forest spoke up. "I have a story too," it said. And when it had finished its story there was another tree and another story, another squirrel and another story. Ivan felt himself to be inside a great matrix, a womb, where he and the entire forest shared a constantly changing and intensely intimate reality.

Deep into the night trees and animals told stories of their past, of the things they had observed, of the things they had heard about. They told stories of the future, how they feared it might be, how they hoped it would be.

It was dawn when Ivan rose to his feet to start back to the world of politics. He knew now at least one way that they might begin. Good reason in controversy would have to wait a while. And so would that old taskmaster, justification. He had a story to tell. And he suspected his colleagues had some too.

When he pulled up his chair at the World Council and the whole assembly drew their attention to him, an old enemy-turned-friend said, "Well Ivan, what have you got for us this time?" The whole assembly laughed heartily. Ivan smiled.

"Hush," he said. "Let's go to the woods. And Listen."

Remarks at International Consumer Electronics Show

Bill Gates
CEO, Microsoft Corporation

Well, good evening and welcome to CES. I'm actually glad to be back at work after the holidays. I spent most of the holidays being beaten by my nieces and nephews on the Xbox. [Laughter.] When I started Microsoft 27 years ago, I had no idea I'd create the ultimate machine to humiliate myself—[laughter]—but there it was and it was a lot of fun.

What I want to talk about tonight is where consumer electronics is going, and in particular the role that software is playing in defining new types of devices and how these devices work together. You'll find that I'm very optimistic about what we'll see, not just in the next decade that I call the digital decade, but even in the next year or two in terms of the advances that take place when great software and hardware come together.

So what are the fundamental hardware trends? You know, consumer electronics historically have been mostly about hardware. How is that changing? Well, first and foremost we have the continued truth of Moore's Law. It may not last forever, but for the next decade we're certainly going to get this doubling in power every 18 months to two years.

And there are two ways to look at Moore's Law. One is to say that the processor in the PC, the $100 to $300 processor, is doubling in power. That's amazing for the PC. It means things like speech recognition, handwriting recognition, linguistic analysis become possible when they wouldn't have been feasible before. It brings entertainment to a whole new level of capability.

But another way to look at it is to say that for a particular level of richness, say screen management or video decoding, the price of that chip is dropping in half every two years. And so this means that we can take microprocessors and put them everywhere. Now, for $4 to $8 the kind of intelligence we get in the microprocessor is far beyond the original PC. And so what it means is that we have multiple devices that are smart and we have protocols, digital protocols, digital standards between those devices allowing them to work together.

This is a real mindset change for the hardware industry because it now means that software and protocols come in, in a very fundamental fashion.

Metcalfe's Law says we're going to connect all these things together. It's very cheap to do it. The value of these things comes solely from their being connected together. So you won't have to simply control a device with the buttons and displays that are on that device, you can turn to your large screen or literally any screen in the house to do those things.

Maxwell's Law—I haven't talked about that for a long time—but what it says is there is a lot of spectrum out there and we'll be able to have lots of bandwidth, certainly inside the home, allowing you to get information, even high-quality video wherever you go. And so these devices will connect, connect in a wireless way and they'll be very, very intelligent.

So that's a new framework for the hardware world.

Let's look at the software world. I said the hardware world started with very much an analog standalone device approach. Well, some of the same things can be said about the software world. The software world definitely had a single device approach. The PC was that device. And it was a miracle device. The whole software industry of course today is 100 times the size it was before the PC came along. The openness of the PC, what we did to evangelize Windows, making sure Windows was the same across different hardware manufacturers, and so that the desire to change and differentiate wasn't there so that users weren't confused when they got that PC device, that was fundamental.

But a lot of the focus was not only on this single device; it was on the scenarios that arose in the office environment. And so use of the PC in the home by and large mirrored what people were doing in the office. The productivity applications, the hardware design, the whole focus was very driven by that market. And there was nothing wrong with that. A lot of people do work at home. Homework is a lot like classic office-productivity work, and the PC, even on this approach, rose to over 60 percent home penetration in the United States.

Well, just like hardware, now we have a different framework to think about. It's about many devices. It's about many different peripherals, some of them with a lot of intelligence that we connect to, and it's about the idea of services, services to make your information immediately available, services to authenticate who you are, so mechanisms like digital rights or group authentication can work on a very easy basis.

All of those things are now part of this framework, and we have to take care of every one of those things to achieve the potential of these devices.

The success of each of these devices will drive the success of the other devices. It will be the people on the streets who will be the most aggressive at using things like the PDAs that will now have telephony and rich connectivity, not just through the wide area wireless network but also through the wireless network, the Wi-Fi network in the home environment—so many devices.

New service standards based on the XML approach are really driving us to think about distributed computing across the Internet in a very new way; very exciting developments there that have accelerated in the last couple of years as everybody's gotten behind this, and some of the key building blocks around XML have been delivered.

Now, consumers and knowledge workers won't know that that service platform, that technology, is there, but they'll see the benefits of it.

For Microsoft, we have two key software products, Windows XP and Windows CE, and those are the software products we adapt to every one of these intelligent devices to make sure we can deliver the integrated experience.

So what's driving the opportunity? The smart devices where the hardware costs are coming down and the intelligence is going up. The fact that digital media means software can add value, we can let people organize things, we can let people control the rights of how information is distributed, we can let people notify other people of what's new, what might be interesting to them.

Wireless connectivity: This is a pillar. For many years we've talked about AC power line or X10-type approaches or running new wires throughout the house. And I'm not saying that those won't be there, but the explosive way that these devices work together will overwhelmingly be the wireless approaches and the standard around Wi-Fi or the so-called 802.11. The costs of the chip are coming down. The breadth of use is going up. And that virtuous cycle that drives higher use means more applications. More applications means more volume, means lower prices, means more use. That virtuous cycle, which we saw for the PC itself, is certainly driving Wi-Fi to critical mass in business, in homes and even in so-called hotspots—hotels, convention centers, copying centers and airports—where you'll have access with the Wi-Fi very, very easily. So that's something that you saw is built in Windows XP and it's even come further since Windows XP has been shipped.

Another key element and probably the top priority at Microsoft, even beyond the key stuff we're doing around usability and new capabilities, is what we call trustworthy computing. This is the idea of taking the need for extreme reliability, knowing that when you install a new application that it won't disturb other things, knowing that your privacy and your security settings will be appropriate without your having to become an expert or your having to go out and get the new software updates manually going across the network. Having that be an understood and accepted thing is important to driving these intelligent devices to new levels. Without that, people will be reluctant and the way they do things simply won't change. They won't see that potential.

So this trustworthiness will have to be an element of all the different devices, which is a substantial challenge, but a challenge that the software industry can meet.

When we talk about integrated experiences, what we mean is that as you move from device to device your information is there for you. If you customize the news page that you care about, when you pick up your screen phone, it comes on to it. If you've said you care about certain traffic, certain stocks, it's always there. If you're using one device, when the system wants to notify you that somebody wants to connect up to you for instant messaging, they know where you are and so you can decide, based on your priorities and who it is, exactly what sort of interaction you want to have with them, but you don't have to give out many addresses for all those different devices, and it's not like phones today where you have to go from one phone number to the next trying to locate that person.

For something like photos, it means that if you take the photos, organize them, then they can show up on all your other devices. You can look at them on the TV set. You can look at them on your PDA device. You can send them off to other people very, very easily.

And so these are big opportunities. I think there is no one that doubts that with the digital approach, software can add value in so many different experiences.

Well, let's take stock, where are we right now? Certainly we're at the very beginning of the decade. This is the decade where all these digital approaches will be common sense, the fact that you organize business appointments through electronic mail, that you coordinate your activities, that you can pick shows and know exactly what that schedule is and have them recorded for you, that as you move around, the music that you care about is available to you.

We've laid a very strong foundation for the digital decade. Although the Internet hype certainly was extreme, particularly in terms of the valuations and some of the new activities, the fact is, Internet popularity continues to go up. Internet traffic is up. Internet shopping is up. And all the key infrastructure pieces were driven forward in the last couple of years in a big way.

PC sales in the fourth quarter are very strong, 130 million units, and growing as that's the PC industry—huge numbers by the standards of any type of device out there.

Big growth in terms of the digital cameras, the music players and so those are there to be used in these new experiences.

Microsoft had three really centerpiece products that were updated recently that for us play a central role. First would be Windows XP. We shipped that in October and already in less than three months we have over 17 million copies of the operating system in use. That's a combination of new copies, which were put onto existing machines and new machines that were shipped that included Windows XP, so a very fast adoption rate, well ahead of anything that we've seen in the past, about 200 percent of what the equivalent was for Windows ME or 300 percent for Windows 98. All the new things we're doing build on the richness of XP.

The second big milestone for us that came a few weeks later in the middle of November was the Xbox launch. And that was a new thing for us. We had to get involved in doing everything end to end to create a breakthrough game platform. Well, it's gone incredibly well. We've sold all that we can make. We've been making them at a furious pace on several continents and the sell-through is over a million and a half units. So from a standing start to a million and a half is pretty incredible. More important than that, though, is the word of mouth and the quality of the games that have been built.

Later tonight we'll give you a glimpse of where we're going with Xbox, but already we've got over three games being bought for every single console sold. That's a record, and it really talks to the fact that the richness of the experience, the breadth of the experiences there is very, very strong. And those games are only going to get better as people take more advantage of what we've built in.

Finally, MSN, our online service, there are a lot of metrics here, but the one I picked is the shopping metric, over a 50 percent increase in shopping during that holiday season. So as ease of use gets out there, as people are using the Internet more and more, there's big growth that's making this a centerpiece, almost in an expected way for people to do things.

Now, one of the things I try to do every year is really capture what's going on out there in terms of how people are looking at these advances, and so this year we went to some experts in Hollywood and asked them to think about the digital decade, try and document for us what the possibilities are and what's going on. So let's take a look at that.

[Videotape presentation.]

[Laughter, applause.]

So how are we going to look at these new experiences? Well, the easiest way is actually to give you a little demo of what we'll see this next year. It's a big year in terms of some neat new things. We've got it divided down into devices: on the go, entertainment, what's going to happen there, and finally Windows at home and how that will change.

The different smart devices are really exploding in volume. The pocket-sized devices are about communications. And here I've put together two categories that historically people have thought of as separate, that is, the screen-based cell phone and the PDA type device. While there will always be the voice-only cell phone devices, it's argued that the difference between a screen-based cell phone and a PDA will become only a matter of emphasis rather than a black and white boundary between two different devices. And so you'll see really the best of both worlds there, the kind of rich communication you expect from the cell phone and some of the richness of applications and experience you've been able to think about with the more powerful PDA devices like the Pocket PC.

The PC itself is constantly evolving. That's the high volume device here. Over the next year you'll see not only some of the things we'll show you tonight but also the tablet PC will be coming out in the second half of next year. And that's a very significant thing because it actually takes the entire PC and gets it into that portable form factor.

The other form factor that we think is important is the big screen and these screen sizes are really the key differentiator. The experience of what you can have on a small device, the desktop-size screen and the big screen, those are the real boundaries that will last even over time. Even as the software and the network and the capabilities converge, the user interface experience of the different screen sizes will have to continue to be optimized for those devices.

For the big screen, it's multiplayer. In the office you might share information, conference together, but you need a user interface that deals with the idea that you're at a distance, you're far away. The PC screen, you've got the keyboard, you're close up, but again it's too big to always have with you and that's where the pocket size comes in. So applications will do user interface specialization to target those devices.

Now, devices without screens will in a sense be peripherals. You'll be able to go to any screen device and go and see their state, understand what's going on, give them commands and there will be a way that those devices, without having any buttons or knobs or screens, will be able to declare themselves and be located and declare their capabilities, so all the different screen devices are connected up.

That's really the dream of this vision, a wireless network, a common way to remote all those capabilities, and then you just pick the size of screen that's appropriate for the task that you're working on at that point.

Now, a key platform I mentioned is Windows CE. We're announcing a major new release of that called Windows CE .NET. This is where we really take the real-time capabilities to a very rich level. All the requirements our customers have had in this real time area we've been able to accommodate with this new release.

We also were able to take the richness, the 802.11 support, authentication support, smart-card capability, different peripherals, networking protocols and benefit from the work we do on Windows on the PC by taking those drivers and that software and customizing them for these smaller devices, making sure we fit into the right memory size, making sure we fit for the small screen and the power budget that these devices have.

We have very broad adoption of these devices. I remember about four years ago, I came to CES and talked about Windows CE and then all the devices were futuristic and we were kind of vague in talking about those. Since then many tens of millions of these devices have shipped and we've been surprised at the variety of devices that people have built around this platform.

We made the development kit, a very rich kit. We put it out there. We've made large parts of the source code available to make it easy to license. People take that and do with it a lot of very, very neat things, and this next version, the CE .NET, will just take that to a new level.

So that's a platform—you can consider it in a sense the little-brother platform next to Windows XP itself—which we custom-tailor also into the so-called embedded XP edition.

Well, I'd like to ask Steven Guggenheimer to come on out and give us a look at what these devices on-the-go look like, what kind of communications things can you do with them, where have the creative hardware companies taken this software power and made it all work together.

Welcome, Steve.

A Statement for Voices Unheard: A Challenge to the National Book Awards

Adrienne Rich, Audre Lorde, and Alice Walker
Writers

At the National Book Award ceremony, Adrienne Rich read the following statement, prepared by herself, Audre Lorde, and Alice Walker—all of whom had been nominated for the poetry award. They agreed that whoever was chosen to receive the award, if any, from among the three, would read the statement.

We, Audre Lorde, Adrienne Rich, and Alice Walker, together accept this award in the name of all the women whose voices have gone and still go unheard in a patriarchal world, and in the name of those who, like us, have been tolerated as token women in this culture, often at great cost and in great pain. We believe that we can enrich ourselves more in supporting and giving to each other than by competing against each other; and that poetry—if it *is* poetry—exists in a realm beyond ranking and comparison. We symbolically join together here in refusing the terms of patriarchal competition and declaring that we will share this prize among us, to be used as best we can for women.

We appreciate the good faith of the judges for this award, but none of us could accept this money for herself, nor could she let go unquestioned the terms on which poets are given or denied honor and livelihood in this world, especially when they are women. We dedicate this occasion to the struggle for self-determination of all women, of every color, identification, or derived class: the poet, the housewife, the lesbian, the mathematician, the mother, the dishwasher, the pregnant teenager, the teacher, the grandmother, the prostitute, the philosopher, the waitress, the women who will understand what we are doing here and those who will not understand yet, the silent women whose voices have been denied us, the articulate women who have given us strength to do our work.

This presentation was given at the National Book Award ceremony, 1974. Reprinted with permission of *Ms.* Copyright © 1974.

Building Community

A Flair for Fashion
A Welcome to New Employees

Erika Fair
Student, Ohio State University

In this presentation, Erika Fair assumed the role of the owner of Erika Fair's Fashion Fair International, welcoming new employees to her company.

Welcome to Erika Fair's Fashion Fair International. I would personally like to express my congratulations and wishes for good luck to each of you. As you know, you were hired because of your flair for fashion and your sense of individuality. This company is built on employees like you.

As each of you knows, my company has a very individual style. Our clothes express the feminine side of a woman. These clothes are playful yet sophisticated, exciting yet subtle, durable yet delicate. Our clothes say, "I'm a professional, a mother, a wife, and even an athlete." Our clothes are versatile. For example, with this belt and these earrings, this outfit says, "Let's go to work, let's give a speech, or even let's have a romantic dinner." Get rid of the belt, throw on a pair of flats, and it says, "I'm ready for a day of shopping or just a day of relaxation."

This is where you come in. You know our reputation, you know what our clothes say and how to wear them. All you have to do is help build this reputation. As buyers, you are skilled enough to know what Erika Fair says and what it doesn't. I expect each of you to assert your individuality when faced with a buying decision but at the same time to be mindful of the company's look.

Look around you—these are your team members. You need to know each other. You need to be able to work with each other as a family unit, to be able to trust one another's judgments, and, at the same time, to be able to accept one another's downfalls.

You are at the top of the line, and I already cherish each of you as a part of the family. If you ever have a problem, feel free to contact me, even at home, if necessary. Think of these headquarters as your home away from home and me as your mom away from mom. I'm here not as a disciplinarian but as an advisor, friend, and confidante.

This presentation was given at Ohio State University, Columbus, Ohio, spring, 1993. Used by permission of Erika Fair.

You were hired because you are the best at what you do, and you all are here because you know that Erika Fair Fashions is the best: The best working with and for the best—what more can we ask for?

Again, I would like to express my sincere congratulations and wishes of good luck to each of you, and I hope that your experience here at Erika Fair Fashions International is rewarding and exciting for you.

Our Lives, One Life

Karen A. Carlton
Professor of English, Humboldt State University

Exactly 30 years ago, I graduated from a small, liberal arts college in southwest Texas and prepared to live in a world I knew and understood. Roles were defined for me: I was engaged to be married; I would teach school so that my young husband could proceed with his studies; we would have children and live happily, safely ever after. In my graduating class of 1963 there were no people of color. All of my professors were men. Sexuality of any sort was a darkly kept secret. There were no divorced couples amongst my friends or even the parents of my friends. There were no single parents. Few people I knew drank alcohol or experimented with drugs. And the word "ecology" was yet to enter the vocabulary of common people. You can see that my reality of 30 years ago was somewhat different from your own today. As a middle class, white and female American, I stepped into a world with social, racial and political boundaries, into a world of absolutes where who was who and what was what and right from wrong were clearly defined.

When my husband and I moved to San Francisco in 1964, you can imagine what happened to us. The world seemed to turn upside down and inside out. You who are parents and grandparents remember the times: The Beatles, the Free Speech and Civil Rights Movements, the Vietnam War, Watts, Hippies, the assassinations, Free Love, and drugs. I think that is when the boundaries of our institutions and cultures began to dissolve, at least for me and people like me. Definitions began to blur and structures seemed to vanish. I felt then like I was in an old black-and-white movie which was suddenly losing its clear story line, its well-developed characters, its predictable ending, its clean focus.

Today we all share a great metaphysical secret, if I may state it so simply: There are no boundaries in the universe. Boundaries are illusions, products not of reality but of the way we map and edit reality. We are reminded daily that we live in a global economy, a global village, that the borders of countries are porous. Money flows around the world in electronic impulses, faxes go everywhere, satellite dishes collect images from all over, and the tapes of revolution can be played at any time or place. All of our major, social issues transcend national lines: AIDS, arms control, terrorism, the environment. As we well know in Humboldt County, the lumber mills of one country, with their emissions that produce acid rain, can denude the trees of the next.

Presented at commencement ceremonies for the College of Arts and Humanities, Humboldt State University, Arcata, California, May 22, 1993. Used by permission of Karen Carlton.

Personal boundaries have dissolved, too. Many of you graduates cannot do as I did 30 years ago after my graduation ceremony, when friends and family socialized. Not all of you can say simply, "These are my parents" or "These are my brothers and sisters" or "This is my fiance." Many of you have stepparents and stepsiblings, half-brothers and sisters, parents of the same gender, or parents who have no biological relationship to you at all. Some of you are married or engaged to the person you live with, many of you are not; some of you are in love with people of the same sex; some of you are single parents; some of you are hermits who live in the woods. And none of this surprises any of us today because we, in the West, have forever moved from that prescriptive age where roles, behaviors and thoughts were fixed by societal norms and expectations.

So much good has come from the dissolution of these imagined boundaries. And so much fear. How exhilarating it is for women and people of color to move into areas so long monopolized by white men! And yet how lonely it is to assume new freedoms and territories without the familiar surroundings, the constant support, the comforting structures of old ways. How liberating it is to choose one's lifestyle, one's family and community, to enjoy the mobility of modern work and leisure. And yet how terrifying and even dangerous it often is to challenge or reshape the traditions of our past. How important it is to be aware of the interrelationships of ideas and organisms, to know, as the Tewa Indians say in one of their prayers, that "your life is my life; our life is one life." And yet how hard this is to remember and feel and *live* when races or religions or genders clash. Complexity, chaos, transformation—these are the watchwords of this day.

The question that presses upon all of us is this: With no boundaries, what will shape and contain our selves, our souls? Without the benefit of authoritarian leadership, without the guidance of old and established institutions, without the forced structures of culture, economics, class, and gender, how will we know who we are and how to be? These are questions, I think, which a university education, particularly a liberal arts education, attempts to address. During your years at HSU, you graduates have been in an environment which has allowed you both the freedom and safety to explore various ways of thinking, being, living. The place of the university, the faculty and staff and friends surrounding you, have permitted many of the benefits and postponed some of the hazards of living with no boundaries.

But now you are leaving this place of wholeness (for that is what a university is: a unified whole) and commencing another life. Outside these halls and this ground, you will have to make your own internal boundaries, forge your own selective communities, establish your own moral order. What will they be? Who will you be? I have a pretty good idea, for I've been watching you, working with many of you, learning with all of you. The German poet Rilke wrote, "The future enters into us, in order to transform itself in us, long before it happens." Your future is in you now, in the choices you have made these last few years at Humboldt State University, in the books you've read, in the papers you've written, in the speeches you've made, in the people you've met, and in the actions you've taken. You have been creating the selves and souls that will endure and even embrace the complexity, chaos and terrible freedom of a universe without boundaries. You've been making yourselves and the future.

Here is a short, short story: Once a group of men and their captain faced a large, terrifying, and unpredictable beast. The men pressed upon the captain and said, "What course of action shall we take?" The captain hesitated to answer at first and then said judiciously: "I think I shall praise it." While I am no captain, I believe it is true that the future is large, terrifying, and unpredictable—that without you and your best selves, it will be a beast.

So just to be safe, let me, for a minute, praise you. Let me act as a mirror and reflect back to you the selves, the souls, and therefore the future I have seen you making: You are generous, compassionate people, devoted to justice and to the well-being of those less privileged than yourselves. Rather than seeking individual power, you work for the empowerment of all. I know that many of you give all together hundreds of hours each week to helping and educating children, young adults, refugees, the homeless, and neglected and abused people. You value collaboration and cooperation; you resist dualism even as you embrace paradox. By celebrating a multidimensional and multicultural view of the world, you recognize and challenge the awful readiness innate within each one of us to fear difference and opposition. You are lovers of the earth and through personal and collective actions you move against ecological destruction. I watch you write essays on recycled paper, and carry your mugs to The Depot for coffee. I hear you call plants, animals and stars by their particular names. You are makers of art, in the service of beauty, interested in creating knowledge as well as acquiring it. You seek ways of knowing which include feeling and being as well as thinking. By holding a worldview which includes the nonvisible, the nonmaterial, the spiritual, you keep body, mind and soul in right relationship. I see your morning Tai Chi, hear your drumming and dancing in the quad. I know your songs, your plays, and I read your poems. Most important, many of you cultivate an inward teacher, a voice of wisdom inside yourselves which will be with you the rest of your lives— in loneliness and alienation, in thoughtful encounters with other people, in dialogue with great ideas and works, in love and in emptiness, in hunger and in richness, in solitude and in community.

Now when you look at yourselves in the mirror, I want you to see something of what I see. I want you to see your own strengths and the beauty of the souls, the future, you are making in this universe with no boundaries. You may have no idea who you will be with, where you will live, or what work you will finally choose, but you can know and live your deepest truths. And *that*, after all, is what matters most for now and tomorrow.

Thirty years ago, I was on the edge of a revolution, a transformation, and didn't know it. You, too, are on the edge of a transformation, a new millennium, but you *do know* it. And because you are working to free yourselves from so many intellectual, psychological, and spiritual boundaries, because you are gifted and able and blessed, I trust you will continue to give your lives to connecting, to serving, to creating, to remembering that Tewa Indian prayer: Your life is my life; my life is your life; our lives are one life.

Commencement Address

Oprah Winfrey
Talk-Show Host

My hat's off to you! My hat's off to you!
[crowd cheers: Go Girl!]
You all have gone girls! I want to say thank you, Dr. Walsh and to the esteemed faculty, to those of you parents, what you have been through, God Bless you, and to the greatest class that has ever graduated from Wellesley. I must say—you are my heart, Dr. Walsh is right. I saw you walking in and I started to weep, and I don't consider myself a weeper, but I guess I must be if I started to weep, because I know what it takes to get through here and I am so proud of all of you for getting through.

Thanks for inviting me to this party, this celebration. I told Dr. Walsh as we were walking in, my graduation was nothing like this. Nobody was having this much fun. When Wendy, Stedman's daughter, Stedman is my beau, my fiancé, don't ask me when we're going to get married, when Stedman's daughter, Wendy, was looking for a school four years ago, no doubt I was far more delighted than she when she chose Wellesley 'cause I knew what she was in for. I had wanted to come to this school. I wanted to be here but I could get no scholarship. I wanted to be here and have lived these past years vicariously through her. I was, as Dr. Walsh said, here with Wendy's father, Stedman, and Wendy's mother, Glinda, on Parents' Day and I was in awe of this place because, see, you all seem to have so much fun, without a keg or anything, and yet you all seemed so serious, so committed to this place with guts and with grace and I saw your sense of integrity and felt your intellect and realized that this was a very special, giving place. Wellesley is a gift to any woman who is willing to open her mind and her heart to it. It is! You are so blessed to have had this, although I know your first year you maybe didn't think it was such a gift because I was there for a lot of those phone calls that Wendy made home. "Daddy [in small girl's voice], this is hard, they just want you to study all the time." Yes, they do. That was the Freshmen Year. About mid-Sophomore Year, though, I think she had several epiphanies and realized what all of you had come to realize here that you do this for yourself, you don't do this for anybody else and that everything you heard about this institution is true—it is a prestigious and powerful place that will wear you out, but what happens is something—that Woman Thing starts to kick in around mid-Sophomore Year. We saw it kick in with Wendy, that Woman Thing that happens. She came here a naive girl from Dallas and Stedman and Glinda, I, and all of those who loved Wendy, are grateful to you Wellesley for the woman in process that you gave us back. We are grateful for that.

This presentation was given at Wellesley College, Wellesley, Massachusetts, May 30, 1997. Available at http://www.wellesley.edu/PublicAffairs/PAhomepage/winfrey.html

You could feel the change about a year and a half after her being here because she went from "Daddy [small girl's voice], this is hard," to "Daddy [adult voice], I won't be able to go on the trip to Africa because I have to study, Daddy." That Woman Thing!

You all know this, that life is a journey and I want to share with you just for a few moments about five things, aren't you glad they aren't ten, five things that have made this journey for me exciting, five lessons that I've learned that if I had gone to Wellesley I could have not made as many mistakes, but five lessons that I've learned that have helped me to make my life better.

First of all, life is a journey. I've learned to become more fully who you are and that is what I love about this institution, it allows women to come to the fullest extent of their possibilities of who they really are and that's what life does—teach you to be who you are. It took me a while to get that lesson, that it really is just about everyday experiences, teaching you, moment in, moment out, who you really are, that every experience is here to teach you more fully how to be who you really are. Because, for a long time I wanted to be somebody else. I mean growing up I didn't have a lot of role models. I was born in 1954. On TV there was only Buckwheat, and I was ten years old before I saw Diana Ross on "The Ed Sullivan Show" with the Supremes and said I want to be like that and it took me a long time to realize I was never going to have Diana Ross' thighs, no matter how many diets I went on, and I was not going to have her hair neither unless I bought some and I came to the realization after being in television and having the news director trying to make me into something that I wasn't and going to New York and allowing myself to be treated less than I should have been—going to a beauty salon, you all know there is a difference between Black hair and White hair. That is the one thing you learn the first week at Wellesley: how did you get your hair to do that? What I learned going to a beauty salon and asking them, after the news director told me that my hair was too thick and my eyes were too far apart and I needed a makeover, sitting in a French beauty salon, allowing them to put a French perm on my black hair and having the perm burn through my cerebral cortex and not being the woman that I am now, so not having the courage to say, this is burning me, and coming out a week later bald and having to go on the air. You learn a lot about yourself when you are Black, and a woman and bald and trying to be an anchorwoman. You learn you are not Diana Ross and that you are not Barbara Walters who I was trying to be at the time.

I had a lot of lessons. I remember going on the air many times and not reading my copy ahead of time. I was on the air one night and ran across the word "Barbados," that may be Barbados to you but it was "Barb-a-does" to me that night and telling the story as an anchor woman about a vote in absentia in California, I thought it was located near San Francisco, and one of the worst, and this is when I broke out of my Barbara shell, because I am sitting there, crossing my legs, trying to talk like Barbara, be like Barbara, and I was reading a story about someone with a "blaze" attitude which, if I had gone to Wellesley, I would have known it was blasé and I started to laugh at myself on the air and broke through my Barbara shell and had decided on that day that laughing was OK even though Barbara hadn't at that time. It was through my series of mistakes that I learned I could be a better Oprah than I could be a better Barbara and I allowed Barbara to be the mentor for me, as she always has been, and I decided then to try to pursue the idea of being myself and I am just thrilled that I get paid so much every day for just being myself, but it was a lesson long in coming, recognizing that I had the instinct that the inner voice that told me that you need to try to find a way to answer to your own truth was the voice I needed to be still and listen to.

One of the other great lessons I learned taught to me by my friend and mentor, Maya Angelou and if you can get this, you can save yourself a lot of time. Wendy and I have had many discussions about this, particularly when it comes to men, although she has a very nice one right now. Remember this because this will happen many times in your life.

When people show you who they are, believe them, the first time. Not the 29th time! That is particularly good when it comes to men situations because when he doesn't call back the first time, when you are mistreated the first time, when you see someone who shows you a lack of integrity or dishonesty the first time, know that that will be followed by many, many, many other times that will at some point in life come back to haunt or hurt you. When people show you who they are, believe them, the first time. Live your life from truth and you will survive everything, everything, I believe even death. You will survive everything if you can live your life from the point of view of truth. That took me a while to get, pretending to be something I wasn't, wanting to be somebody I couldn't, but understanding deep inside myself when I was willing to listen, that my own truth and only my own truth could set me free. Turn your wounds into wisdom. You will be wounded many times in your life. You'll make mistakes. Some people will call them failures but I have learned that failure is really God's way of saying, "Excuse me, you're moving in the wrong direction." It's just an experience, just an experience.

I remember being taken off the air in Baltimore, being told that I was no longer being fit for television and that I could not anchor the news because I used to go out on the stories and my own truth was, even though I am not a weeper, I would cry for the people in the stories, which really wasn't very effective as a news reporter to be covering a fire and crying because the people lost their house [pretending to cry as she said this]. And it wasn't until I was demoted as an on-air anchorwoman and thrown into the talk show arena to get rid of me, that I allowed my own truth to come through. The first day I was on the air doing my first talk show back in 1978, it felt like breathing, which is what your true passion should feel like. It should be so natural to you. And so, I took what had been a mistake, what had been perceived as a failure with my career as an anchorwoman in the news business and turned it into a talk show career that's done OK for me!

Be grateful. I have kept a journal since I was 15 years old and if you look back on my journal when I was 15, 16, it's all filled with boy trouble, men trouble, my daddy wouldn't let me go to Shoney's with Anthony Otie, things like that. As I've grown older, I have learned to appreciate living in the moment and I ask that you do, too. I am asking this graduating class, those of you here, I've asked all of my viewers in America and across the world to do this one thing. Keep a grateful journal. Every night list five things that happened this day, in days to come that you are grateful for. What it will begin to do is to change your perspective of your day and your life. I believe that if you can learn to focus on what you have, you will always see that the universe is abundant and you will have more. If you concentrate and focus in your life on what you don't have, you will never have enough. Be grateful. Keep a journal. You all are all over my journal tonight.

Create the highest, grandest vision possible for your life because you become what you believe. When I was little girl, Mississippi, growing up on the farm, only Buckwheat as a role model, watching my grandmother boil clothes in a big, iron pot through the screen door, because we didn't have a washing machine and made everything we had. I watched her and realized somehow inside myself, in the spirit of myself, that although this was segregated Mississippi and I was "colored" and female, that my life could be bigger, greater than what I saw.

I remember being four or five years old, I certainly couldn't articulate it, but it was a feeling and a feeling that I allowed myself to follow. I allowed myself to follow it because if you were to ask me what is the secret to my success, it is because I understand that there is a power greater than myself, that rules my life and in life if you can be still long enough in all of your endeavors, the good times, the hard times, to connect yourself to the source, I call it God, you can call it whatever you want to, the force, nature, Allah, the power. If you can connect yourself to the source and allow the energy that is your personality, your life force to be connected to the greater force, anything is possible for you. I am proof of that. I think that my life, the fact that I was born where I was born, and the time that I was and have been able to do what I have done speaks to the possibility. Not that I am special, but that it could be done. Hold the highest, grandest vision for yourself. Just recently we followed Tina Turner around the country because I wanted to be Tina, so I had me a nice little wig made and I followed Tina Turner because that is what I can do and one of the reasons I wanted to do that is Tina Turner is one of those women who have overcome great obstacles, was battered in her life, and like a phoenix rose out of that to have great legs and a great sense of herself. I wanted to honor other women who had overcome obstacles and to say that Tina's life, although she is this great stage performer, Tina's life is a mirror of your life because it proves that you can overcome.

Every life speaks to the power of what can be done. So I wanted to honor women all over the country and celebrate their dreams and Tina's tour was called the Wildest Dreams Tour. I asked women to write me their wildest dreams and tell me what their wildest dreams were. Our intention was to fulfill their wildest dreams. We got 77,000 letters, 77,000. To our disappointment we found that the deeper the wound the smaller the dreams. So many women had such small visions, such small dreams for their lives that we had a difficult time coming up with dreams to fulfill. So we did fulfill some. We paid off all the college debt, hmmm, for a young woman whose mother had died and she put her sisters and brothers through school. We paid off all the bills for a woman who had been battered and managed to put herself through college and her daughter through college. We sent a woman to Egypt who was dying of cancer and her lifetime dream was to sit on a camel and use a cell phone. We bought a house for another woman whose dream had always been to have her own home but because she was battered and had to flee with her children one night, had to leave the home seventeen years ago. And then we brought the other women who said we just wanted to see you, Oprah, and meet Tina, that was their dream! Imagine when we paid off the debt, gave the house, gave the trip to Egypt, the attitudes we got from the women who said I just want to see you. And some of them afterwards were crying to me saying that we didn't know, we didn't know, and this is unfair, and I said, that is the lesson: you needed to dream a bigger dream for yourself. That is the lesson. Hold the highest vision possible for your life and it can come true.

I want to leave you with a poem that I say to myself sometimes when I am feeling a little down, although I really don't get down a lot because I know that every experience when it happens, something difficult comes into my life, I say what is it you're here to teach me and what I try to do in my life is to get God on the whisper. He always whispers first. Try to get the whisper before the earthquake comes because the whisper is always followed by a little louder voice, then you get a brick I say, and then sometimes a brick wall, and then the earthquake comes. Try to get it on the whisper. But Maya Angelou wrote a poem and I don't know a poem more fitting than Phenomenal Woman for this crowd because you are and these words are for you.

She says, "Pretty women, honey, they wonder just where my secret lies 'cause I'm not cuter, built to suit a fashion model size but when I start to tell them, they say, Girl, you're telling lies and I said, no, honey, it's in the reach of my arms, it's in the span of my hips, it's in the stride of my stepping, it's in the curl of my lips, 'cause I'm a woman, honey, phenomenally, phenomenal, phenomenal woman. Sometimes I walk into a room just as cool as you please and to a man the fellows either stand up or fall down on their knees. And then they start swarming all around me like a hive of honey bees and I said whoopcha must be this fire in my eyes, could be the flash of my teeth or the swing of my waist or just the joy in my feet, all I know is I'm a woman, you're a woman, we are women, honey, phenomenally, phenomenal women. Now you understand why my head's not bowed, you won't see me dropping about or when you see me coming, it ought to make you proud, sister girl, I say, it's the bend of my hair, it's in the palm of my hands, the need for your care 'cause I'm a woman, you're a woman, we just women, we phenomenal, phenomenally phenomenal, phenomenal women." That's you, Wellesley, that's you. God Bless You!

Seeking Adherence

Who Is a True Friend?

Christa C. Porter
Student, Ohio State University

In this presentation, Christa C. Porter assumed the role of a teacher of a high-school Sunday school class.

Good morning, y'all.

Class members: Good morning.

Today, we're going to talk about something you all know a lot about; I hope we'll get some new ideas on the subject that will stay in your heads when you leave and get on the church bus. We're going to talk about friendship. Anybody here have friends?

Class members: Yes.

What is your definition of a true friend? Someone give me a definition of a true friend.

Class member: Somebody who's loyal and who can be trusted.

OK! Somebody else?

Class member: Somebody you can talk with.

All right. Anyone else?

Class member: Someone to do things with and have fun with.

OK. Everyone has their own definition of a friend. I'd like to add mine to the list. One of my definitions is that a friend is someone who will respect what I say. Even if my opinions are different from theirs, they'll still respect me and won't call me stupid. A friend is also someone I can call at 3:00 in the morning and say, "I need somebody to talk to," and she'll talk to me. That's what I consider a friend. Even if she has to wake up at 3:00 in the morning, she's willing to talk to me when I need help.

The Bible has some things to say about friends. Proverbs 18:24 says a friend is closer than any brother. Proverbs 27:10: Far better is the neighbor that is nearer than a brother that is far off. And greater love hath no man than this that a man lay down his life for his friend.

OK, you've given me your definitions of a friend, I've given you my definition, and I've given you some of what the Bible says about friends. We've been looking at friendship from our perspective here—of what friends do for us. How about looking at friendship from the other side?

This presentation was given at Ohio State University, Columbus, Ohio, spring, 1993. Used by permission of Christa C. Porter.

How can we be a good friend? Would I wake up at 3:00 in the morning for my friend—to listen to her? If your friend were stranded 20 miles away, would you go pick her up? So, a lot of times, we think about what we want our friends to do, but we never think about what we would do for our friends.

One of the ways in which we can be good friends to others is by being trustworthy, which Regina mentioned in her definition of a friend. Can I keep a secret? Can I be trusted? Trust. That's a common word that is used in the definition of a friend. You've probably all had the experience of having friends talk about you behind your back, they say bad things about you, they tell your business to everyone. The Bible recognizes this potential problem. Proverbs 18:24 says that he that maketh many friends doeth it to his own destruction. A prime example: If you tell your friend something, your friend could have a friend who has a friend who has a friend. And the next thing you know, your business is around the whole school.

Help me out here—you stand up. Now pick out somebody real quick who's your friend. OK, now you pick out somebody who's your friend, and you stand up. One more time—you pick out someone who is your friend. Now, I could tell her about my conversation with a guy from school, she could tell her something, and she could tell him something, and he then tells it to his friend, over here. And by the time it gets back to me, according to the story, I've had a date with this guy, we've had sex, I got pregnant, and I had an abortion—all that from just telling one person one thing. That's what happens when you have a lot of friends, especially the kind who aren't trustworthy.

The whole point of this is the person you can really have trust in is God. You don't have to worry about Him coming down and saying, "Guess what she did last night?" He's going to be there for you regardless, he's going to listen to you, and he's going to give you the best advice. Our friends can be wonderful, but God is the best friend of all.

Statement in Opposition to S. J. Resolution 23, Authorizing the Use of Military Force

Barbara Lee
Member, U.S. House of Representatives

Barbara Lee was the only member of Congress to vote against a resolution authorizing President George W. Bush to use military force against those associated with the September 11, 2001, terrorist attacks. Lee gave this presentation prior to the vote in the House of Representatives.

Mr. Speaker, I rise today with a heavy heart, one that is filled with sorrow for the families and loved ones who were killed and injured in New York, Virginia, and Pennsylvania. Only the most foolish or the most callous would not understand the grief that has gripped the American people and millions across the world. This unspeakable attack on the United States has forced me to rely on my moral compass, my conscience, and my God for direction.

September 11 changed the world. Our deepest fears now haunt us. Yet I am convinced that military action will not prevent further acts of international terrorism against the United States.

I know that this use-of-force resolution will pass although we all know that the President can wage a war even without this resolution. However difficult this vote may be, some of us must urge the use of restraint. There must be some of us who say, let's step back for a moment and think through the implications of our actions today—let us more fully understand its consequences.

We are not dealing with a conventional war. We cannot respond in a conventional manner. I do not want to see this spiral out of control. This crisis involves issues of national security, foreign policy, public safety, intelligence gathering, economics, and murder. Our response must be equally multi-faceted.

We must not rush to judgment. Far too many innocent people have already died. Our country is in mourning. If we rush to launch a counterattack, we run too great a risk that women, children, and other non-combatants will be caught in the crossfire. Nor can we let our justified anger over these outrageous acts by vicious murderers inflame prejudice against all Arab Americans, Muslims, Southeast Asians, or any other people because of their race, religion, or ethnicity.

Finally, we must be careful not to embark on an open-ended war with neither an exit strategy nor a focused target. We cannot repeat past mistakes.

This presentation was given in the House of Representatives, U.S. Congress, Washington, DC, September 14, 2001.

In 1964, Congress gave President Lyndon Johnson the power to "take all necessary measures" to repel attacks and prevent further aggression. In so doing, this House abandoned its own constitutional responsibilities and launched our country into years of undeclared war in Vietnam. At that time, Senator Wayne Morse, one of two lonely votes against the Tonkin Gulf Resolution, declared, "I believe that history will record that we have made a grave mistake in subverting and circumventing the Constitution of the United States. . . . I believe that within the next century, future generations will look with dismay and great disappointment upon a Congress which is now about to make such a historic mistake."

Senator Morse was correct, and I fear we make the same mistake today. And I fear the consequences. I have agonized over this vote. But I came to grips with it in the very painful yet beautiful memorial service today at the National Cathedral. As a member of the clergy so eloquently said, "As we act, let us not become the evil that we deplore."

Winning the Cultural War

Charlton Heston
Actor and President of the National Rifle Association of America

I remember my son when he was five, explaining to his kindergarten class what his father did for a living. "My Daddy," he said, "pretends to be people."

There have been quite a few of them. Prophets from the Old and New Testaments, a couple of Christian saints, generals of various nationalities and different centuries, several kings, three American presidents, a French cardinal and two geniuses, including Michelangelo. If you want the ceiling re-painted I'll do my best. There always seem to be a lot of different fellows up here. I'm never sure which one of them gets to talk. Right now, I guess I'm the guy.

As I pondered our visit tonight it struck me: If my Creator gave me the gift to connect you with the hearts and minds of those great men, then I want to use that same gift now to re-connect you with your own sense of liberty . . . your own freedom of thought . . . your own compass for what is right.

Dedicating the memorial at Gettysburg, Abraham Lincoln said of America, "We are now engaged in a great Civil War, testing whether this nation or any nation so conceived and so dedicated can long endure."

Those words are true again. I believe that we are again engaged in a great civil war, a cultural war that's about to hijack your birthright to think and say what resides in your heart. I fear you no longer trust the pulsing lifeblood of liberty inside you . . . the stuff that made this country rise from wilderness into the miracle that it is.

Let me back up. About a year ago I became president of the National Rifle Association, which protects the right to keep and bear arms. I ran for office, I was elected, and now I serve . . . I serve as a moving target for the media who've called me everything from "ridiculous" and "duped" to a "brain-injured, senile, crazy old man." I know . . . I'm pretty old but I sure Lord ain't senile.

As I have stood in the crosshairs of those who target Second Amendment freedoms, I've realized that firearms are not the only issue. No, it's much, much bigger than that.

I've come to understand that a cultural war is raging across our land, in which, with Orwellian fervor, certain acceptable thoughts and speech are mandated.

For example, I marched for civil rights with Dr. King in 1963—long before Hollywood found it fashionable. But when I told an audience last year that white pride is just as valid as black pride or red pride or anyone else's pride, they called me a racist.

This presentation was given at the Harvard Law School Forum, Boston, Massachusetts, February 16, 1999. Used with permission.

I've worked with brilliantly talented homosexuals all my life. But when I told an audience that gay rights should extend no further than your rights or my rights, I was called a homophobe.

I served in World War II against the Axis powers. But during a speech, when I drew an analogy between singling out innocent Jews and singling out innocent gun owners, I was called an anti-Semite.

Everyone I know knows I would never raise a closed fist against my country. But when I asked an audience to oppose this cultural persecution, I was compared to Timothy McVeigh.

From *Time* magazine to friends and colleagues, they're essentially saying, "Chuck, how dare you speak your mind. You are using language not authorized for public consumption!"

But I am not afraid. If Americans believed in political correctness, we'd still be King George's boys—subjects bound to the British crown.

In his book, "The End of Sanity," Martin Gross writes that "blatantly irrational behavior is rapidly being established as the norm in almost every area of human endeavor. There seem to be new customs, new rules, new anti-intellectual theories regularly foisted on us from every direction. Underneath, the nation is roiling. Americans know something without a name is undermining the nation, turning the mind mushy when it comes to separating truth from falsehood and right from wrong. And they don't like it."

Let me read a few examples. At Antioch College in Ohio, young men seeking intimacy with a coed must get verbal permission at each step of the process from kissing to petting to final copulation . . . all clearly spelled out in a printed college directive.

In New Jersey, despite the death of several patients nationwide who had been infected by dentists who had concealed their AIDS—the state commissioner announced that health providers who are HIV-positive need not . . . need not . . . tell their patients that they are infected.

At William and Mary, students tried to change the name of the school team "The Tribe" because it was supposedly insulting to local Indians, only to learn that authentic Virginia chiefs truly like the name.

In San Francisco, city fathers passed an ordinance protecting the rights of transvestites to cross-dress on the job, and for transsexuals to have separate toilet facilities while undergoing sex change surgery.

In New York City, kids who don't speak a word of Spanish have been placed in bilingual classes to learn their three R's in Spanish solely because their last names sound Hispanic.

At the University of Pennsylvania, in a state where thousands died at Gettysburg opposing slavery, the president of that college officially set up segregated dormitory space for black students.

Yeah, I know . . . that's out of bounds now. Dr. King said "Negroes." Jimmy Baldwin and most of us on the March said "black." But it's a no-no now. For me, hyphenated identities are awkward . . . particularly

"Native-American." I'm a Native American, for God's sake. I also happen to be a blood-initiated brother of the Miniconjou Sioux. On my wife's side, my grandson is a thirteenth generation native American . . . with a capital letter on "American."

Finally, just last month . . . David Howard, head of the Washington D.C. Office of Public Advocate, used the word "niggardly" while talking to colleagues about budgetary matters. Of course, "niggardly" means stingy or scanty. But within days Howard was forced to publicly apologize and resign.

As columnist Tony Snow wrote: "David Howard got fired because some people in public employ were morons who (a) didn't know the meaning of 'niggardly,' (b) didn't know how to use a dictionary to discover the meaning, and (c) actually demanded that he apologize for their ignorance."

What does all of this mean? It means that telling us what to think has evolved into telling us what to say, so telling us what to do can't be far behind.

Before you claim to be a champion of free thought, tell me: Why did political correctness originate on America's campuses? And why do you continue to tolerate it? Why do you, who're supposed to debate ideas, surrender to their suppression?

Let's be honest. Who here thinks your professors can say what they really believe? It scares me to death, and should scare you too, that the superstition of political correctness rules the halls of reason.

You are the best and the brightest. You, here in the fertile cradle of American academia, here in the castle of learning on the Charles River, you are the cream. But I submit that you, and your counterparts across the land, are the most socially conformed and politically silenced generation since Concord Bridge.

And as long as you validate that . . . and abide it . . . you are—by your grandfathers' standards—cowards.

Here's another example. Right now at more than one major university, Second Amendment scholars and researchers are being told to shut up about their findings or they'll lose their jobs. Why? Because their research findings would undermine big-city mayors' pending lawsuits that seek to extort hundreds of millions of dollars from firearm manufacturers.

I don't care what you think about guns. But if you are not shocked at that, I am shocked at you. Who will guard the raw material of unfettered ideas, if not you? Who will defend the core value of academia, if you supposed soldiers of free thought and expression lay down your arms and plead, "Don't shoot me."

If you talk about race, it does not make you a racist. If you see distinctions between the genders, it does not make you a sexist. If you think critically about a denomination, it does not make you anti-religion. If you accept but don't celebrate homosexuality, it does not make you a homophobe.

Don't let America's universities continue to serve as incubators for this rampant epidemic of new McCarthyism.

But what can you do? How can anyone prevail against such pervasive social subjugation?

The answer's been here all along. I learned it 36 years ago, on the steps of the Lincoln Memorial in Washington, D.C., standing with Dr. Martin Luther King and two hundred thousand people.

You simply . . . disobey. Peaceably, yes. Respectfully, of course. Nonviolently, absolutely. But when told how to think or what to say or how to behave, we don't. We disobey social protocol that stifles and stigmatizes personal freedom.

I learned the awesome power of disobedience from Dr. King . . . who learned it from Gandhi, and Thoreau, and Jesus, and every other great man who led those in the right against those with the might.

Disobedience is in our DNA. We feel innate kinship with that disobedient spirit that tossed tea into Boston Harbor, that sent Thoreau to jail, that refused to sit in the back of the bus, that protested a war in Viet Nam.

In that same spirit, I am asking you to disavow cultural correctness with massive disobedience of rogue authority, social directives and onerous law that weaken personal freedom.

But be careful . . . it hurts. Disobedience demands that you put yourself at risk. Dr. King stood on lots of balconies.

You must be willing to be humiliated . . . to endure the modern-day equivalent of the police dogs at Montgomery and the water cannons at Selma.

You must be willing to experience discomfort. I'm not complaining, but my own decades of social activism have taken their toll on me. Let me tell you a story.

A few years back I heard about a rapper named Ice-T who was selling a CD called "Cop Killer" celebrating ambushing and murdering police officers. It was being marketed by none other than Time/Warner, the biggest entertainment conglomerate in the world.

Police across the country were outraged. Rightfully so—at least one had been murdered. But Time/Warner was stonewalling because the CD was a cash cow for them, and the media were tiptoeing around it because the rapper was black. I heard Time/Warner had a stockholders meeting scheduled in Beverly Hills. I owned some shares at the time, so I decided to attend.

What I did there was against the advice of my family and colleagues. I asked for the floor. To a hushed room of a thousand average American stockholders, I simply read the full lyrics of "Cop Killer"—every vicious, vulgar, instructional word.

"I GOT MY 12 GAUGE SAWED OFF,
I GOT MY HEADLIGHTS TURNED OFF,
I'M ABOUT TO BUST SOME SHOTS OFF,
I'M ABOUT TO DUST SOME COPS OFF . . ."

It got worse, a lot worse. I won't read the rest of it to you. But trust me, the room was a sea of shocked, frozen, blanched faces. The Time/Warner executives squirmed in their chairs and stared at their shoes. They hated me for that.

Then I delivered another volley of sick lyric brimming with racist filth, where Ice-T fantasizes about sodomizing two 12-year old nieces of Al and Tipper Gore.

"SHE PUSHED HER BUTT AGAINST MY . . ."

Well, I won't do to you here what I did to them. Let's just say I left the room in echoing silence. When I read the lyrics to the waiting press corps, one of them said "We can't print that." "I know," I replied, "but Time/Warner's selling it."

Two months later, Time/Warner terminated Ice-T's contract. I'll never be offered another film by Warners, or get a good review from *Time* magazine. But disobedience means you must be willing to act, not just talk.

When a mugger sues his elderly victim for defending herself . . . jam the switchboard of the district attorney's office.

When your university is pressured to lower standards until 80% of the students graduate with honors . . . choke the halls of the board of regents.

When an 8-year-old boy pecks a girl's cheek on the playground and gets hauled into court for sexual harassment . . . march on that school and block its doorways.

When someone you elected is seduced by political power and betrays you . . . petition them, oust them, banish them.

When *Time* magazine's cover portrays millennium nuts as deranged, crazy Christians holding a cross as it did last month . . . boycott their magazine and the products it advertises.

So that this nation may long endure, I urge you to follow in the hallowed footsteps of the great disobediences of history that freed exiles, founded religions, defeated tyrants, and yes, in the hands of an aroused rabble in arms and a few great men, by God's grace, built this country.

If Dr. King were here, I think he would agree.

Thank you.

Discovering Knowledge and Belief

Arcata Town Meeting

In response to the start of the Gulf War in January, 1991, the Arcata City Council approved a resolution declaring the city "a sanctuary for all persons who for moral, ethical or religious reasons cannot partici- pate in military action." The public debate spurred by the resolution prompted the Council to call a town meeting at which citizens could express their views. The meeting began with the Council's vote to rescind the resolution; it ended with Council members agreeing to con- sider, at their next meeting, whether or not to take future action in regard to the war. Because no council member offered a proposed reso- lution for the agenda, however, no further formal action was taken. Selected excerpts from the testimony are presented here.

Victor Schaub [mayor]: Welcome to this special meeting of the Arcata City Council. . . . This meeting has a special agenda. It is an official meet- ing of the City Council, and the item on the agenda is as follows: "Public discussion of resolution 901–49. Resolution of the City Council of the city of Arcata to be a sanctuary for all persons who for moral, ethical or reli- gious reasons cannot participate in military action." The Council will make some comments after which the meeting, the public discussion part of the meeting, will be facilitated by Mr. Bryan Gaynor, who is our city attorney. There are set rules for how the discussion will proceed, and Mr. Gaynor will announce those rules and explain them after we have done some initial things here. . . . At this time, I will entertain comments from the Council members before we proceed with the discussion portion of the agenda. First, I'll call on Council member Pennisi.

Sam Pennisi: Thank you, Mr. Mayor. I've been doing a lot of soul searching, as I think many of us have been doing, and maybe many of you have been doing this week, I don't know. I've got a couple of com- ments that will be very brief that I'd like to express to you. A little bit of this I said on Saturday, but this is a different group, and I'd like to take this opportunity. This past week has not been pleasant for you or me, and I wish to apologize personally, as one Council member, for this conflict that we are in this evening. When the sanctuary resolution was passed, I honestly thought we were declaring that there should always be a place in our hearts during times of conscription and war for conscientious objec-

This testimony was presented to the Arcata City Council, Arcata, California, January, 1991. Used with permission of the participants.

tors and that we had hoped that a peaceful solution might still be achieved in the Gulf. We were only three hours into the war when our Council meeting started last time. Obviously, I was wrong. I think wording was a problem and other things, and I won't go into details here. That's what we're here to hear about tonight. I was also wrong in not demanding a public meeting or questioning the wisdom of deciding on this issue for our community at all. For these things, too, I offer my apologies. I want to take this opportunity to state my personal, absolute support for the men and women who have been asked to fight, and perhaps die, for a war in which this country has seen fit to participate. And I emphasize this country. It went through the UN resolution, it went through Congressional debate; in my lifetime, I've never been witness to that. If we learned anything from the Vietnam conflict, it is to clearly separate the people who must go to war from the civil policies that find a need for war. I trust any war protester can appreciate the need for this distinction, and I can't emphasize that distinction enough. The tragedy of this resolution, in my opinion, is that we've divided this community unnecessarily, and for my part in that, I, too, am sorry. I have some ideas that might guide future larger-than-Arcata issues, but I want to hear this meeting's input before I finalize these ideas and make specific proposals, and I thank you all for coming this evening.

Victor Schaub: I, too, wish to publicly acknowledge the error of having adopted this resolution—of taking any action, especially on an issue as important as this. We allow public discussion about what color to paint a water tank in somebody's neighborhood, and I acknowledge the error of not having allowed public discussion. I dare say that each of the Council members recognized this error Thursday morning, if not Wednesday night, before the barrage of phone calls and other contacts that we have received. However, I wish to call to mind the quote of John Kennedy regarding the Bay of Pigs when he said, "An error does not become a mistake until you refuse to admit it." And we're admitting the error that we did not allow public discussion.

I want to remind us all of the things that we have in common. We all, those who support the resolution and those who are opposed, we all condemn the actions of Saddam Hussein. We have that in common. We all support the well-being of our troops and the efforts they are required to undertake. We have that in common. And we all have the desire for peace. We know that. We all have that in common. The debate is over how best to achieve that. I would like tonight to be a positive experience for our community—a night in which we can learn that we can have public discussion about an issue as serious as this and that it can be constructive and that we can have this discussion in a peaceful manner. I think we have an opportunity to demonstrate to the larger community, of which we are a part, that the issues of war and peace can be discussed publicly and peacefully.

Now, since we have all acknowledged that it was inappropriate for us to take action without public discussion, it wouldn't seem inappropriate, to me at least, to wipe the slate clean and to start right now having a public discussion of war and peace. It wouldn't seem inappropriate at this time for the mayor to entertain a motion to facilitate the beginning of that process—of that public discussion—by entertaining a motion to rescind the resolution that is before us so that we can then conduct public discussion and make a decision as to whether or not to adopt this or some other resolution. So at this time, I will entertain a motion from any Council member who desires to make one.

Bob Ornelas: I move that we rescind the Arcata sanctuary resolution number 901–49.

Audience: [cheers and applause]

Bob Ornelas: And that we provide the opportunity for this town to develop a statement regarding the Persian war.

Victor Schaub: Is there a second to the motion?

Sam Pennisi: I second it.

Victor Schaub: Okay, the motion has been made by Council member Ornelas to rescind resolution number 901–49 and to commence a public discussion of what, if any, statement to make concerning the Persian Gulf war, and the motion has been seconded by Council member Pennisi. Is there a need for further discussion? Are we ready to vote? All in favor say aye.

Council members: Aye.

Victor Schaub: The vote is unanimous. Okay, at this point, then, we will commence the process of public discussion on this issue. At the end of the discussion, we will make whatever decision that we can make given what is on the written and posted agenda. To facilitate this process, I'm going to turn the meeting over to Mr. Bryan Gaynor: Bryan.

Bryan Gaynor: Thank you, Mr. Mayor. First of all, a set of rules of conduct for conducting this meeting has been prepared for you, and they are available at the door. I hope that each of you has had an opportunity to pick up a set of these rules and has familiarized yourself with them. I want to ask if the people who are outside can hear me clearly. [Crowd noise is heard.] I'll take that for a yes. And we can hear you. So, these rules are intended to provide an atmosphere in which the diversity of opinion that is present in this room and outside this room can be expressed and heard by all the participants of this meeting. . . .

If you would like to speak, and of course everyone is encouraged to speak, you must obtain at the door of this hall one of the color-coded cards. If you are an Arcata resident or an Arcata businessperson, you should obtain a yellow card. If you are not an Arcata resident or businessperson and you wish to speak, please obtain one of the red-colored cards. The reason for this is we wish to hear from everyone, but this is a city-of-Arcata issue and, accordingly, Arcata residents and businesspersons will be given priority. That is, they'll be allowed to speak first. This doesn't mean that others from outside of Arcata will not be allowed to speak. Rather, it's merely to reflect the priorities of the Council. . . .

We're asking that people who intend to speak be in the line that is on the left-hand side of the hall from my perspective, the right-hand side of the hall from the perspective of you in the audience. We ask that 10 speakers be in line ready to make their comments. Accordingly, when you come to the microphone to speak, we ask that you state your name and the fact that you're a resident of Arcata, if that is the case, or otherwise if you're not, and that you also indicate what your speaker number is. That way, the next person will know that he or she should be ready to come to the microphone. We hope, by following these procedures, that we can move expeditiously and allow the maximum number of people to be heard. Each speaker will be allowed one opportunity to address the Council, and each speaker will be limited to three minutes. . . .

I want to point out to everyone that this meeting is going to be broadcast subject to a two-hour time delay on channel 31. A video repeat will occur on January 26, Saturday, at 1:00 P.M.; again on January 30, Wednesday, at 7:00 P.M.; and on February 2, Saturday, at 1:00 P.M. Please address your remarks to the City Council. Personal attacks and name-calling are not appropriate, nor is the interruption of any speaker. Please follow these rules, and please let us hear your comments. . . . So, will the first speaker please identify himself?

Robert Thomas: Thank you, Mr. Gaynor. Mr. Chairman, fellow Council members. My name is Robert Thomas. I am a co-owner of Joe Costa Trucking. We are located in the city of Arcata, California. I'd just like to say that I've been a member of this community for the past 15 years. My wife's family has been here for almost a century. I'm sure there has never been an issue that has divided the community as deeply as the resolution that was passed last week. And I would like to commend the City Council for the position they've taken tonight, and I would just like to say that I hope that this never happens again. I've addressed many public forums recently but none with as serious implications as this one has had. I represent a company that has approximately 100 families in the Arcata community. Many of them have loved ones in the Middle East, and many of them feel very strongly about the support that we show and provide for those family members. My comments obviously are not what I intended them to be because of the action that was just taken by the City Council. But I can tell you this: an overwhelming number of phone calls came into the city during the past 5 or 6 days, 75 percent of which opposed the pass of the resolution. And I would just like to say, once again to reiterate, that I commend you for what you've done this evening, and I would hope that a resolution similar to the one you passed will never be passed again. Thank you very much.

Bill Hanley: I'm number 91. My name is Bill Hanley. I thank the Council and everybody for going for the sanctuary. I just think it's lame to

be out killing people in this day and age when we're supposed to be leading the world and world leaders, and we can't come up with a damn idea,
another way around this. The only way to do it is to kill somebody. It's
stupidity, and I applaud the Council. I wish you didn't rescind the resolution, and I hope you come up with another one. I don't think everyone
has had the chance to speak yet tonight, and I think you need another
night of discussion. Thanks.

Elizabeth Comet: [Gives peace sign to audience before beginning to
speak.] Hi, my name is Elizabeth Comet, and I live at 1227 Old Arcata
Road, and I'm number 94. God, I'm really nervous. I think the question is
no longer whether war is appropriate or correct or not. That doesn't make
any difference any more. It's now a question of choice—the choice to kill,
to fight a war when you're not sure why we are at war. My father was a
Marine. My grandfather was a Flying-Tiger in World War II, and I've seen
what happens to people who fight in wars. Friends, to choose to fight in a
war is a very serious decision. To see people die, to kill other human
beings, is a very important decision, whether it's for your country or for
whatever reason. It's a heavy decision to make. I don't think there's anybody ever who has the right to tell you whether you have to kill other people. We have a country where we kill people to show people who kill
people that killing people is wrong. This country gives people the death
penalty to show other people that killing people is wrong, and now we're
telling you that you have the choice—you either kill or you go to jail.
That's crazy. This is insane. I was talking to my friend before this war
broke out about going to Costa Rica this summer, and it's something I've
always wanted to do. It's my summer, it's what I want to do this summer,
but you know what? Now that this war has broken out, I'm going to go to
Costa Rica this summer, and if my friends are drafted, I don't think I'll ever
come back because I could not feel proud to be a member of a country that
tells you either to kill other people or you go to prison. That's crazy.

Ron Grace: Good evening, ladies and gentlemen, City Councilmen.
My name is Ron Grace. I'm a business owner here in Arcata. I was a resident here in Arcata for about 7 years. I presently live in McKinleyville. I
am a proud member of the Arcata volunteer fire department. I am a
proud parent of two students who graduated from Arcata High. My son
is currently in Saudi Arabia. Many people tonight have voiced their opinion on a lot of different issues, many of which are not the reason why
we're here tonight. But the real reason we are here tonight is your actions
taken last week. The objective of tonight's meeting is to decide if we
should pass a resolution similar to the one the Humboldt County Board
of Supervisors passed. You have offended a small group of radicals. I am
pleased that you rescinded your resolution, but you must pass a resolution in support of our servicemen in the Gulf and all over the world. Two
groups are here tonight, one that will be here in Arcata for a short period
of time—students and activists. The other will be here a long time—busi-

nesspeople and long-time residents—the silent majority, as many have said tonight. So you must consider this in your discussion of further passing another resolution. I ask you to uphold your oath of office, support the U.S. President and the Congressional action, and support the will of the citizens of Arcata or resign.

Frank Hollyman: Thank you. Good evening. My name is Frank Hollyman. I've lived in Arcata for 24 years. I am proud to say that I am from Arcata, even though I do disagree with what the Council did, but I would like to say this: It's been a pleasure to be in Arcata. I think there's an even ground that we all need to seek here, but we all need to have voice in order to seek that even ground, and we weren't granted that, I don't believe, in this case. I don't want you to make decisions for me unless you have my input. I can't make that decision for you, but I do ask you to search your soul and come up with an answer that fits for you but, more importantly, fits for Arcata, the city whom you represent. As I've said before, I've grown up in Arcata, I'm proud of Arcata. I have two sons I am raising in Arcata, and I hope that when they reach the draft age, there isn't a draft. But if there is, I hope that they will find it in their hearts to go and defend their country as the people we have over there today are defending their country. I hope they get the support from their town, which hopefully at that time will be Arcata. I was a Marine. I'm proud to say I was a Marine, and if I get called upon, I will go—not that I really want to go. I don't want to kill anybody. I don't think anybody here wants that. I think everybody wants peace. But we also want representative government, and all I'm asking you is give us a chance to have that representation. I also applaud your efforts to rescind this bill or this ordinance number 901–49, and I ask that instead of tearing apart Arcata, it might be a good idea to listen a little more attentively before decisions such as this are made in the future. Thank you.

James Moray: My name is James Moray. I'm a very new resident of Arcata. I think we've had a lot of requests here tonight for the City Council to resign, and there have been a lot of people saying they're ashamed to be living in Arcata because of this resolution. I think that's really ridiculous and terrible. They did not cause this split and this conflict. George Bush did. This war did. This war is causing us to fight each other and not realize that we all need to uphold our right to make a choice and live and decide for ourselves what we want to do. The draft violates the right to choose. I understand the people who are objecting to the fact that the City Council might have made this resolution hastily without input from the public, but if you're concerned with the democratic ideal, you should be here in support of people's right to make a choice for themselves. There's a very basic choice, whether you want to go thousands of miles, be commanded by George Bush and kill people and possibly be killed. I mean that's a very basic decision there, and I can't imagine why a community so concerned with democracy wouldn't want people to have that choice. That's really all I have to say.

Shacoti Walsch: Hello, my name is Shacoti Walsch, and I am a resident of Arcata, a student, and a mother. I've heard a lot of different things tonight, and I really do not understand, after reading this resolution, what in the world you can possibly be sorry for. You should be proud of yourselves, and if it is a democratic process that is to be encouraged here tonight, then I ask that it truly be a democratic process. If it means taking a vote of every citizen of Arcata, then we take a vote, but democracy should not be outweighed by money and power again. I really ask that. One thing I keep hearing over and over again is that we all seem to be united on our right to freedom. I do look for the things that we can be united on. George Bush has convinced a good part of this country that we are in Iraq for freedom, but I want to ask you something. Search your minds and souls and look. Where were we when the students in China were shot down if this is over freedom? Where were we when 700 Black babies were killed one morning for their rights of freedom in South Africa? Where were we? This is not over freedom, unfortunately, but if we can be united on the right to freedom, let's bring the issue back home. In the Constitution, it says we have the right to the pursuit of life, liberty, and happiness—the freedom to pursue life, liberty, and happiness. How can any of us be happy killing another human being? That's murder. I applaud you with my heart and my mind and my whole being for being the forerunners of such a resolution. We live in a changing time, and it is time to drop the old blind patriotism and pull the truth out from within ourselves of what it means to be free human beings, and freedom means to have a choice of whether to go to war or not go to war. Remember, the draft takes away our freedom. Thank you.

Focus-Group Discussion of *The Lantern*

Randi Lewis
Student, Ohio State University

In this presentation, Randi Lewis uses a focus group to generate feed-back for the staff of the student newspaper at Ohio State University, The Lantern. *Her words are included below, although the answers her audience gave are not.*

In public relations, we do a lot of focus groups to find out who our audience is, what they think about a product, or what they like about a product or service. As students at OSU, I'm assuming most of you read *The Lantern*, so that will be the focus of this discussion today. I'd like to begin by welcoming you all to this focus group. Thank you for taking time out of your busy schedules to participate in this session. I will be asking several open-ended questions about *The Lantern* and would like you to be honest in answering them.

There are several goals we are trying to accomplish by conducting this focus group. First, we'd like to find out the aspects you like and dis-like about our student newspaper. Second, we want to hear what you think about the stories we've been running the past three quarters. Last, we want to get some suggestions from you—the students who read our paper—on how we can serve you better. The paper is here for you, and we want to do the best job that we can in meeting your needs.

Before we begin the discussion, I would like to give you a little bit of background about *The Lantern*. It is a student-run newspaper that is written and put together entirely by journalism students in the news and public relations tracks. The paper is published every day, Monday through Friday, during autumn, winter, and spring quarters and bi-weekly during the sum-mer quarter. It is funded and supported totally by advertising dollars.

With this background in mind, let's get started with the focus-group questions. You can raise your hand or jump right in, whatever you're most comfortable doing. I'm going to be taking notes while you're talking in order to get your suggestions down.

- How many of you read *The Lantern* on a regular basis?
- How many of you read it more than 3 times a week?
- How many of you read *The Lantern* as a primary source for your news?
- What are the sections you flip to first or the ones you read most often?
- What about sports? Do you feel we should be including more arti-cles about sports—not just those at OSU but nationally?

This presentation was given at Ohio State University, Columbus, Ohio, spring, 1993. Used by permission of Randi Lewis.

- What about the editorial page/letters to the editor? Do you all read that section? What do you think about that section?
- What are some of the stories that stood out for you in *The Lantern* over the past three quarters? Why do you remember those stories in particular?
- What are some of the things you like about *The Lantern*?
- What are some of the things you dislike about *The Lantern*?
- You've given me several valuable suggestions for *The Lantern*. There is one specific question I'd like to ask you. Do you feel we should print Associated Press (or AP) articles in *The Lantern*? There are two schools of thought in journalism. Some think that we should have totally student-written articles—no AP articles whatsoever. Others argue that, for many students, this is their only source of news, so we need to include a balance between AP and student-written articles about campus. What's your feeling on that?

This has been a very productive discussion, but unfortunately, I need to wrap up here. Let me summarize the main ideas you've given me: We need more accurate reporting, more careful attention to grammar and spelling, a more professional look generally, and more in-depth coverage of OSU sports. In terms of AP articles, you believe they are appropriate to include not as major sources of news but to acknowledge certain world events—such as when a prominent person dies. All of these suggestions are extremely valuable.

I want to thank you all for participating in this focus-group discussion. As I said before, you, the students, are the primary audience that we're trying to serve, so your input is greatly appreciated. I want you to know all of your suggestions will be carefully considered by *The Lantern* staff. Thank you all again.

ENDNOTES

Chapter One

[1] "Population: U.S. Ever More Multi-Ethnic," *World News*, 2 October 1999; available from www.oneworld.org/ips2/oct99/14_15_051.html.

[2] Todd S. Purdum, "California Census Confirms Whites Are in Minority," *New York Times*, 30 March 2001; available from www.nytimes.com/2001/03/30/national/30CALI.html.

[3] Margie Mason, "Census Gives a Picture, Although Incomplete, of Gay Couples," *The Record* [New Jersey], 8 August 2001; available from www.bergen.com/faith/gays8200108086.htm.

[4] The terms *conquest* and *conversion* to describe modes of rhetoric were developed by Sally Miller Gearhart in "The Womanization of Rhetoric," *Women's Studies International Quarterly* 2 (1979): 196. The terms *advisory rhetoric* and *invitational rhetoric* and the general schema for the modes of rhetoric were developed by Sonja K. Foss and Cindy L. Griffin in an early draft of "Beyond Persuasion: A Proposal for an Invitational Rhetoric," *Communication Monographs* 62 (March 1995): 2–18. The term *benevolent rhetoric* was developed by Barbara J. Walkosz in a conversation with Sonja K. Foss, 1999.

[5] Suzette Haden Elgin, *How to Disagree Without Being Disagreeable: Getting Your Point Across with the Gentle Art of Verbal Self-Defense* (New York: John Wiley, 1997), 80.

[6] Much of this description of invitational rhetoric is from Foss and Griffin, 2–18.

[7] James S. Baumlin and Tita French Baumlin, "Rogerian and Platonic Dialogue in—and Beyond—the Writing Classroom," in *Rogerian Perspectives: Collaborative Rhetoric for Oral and Written Communication*, ed. Nathaniel Teich (Norwood, NJ: Ablex, 1992), 128.

[8] Deborah Tannen, *The Argument Culture: Stopping America's War of Words* (New York: Ballantine, 1998), 14.

[9] Tannen, 3.

[10] Suzette Haden Elgin, "Peacetalk 101," 2000, preface; available from www.forlovingkindness.org/peacetalk1.html.

[11] Tannen, 20.

[12] Carl R. Rogers, *A Way of Being* (Boston: Houghton Mifflin, 1980), 143.

[13] Annette Simmons, *A Safe Place for Dangerous Truths: Using Dialogue to Overcome Fear & Distrust at Work* (New York: American Management Association, 1999), 99.

[14] Martha C. Nussbaum, *Cultivating Humanity: A Classical Defense of Reform in Liberal Education* (Cambridge: Harvard University Press, 1997), 10–11.

[15] The term *trial empathy* is suggested by Heinz Kohut, *The Restoration of the Self* (New York: International Universities Press, 1977), 168; *trial identification* comes from Stanley L. Olinick, "A Critique of Empathy and Sympathy," in *Empathy I*, ed. Joseph Lichtenberg, Melvin Bornstein, and Donald Silver (Hillsdale, NJ: Lawrence Erlbaum, 1984), 137–66; and *transient identification* is a label proposed by James H. Spencer, Jr., "Discussion," in *Empthy I*, ed. Joseph Lichtenberg, Melvin Bornstein, and Donald Silver (Hillsdale, NJ: Erlbaum, 1984), 37–42.

[16] Gearhart, "The Womanization of Rhetoric," 195.

[17] Ursula K. LeGuin, "Bryn Mawr Commencement Address (1986)," in *Dancing at the Edge of the World: Thoughts on Words, Women, Places* (New York: Grove, 1989), 150–51.

[18] Sonia Johnson, *The Ship That Sailed into the Living Room: Sex and Intimacy Reconsidered* (Estancia, NM: Wildfire, 1991), 162.

[19] Starhawk, *Truth or Dare: Encounters with Power, Authority, and Mystery* (San Francisco: Harper & Row, 1987), 9–10.

[20] Stanley A. Deetz, "Communication in the Age of Negotiation," *Journal of Communication* 47 (Autumn 1997): 130.

[21] Simmons, 20.

[22] Jerry Hicks and Esther Hicks, Workshop audiotape G-5-9-92A (San Antonio: Abraham-Hicks Publications, 1992).

[23] Myles Horton with Judith Kohl and Herbert Kohl, *The Long Haul: An Autobiography* (New York: Doubleday, 1990), 16.

[24] Gearhart, "The Womanization of Rhetoric," 198.

[25] Dennis A. Lynch, Diana George, and Marilyn M. Cooper, "Moments of Argument: Agonistic Inquiry and Confrontational Cooperation," *College Composition and Communication* 48 (February 1997): 80.

[26] Carl R. Rogers, *On Becoming a Person: A Therapist's View of Psychotherapy* (Boston: Houghton Mifflin, 1961), 333.

[27] Simmons, 57.

[28] Simmons, 45.

[29] Martin Buber, *Between Man and Man*, trans. Ronald Gregor Smith (New York: Macmillan, 1965), xiv.

[30] Sally Miller Gearhart, quoted in Eric Mills, "Enriching and Expanding the Animal Movement: Dr. Sally Gearhart Talks about Sexism, Racism and Coalition-Building," *Agenda* 111 (September/October 1983): 5.

[31] Charles Simic, quoted in Tannen, 7–8.

[32] Janice Moulton, "A Paradigm of Philosophy: The Adversary Method," in *Discovering Reality: Feminist Perspectives on Epistemology, Metaphysics, Methodology, and Philosophy of Science*, ed. Sandra Harding and Merrill B. Hintikka (Boston: D. Reidel, 1983), 151.

[33] For an example of Judge Kass's approach, see *Mediation*, videotaped presentation by Kass to divorcing parents, prepared by the District Court of the Second Judicial District, Albuquerque, NM, June, 1990.

[34] Sonia Johnson is one theorist who develops this idea. See Sonia Johnson, *Going Out of Our Minds: The Metaphysics of Liberation* (Freedom, CA: Crossing, 1987), 27.

[35] Jerry Hicks and Esther Hicks, "Limiting Beliefs and the Art of Allowing," *The Science of Deliberate Creation* 17 (July/August/September 2001): 6.

[36] Kate Zernike, "Program DAREs to Start Over Again," *The Denver Post*, 15 February 2001, pp. A1, A17.

[37] Carol Kreck, "Anti-Drug Focus Goes One-on-One," *The Denver Post*, 4 December 2000, pp. B1, B3.

[38] Sonia Johnson, *Wildfire: Igniting the She/Volution* (Albuquerque: Wildfire, 1989), 251.

[39] Johnson, *Wildfire*, 37.

[40] Bell hooks does not capitalize the initial letters of her name.

[41] Bell hooks, *Teaching to Transgress: Education as the Practice of Freedom* (New York: Routledge, 1994), 48.

[42] Gloria Anzaldúa, *Borderlands/La Frontera: The New Mestiza* (San Francisco: Aunt Lute, 1987), 70.

Chapter Two

[1] Lloyd F. Bitzer, "The Rhetorical Situation," *Philosophy and Rhetoric* 1 (Winter 1968): 1–14.

[2] Bitzer, 2.

[3] Kenneth Burke, *The Philosophy of Literary Form: Studies in Symbolic Action* (Berkeley: University of California Press, 1973), 109.

[4] Burke, 1.

[5] Richard M. Weaver, *Language is Sermonic: Richard M. Weaver on the Nature of Rhetoric*, ed. Richard L. Johannesen, Rennard Strickland, and Ralph T. Eubanks (Baton Rouge: Louisiana State University Press, 1970), 222.

[6] Weaver, 224.

[7] See, for example, Satoshi Ishii, "Thought Patterns as Modes of Rhetoric: The United States and Japan," *Communication* 11 (December 1982): 81–86, 97–102; Yoshitaka Miike, "Theorizing Culture and Communication in the Asian Context: An Assumptive Foundation," *Intercultural Communication Studies* 11 (2002): 1–21; David Y. F. Ho, "Selfhood and Identity in Confucianism, Taoism, Buddhism, and Hinduism: Contrasts with the West," *Journal for the Theory of Social Behavior* 25 (1995): 115–39; Harry Irwin, *Communicating with Asia: Understanding People and Customs* (New South Wales, Aust.: Allen & Unwin, 1996); and Jan Servaes, "Reflections on the Differences in Asian and European Values and Communication Modes," *Asian Journal of Communication* 10 (2000): 53–70.

[8] Burke, 146.

[9] Mary Alice Speke Fredig, "Exploring the Social Construction of Complex Self-organizing Change" (Ph.D. diss., Benedictine University, 2001), 181.

[10] Nelle Morton, *The Journey is Home* (Boston: Beacon, 1985), 202–07.

Chapter Three

[1] These conditions are derived, in part, from Sonja K. Foss and Cindy L. Griffin, "Beyond Persuasion: A Proposal for an Invitational Rhetoric," *Communication Monographs* 62 (March 1995): 2–18.

[2] For a discussion of how feeling free to talk affects participation in civic life, see Robert O. Wyatt, Joohan Kim, and Elihu Katz, "How Feeling Free to Talk Affects Ordinary Political Conversation, Purposeful Argumentation, and Civic Participation," *Journalism and Mass Communication Quarterly* 77 (Spring 2000): 99–114.

[3] Mary Alice Speke Ferdig, "Exploring the Social Construction of Complex Self-organizing Change: A Study of Emerging Change in the Regulation of Nuclear Power" (Ph.D. diss., Benedictine University, 2001), 187.

[4] Annette Simmons, *A Safe Place for Dangerous Truths: Using Dialogue to Overcome Fear & Distrust at Work* (New York: American Management Association, 1999), 80.

[5] Simmons, 82.

[6] Simmons, 80–81.

[7] Michael P. Nichols, *The Lost Art of Listening* (New York: Guilford, 1995), 250.

[8] Nichols, 13.

[9] Sally Miller Gearhart, "Womanpower: Energy Re-Sourcement," in *The Politics of Women's Spirituality: Essays on the Rise of Spiritual Power within the Feminist Movement*, ed. Charlene Spretnak (Garden City, NY: Doubleday, 1982), 95.

[10] Bill Amend, *FoxTrot*, *The Albuquerque Journal*, 12 January 2002, p. F3.

[11] Suzette Haden Elgin, *How to Disagree Without Being Disagreeable: Getting Your Point Across with the Gentle Art of Verbal Self-Defense* (New York: John Wiley, 1997), 145–46.

Chapter Four

[1] Elizabeth Kirk, quoted in Andrew Harnack and Eugene Kleppinger, *Online!: A Reference Guide to Using Internet Sources* (New York: Bedford/St. Martin's, 2000), 51–64.

Chapter Five

[1] Christine Todd Whitman, "Statement of Governor Christine Todd Whitman, Administrator, U. S. Environmental Protection Agency, Before the Subcommmittee on VA, HUD, and Independent Agencies of the Committee on Appropriations, 28 November 2001; available at http://yosemite.epa.gov/administrator/speeches.nsf/cb7284cd464285f8852564457777006faf39/175.

[2] David Boaz, "The Public School Monopoly: America's Berlin Wall," *Vital Speeches of the Day* 58 (1 June 1992): 507–11.

[3] Richard R. Kelley, "Prospering in '92: How to Avoid a Cold When the World is Sneezing," *Vital Speeches of the Day* 58 (1 June 1992): 333–36.

[4] The motivated sequence was developed by Alan Monroe. See Bruce E. Gronbeck, Raymie E. McKerrow, Douglas Ehninger, and Alan H. Monroe, *Principles and Types of Speech Communication*, 12th ed. (New York: HarperCollins College, 1994), 193–223.

[5] Sally Miller Gearhart, "Whose Woods These Are" (paper presented at the annual meeting of the Western Speech Communication Association Convention, Portland, OR, February 1980).

[6] Jimmy Carter, "Tribute to Hubert Humphrey," December 1977; available at http://www.historyplace.com/speeches/carter.htm.

Chapter Six

[1] George W. Bush, "State of the Union," *The Denver Post*, 29 January 2002, p. A4.

[2] Harvey Milk, "Milk Forum: My Concept of a Legislator," *Bay Area Reporter*, 27 May 1976, n.p.

[3] Patricia Roberts Harris, "The Law and Moral Issues," in *American Public Discourse: A Multicultural Perspective*, ed. Ronald K. Burke (Lanham, MD: University Press of America, 1992), 84.

[4] Bill Gates, "Remarks at the 2002 International Consumer Electronics Show, 7 January 2002; available from http://www.microsoft.com/billgates/speeches/2002/01-07ces.asp.

[5] *Merriam-Webster's Collegiate Dictionary*, 10th ed. (Springfield, MA: Merriam-Webster, 1998), 137.

[6] Cal Ripken, Jr., "Address at Camden Yards on the Occasion of Final Appearance as an Orioles Player (10-06-01)"; available from http://www.americanrhetoric.com/speeches/calripkenjr.htm.

[7] Sonia Johnson, *Going Out of Our Minds: The Metaphysics of Liberation* (Freedom, CA: Crossing, 1987), 316–17.

[8] Mary Catherine Bateson, *Composing a Life* (New York: Penguin, 1989), 240.

[9] Gwen Moffat, quoted in Nina Winter, *Interview with the Muse: Remarkable Women Speak on Creativity and Power* (Berkeley: Moon, 1978), 123.

[10] Alan Alda, "Commencement Address at Drew University," in *Contemporary American Speeches: A Sourcebook of Speech Forms and Principles*, 6th ed., ed. Richard L. Johannesen, R. R. Allen, and Wil A. Linkugel, 6th ed. (Dubuque: Kendall/Hunt, 1988), 11.

[11] Charlton Heston, "Winning the Cultural War," Harvard Law School Forum, 16 February 1999; available from http://nramemberscouncils.com/harvard1.shtml.

[12] Spiro T. Agnew, "Television News Coverage," in *Contemporary American Voices: Significant Speeches in American History, 1945–Present*, ed. James R. Andrews and David Zarefsky (New York: Longman, 1992), 270.

[13] John F. Kennedy, "Inaugural Address," in *Three Centuries of American Rhetorical Discourse: An Anthology and a Review*, ed. Ronald F. Reid (Prospect Heights, IL: Waveland, 1988), 713.

[14] George W. Bush, "Statement by the President in His Address to the Nation," 11 September 2001; available from http://www.whitehouse.gov/news/releases/2001/09/20010911-16 html.

[15] Walt Bresette, "We Are All Mohawks," *Green Letter* [Winter 1990]: 50.

[16] Annie Dillard, *The Writing Life* (New York: HarperCollins, 1989), 16.

[17] Andrei Codrescu, "What Central-European Artists & Writers Can Do for Us, with Remarks on Missouri," *Artlogue* [Missouri Arts Council] 12 (March 1991): 7.

[18] Garrison Keillor, *Lake Wobegon Days* (New York: Viking, 1985), 13–14.

[19] Chief Weninock, quoted in T. C. McLuhan, ed., *Touch the Earth: A Self-Portrait of Indian Existence* (New York: Touchstone, 1971), 10.

[20] Patti P. Gillespie, "1987 Presidential Address: Campus Stories, or The Cat Beyond the Canvas," *Spectra* [Speech Communication Association] (January 1988): 3.

[21] Maggie Sale, "Call and Response as Critical Method: African-American Oral Traditions and *Beloved*," *African American Review*, 26 (1992): 44.

[22] William Shakespeare, *As You Like It*, II, vi, 139.

[23] Mother Teresa, "Mother Teresa on Family Values and Abortion," National Prayer Breakfast, Washington, D. C., 5 February 1994; available from http://www.drini.com/motherteresa/own_words/abortion1.html.

[24] Barbara Brown Zikmund, "What is Our Place?," in *And Blessed Is She: Sermons by Women*, ed. David Albert Farmer and Edwina Hunter (San Francisco: Harper & Row, 1990), 233.

[25] Janet Hughes, statement presented at the opening of the Missouri Visual Artists' Biennial, University of Missouri, Columbia, 5 March 1993.

[26] Ted Koppel, "The Vannatizing of America," in *Representative American Speeches 1987–1988*, vol. 60, ed. Owen Peterson (New York: H. W. Wilson, 1988), 50.

[27] Koppel, 52.

[28] Heston.

[29] Isidore Okpewho, *African Oral Literature: Backgrounds, Character, and Continuity* (Bloomington: Indiana University Press, 1992), 53.

[30] Jesse Jackson, "The Rainbow Coalition," in *Contemporary American Public Discourse*, 3rd ed., ed. Halford Ross Ryan (Prospect Heights, IL: Waveland, 1992), 325.

[31] Jackson, "The Rainbow Coalition," 320.

[32] Diane Stein, *Casting the Circle: A Woman's Book of Ritual* (Freedom, CA: Crossing, 1990), 178.

[33] Michael L. Hecht, Mary Jane Collier, and Sidney A. Ribeau, *African American Communication: Ethnic Identity and Cultural Interpretation* (Newbury Park, CA: Sage, 1993), 99.

[34] Barbara Kingsolver, *The Bean Trees* (New York: Harper Perennial, 1988), 163.

[35] David E. Thigpen, "A New Kind of Homeless," *Time*, 31 December 2001/7 January 2002, 30.

[36] J. D. Salinger, *The Catcher in the Rye* (New York: Bantam, 1951), 58.

Chapter Seven

[1] Peggy Dersch, "Do You Think You Know Me?," in *Contemporary American Speeches: A Sourcebook of Speech Forms and Principles*, 7th ed., ed. Richard L. Johannesen, R. R. Allen, and Wil A. Linkugel (Dubuque: Kendall/Hunt, 1992), 232.

[2] Kahlil Gibran, *The Prophet* (New York: Alfred A. Knopf, 1923), 16–17.

[3] Terry Russell and Renny Russell, *On the Loose* (San Francisco: Sierra Club, 1967), 45.

[4] Melodie Lancaster, "The Future We Predict Isn't Inevitable: Reframing Our Success in the Modern World," *Vital Speeches of the Day* 58 (1 August 1992): 636.

[5] Theodore Hesburgh, Alumni Reunion Talk, audiotape of speech, presented at University of Notre Dame, South Bend, 1983.

[6] Kim Woo Choong, "The Korea-America Friendship," *Vital Speeches of the Day* 58 (1 October 1992): 738.

[7] George W. Bush, "State of the Union," *The Denver Post*, 30 January 2002, p. A4.

[8] Karen A. Carlton, "Our Lives, One Life," commencement speech, College of Arts and Humanities, Humboldt State University, Arcata, CA, 22 May 1993.

[9] George C. Fraser, "Excellence, Education and Perceptions: An African American Crisis," in *Vital Speeches of the Day* 58 (15 November 1991): 78.

[10] Huey P. Long, "Sharing Our Wealth," in *American Voices: Significant Speeches in American History: 1640–1945*, ed. James Andrews and David Zarefsky (New York: Longman, 1989), 449.

[11] Dan George, quoted in T. C. McLuhan, ed., *Touch the Earth: A Self-Portrait of Indian Existence* (New York: Touchstone, 1971), 162.

[12] Edward M. Kennedy, "Tribute to John F. Kennedy, Jr.," 23 July 1999; available from http://www.historyplace.com/speeches/ted-kennedy-jfk-jr.htm.

[13] Barbara Jordan, "Democratic Convention Keynote Address," in *Contemporary American Public Discourse*, 3rd ed., ed. Halford Ross Ryan (Prospect Heights, IL: Waveland, 1992), 278.

[14] Christine D. Keen, "May You Live in Interesting Times: The Workplace in the '90s," in *Vital Speeches of the Day* 58 (15 November 1991): 83–86.

[15] Richard W. Carlson, "When Words Collide: Legal Ethics and the Coming Information Wars," *Vital Speeches of the Day* 54 (15 July 1988): 583.

[16] Fraser, 78–79.

[17] Richard L. Weaver II, "Self Motivation: Ten Techniques for Activating or Freeing the Spirit," *Vital Speeches of the Day* 57 (1 August 1991): 623.

Chapter Eight

[1] Umberto Eco, *The Open Work*, trans. Anna Cancogni (Cambridge: Harvard University Press, 1989), 166.

[2] Bill Gates, "Remarks at the 2002 International Consumer Electronics Show," 7 January 2002; available from http://www.microsoft.com/billgates/speeches/2002/01-07ces.asp.

[3] Edward M. Kennedy, "Tribute to John F. Kennedy, Jr.," 23 July 1999; available from http://www.historyplace.com/speeches/ted-kennedy-jfk-jr.htm.

[4] Gates.

[5] Michele Kurtz, "Sentence for Junta May Hinge on Past," *Boston Globe*, 25 January 2002, p. B1.

Chapter Nine

[1] Suzette Haden Elgin, *The Last Word on the Gentle Art of Verbal Self-Defense* (New York: Prentice Hall, 1987), 143.

[2] Elgin, 142.

[3] Albert Ellis and Robert A. Harper, *A New Guide to Rational Living* (North Hollywood, CA: Melvin Powers, 1975), 146.

[4] This discussion of irrational anxiety is adapted from Ellis and Harper, pp. 145–57.

[5] Elgin, 149.

[6] Adapted from Elgin, 166.

[7] For an account of the history of women speakers in the United States, see Karlyn Kohrs Campbell, *Man Cannot Speak for Her: A Critical Study of Early Feminist Rhetoric*, vol. 1 (New York: Greenwood, 1989).

INDEX